# $\mathcal{O}$RNAMENTAL GRASSES

## Roger Grounds

*Published in association with the Hardy Plant Society*

CHRISTOPHER HELM

*London*

© 1989 Roger Grounds

Line illustrations by Helen Senior

Christopher Helm (Publishers) Ltd, Imperial House,
21–25 North Street, Bromley, Kent BR1 1SD

ISBN 0-7470-1219-9

A CIP catalogue record for this book
is available from the British Library

Forthcoming books in the Christopher Helm
HARDY PLANT series:

CAMPANULAS *Peter Lewis and Margaret Lynch*

MECONOPSIS *James Cobb*

HARDY EUPHORBIAS *Roger Turner*

ALLIUMS *Dilys Davies*

DIANTHUS *Richard Bird*

Typeset by Paston Press, Loddon, Norfolk

Printed and bound in Great Britain by
Biddles Ltd, Guildford and King's Lynn

# Contents

# Colour Plates

# Figures

# Acknowledgements

Many people have helped me produce this much expanded and improved version of my book on Ornamental Grasses, and I am happy to thank them.

First, I should like to thank the Hardy Plant Society for inviting me to revise my book: Graham Rice for acting as go-between and getting the book off the ground: and everyone at Christopher Helm for turning my MS. into such a pleasing book. I should also like to thank Jane Leitch for turning my now terrible handwriting into a decent typescript and Helen Senior for enriching the book with her enchanting line drawings.

I am grateful to John Bond, VMH, Keeper of the Gardens at Windsor Great Park, for many interesting discussions about grasses in the looser sense over the years, and in particular for information about two unusual *Miscanthus* species growing at the Savill Gardens; to Tony Schilling, Deputy Curator of the Royal Botanic Garden, Wakehurst Place, for information about *Miscanthus nepalensis*: to Dr S. M. Walters, former Director of Cambridge Botanic Gardens, for information about various carices; to David McClintock, again for information about carices; to Roy Lancaster, VMH for information concerning a nomenclatural problem and for the gift of an enchanting grass he collected in the Himalayas and which I am still unable to identify; to Piers Trehane for print-outs of the names and authors he would be adopting in the *Index Hortensis*, and for much general encouragement; to Dr Brent Elliott for useful background information from the Royal Horticultural Society's Lindley Library; to Peter Barnes, the Royal Horticultural Society's Botanist at Wisley, again for help with carices; to Peter Addington who read the section on bamboos and made many helpful suggestions; to Graham Hutchins, County Park Nurseries, for information about grasses from New Zealand and the Falkland Islands; to Nigel Taylor, Hoecroft Plants, for information on several grasses in his list; to Dr Ullrich Fischer for much help over grasses of German origin; to Thomas Cope and Dr D. A. Simpson, both of the Royal Botanic Gardens, Kew, for help with some nice problems of identity and naming; and to Dr C. D. Pigott, Director of Cambridge Botanic Gardens, for permitting Helen Senior to draw grasses there.

In 1987 Diana and I went to America and one of the main purposes of that visit was to study grasses there. That visit has greatly enriched this book. I should like to thank many people for their kindness and their generous

vi

hospitality, especially Dr & Mrs Harold Peck and Dr & Mrs Warren I. Pollock for their hospitality and kind introductions; Dr Darrell Apps, formerly Director of Education at Longwood Gardens, who was the prime mover in my visit to Longwood; Tom Brinda, formerly Continuing Education Coordinator, for organising my day at Longwood efficiently; and Rick Darke the Curator of Plants, for a fascinating guided tour and for subsequent information about several grasses. My very particular thanks also to Kurt and Hannah Bluemel, Kurt Bluemel Inc., for their hospitality and for a most enjoyable and rewarding day spent at their nursery and garden; and to Wolfgang von Oehme, Oehme & Van Sweden Associates Inc. for a guided tour of their landscape plantings of grasses in the city of Washington, DC.

And last, and most importantly, my thanks to Diana for encouraging me to undertake these revisions and for her endless help.

# *Author's Note*

In the description of grasses, sedges and bamboos specific terminology is used which may be unfamiliar and which may at first sight appear confusing. I have tried throughout this book to write in plain English but the very nature of the plants which are the subject of the book is such that this is not entirely possible. Because grasses are different from other plants, and because in particular, their flowers are different from other plants, one has to use the terms which properly belong to the organs one is describing. A spikelet is a spikelet: it would be misleading to try to describe it in terms of a normal flower.

Having said that, the terminology which does apply to grasses is not difficult to master. One can get by on perhaps five or six new words — spikelet, rachilla, glume, lemma and awn being the most important.

Chapter Two is devoted to explaining these terms. The diagrams on pages 31 and 33 also provide a ready-reference, and there is a glossary at the end of the book as well. In the end the most surprising thing about these terms is how quickly one becomes familiar with them.

# 1 *The Diversity of Grasses*

Grasses have a grace and beauty that no other group of plants can match, and a diversity of size, form and habit that makes them suitable for a great variety of ornamental garden uses. Yet their ornamental and decorative potential has as yet hardly been recognised, let alone exploited. It comes out again and again in conversation, with both gardeners, and other garden designers, that this absence of grasses in our gardens arises largely because people do not know how to use grasses in gardens, and are perhaps afraid to experiment. People ask me 'Where do you grow your grasses?' as though their expectation is that one grows grasses in a place set apart so that they will not contaminate other plantings. Yet the way to grow grasses to best effect is simply to regard them as perennials like any other perennials, and use them as you would use other perennials, for their flowers or foliage. Many are also suitable for picking and drying, and these may conveniently be grown in the reserve garden if one has one.

Grasses range in size from miniatures so small that they need to be nurtured in an alpine house or sink garden, to invasive giants whose stems are so toughened with silica that they will blunt even the sharpest blade. Between these extremes there are grasses suitable for gardens of every size and shape, and for every garden situation. There are hummock-forming species suitable for the front of a border. There are invasive ground-covering grasses and non-invasive grasses that look at their most elegant grown in a mixed border. Then there are grasses so large that they are often listed by nurserymen as shrubs, ideal for the backs of borders or for screening or hedging. Some of the largest and most dramatic grasses are excellent when used instead of shrubs as specimen plants. And among all these are grasses best suited to full sun and others that do best in full shade, though most tolerate a little of each. There are grasses for rock gardens and screes or sinks, and others for bog gardens. Some like to have their feet in water, while others need a really hot, dry position if they are to survive at all. The great majority are meadow plants, ideal for the rich soil of a mixed border, but many are woodland plants, associating well with the sort of plants usually grown in woodland. Some need peat-bed conditions; others dry, gravelly soils. In general, however, the grasses are not too fussy about soil, and this is undoubtedly one of the reasons why they have been, in evolutionary terms, one of the most successful groups of plants ever.

The true grasses are all members of the family Gramineae, but when we talk of grasses in a gardening context we are more usually using the word in a loose sense, to include other groups of plants of similar grassy appearance — sedges, rushes, woodrushes or even the cat-tails — though in systematic or evolutionary terms these are not remotely related to the true grasses. They do however contribute much to the sheer diversity of grasses. *Cymophyllus fraseri*, for instance, is a sedge with saw-edged leaves as much as 5 cm across and 20 cm long, broad and flat, looking for all the world like the leaves of tulips newly emerged; while there are other sedges, such as *Carex comans*, which have leaves that are thin, flexuous and almost tubular in section. The great majority, of course, have more typically grass-like leaves, yet the more closely one looks at grasses the more difficult it is to define quite what is a typical leaf of grass. The leaves of *Festuca punctoria* are as stiff and prickly as the spines of a hedgehog, while those of *Scirpus cernuus* are as soft as silk. The long leaf blades of the pampas grass, *Cortaderia selloana*, are covered in tiny hairs so stiff that they will cut your flesh if you are imprudent enough to run your hand along the blade, while the short blades of *Alopecurus lanatus* are covered in a soft, woolly conglomeration of hairs. The leaves of *Juncus acuta* or *J.maritinum*, the hard rush, are tubular in section, and not only stiff but tough tipped with a point that can pierce the skin. The leaves of many other rushes grow straight up out of the ground, vertically, but those of one particularly delightful sedge, *Carex buchanani*, end in a little curly twist. The leaves of *Juncus effusus* 'Spiralis' take matters to extremes and are curled and twisted very much in the manner of the corkscrew hazel, *Corylus avellana* 'Contorta'. The variations are almost endless.

Nor are the leaves of grass merely green. There are grasses whose leaves are either variegated purple, red, bronze, brown, orange or wholly yellow, cream, white or blue. Often, if the variegation is a white one, there is an overlying tint of pink as well. There are plants like *Festuca caesia*, one of the bluest of all blue grasses, whose leaves seem to have a metallic sheen about them, and others like *F. glacialis* whose leaves seem to have been frozen for ever somewhere between the most delicate blue and the most delicate green; and still others, like the seaside grass *Elymus arenarius*, whose rich blue leaves seem to have an almost leaden heaviness in their colouring. At the other extreme of the colour scale, there are plants with bright yellow leaves, like Bowles's golden grass, *Milium effusum* 'Aureum', a singularly striking plant when grown in semi-shade where the sun can strike the leaves against a darker background. Other grasses like *Pennisetum setaceum* 'Rubra' have leaves of horticultural purple. Plants such as *Carex petriei* and *Uncinia unciniata* strike out in a new direction, having leaves of an exceptionally brilliant copper-red, while *Carex buchanani* has leaves of a curious weathered copper colour. Most brilliant of all perhaps is *Imperata cylindrica*, Japanese blood grass, whose leaf tips are stained crimson in spring, the crimson spreading across the whole leaf by late summer so that by autumn, when seen with the sun beyond it, it glows as if on fire.

There is diversity, too, in the form of the plants. Some are low-growing, ground-covering plants that form low mats, while others form tight-knit hummocks. Some grow into large mounds while others reach straight upwards in a narrowly erect form, having something of the disciplined rigidity of a guardsman on parade. Others start off by growing upwards, but then spread outwards as though spilling over the sides of some invisible vase that constricts them for only three-quarters of their height. Many grasses could only be said to be irregular in form, each stem usually growing more or less upright, but the whole plant growing from a mass of subterranean runners forming an amorphous patch usually lower at the edge than at the centre of the patch. Others, like *Phragmites australis*, the common reed, form in nature large stands, every plant growing much the same height over vast, uninterrupted hectares.

The flowers of grass (in the looser sense) can vary in colour from greens and whites to pinks, purples, blues and browns, and the shapes of the inflorescences can vary endlessly from the plumes of the pampas grass to the many-fingered spikes of *Cynodon dactylon*; from the dense, ovoid head of *Lagurus ovatus* to the long, cylindrical spike of *Phleum pratense*; from the loose cyme of *Luzula sylvatica* to the tight, solitary spikelet of *Scirpus setaceus*; from the graceful, loose, drooping panicle of *Briza minor* to the tight, one-sided spike of *Nardus stricta*; from the single-headed cat-tails, reed-maces or bulrushes to the three-headed flowers of many sedges.

Many highly decorative grasses are so common that you can find them on the roadsides: others are so rare that you will only be able to obtain them with the greatest difficulty. The great majority, however, can be obtained from nurserymen, while many of the less common species can be grown from seed.

# 2  *The Garden Uses of Grasses*

If you look around at the world you cannot fail to be impressed by the fact that grasses vastly outnumber all other plants put together, in almost every aspect of the landscape. If you look, by contrast, at most gardens, you will be equally impressed by the singular lack of grasses in proportion to other plants. There is, of course, no reason why the proportions of plants in a garden should reflect the balance of species in the wild. A garden is, after all, a work of art, and not an imitation of nature. But it is surprising how little grasses are used.

Since the one part of a garden to which most people readily admit grasses is the lawn, it is interesting to take a fresh look at lawns and see whether they in fact need to be the baize-green of a billiard table. Undoubtedly, if you want to play bowls on it, this type of lawn is the ideal. But from a decorative point of view there may be other possibilities. To start with, typical lawn grasses seldom grow well under trees, even those mixes that are supposed to do well in shade. Instead of persevering at trying to grow a fine lawn under trees, it might be better simply to settle for grass under the trees—a grass that does not need mowing, merely lightly trimming over once a year and tidying around the edges. One of the best grasses for such a situation would be *Deschampsia caespitosa*, a delightfully refined grass, with dark green leaves and the most airy imaginable flower-heads borne in late summer. A word of warning though: it does seed itself with tremendous freedom. Another good grass for such a situation would be *Milium effusum*, the wood mellic—ideal because it is a woodland grass anyway. Even more dramatic, had one the courage to use it, would be its golden form, Bowles's golden grass, *M.effusum* 'Aureum', whose golden leaves light up the shade under trees to perfection. This normally flowers around May or June, and if trimmed over the top with shears looks neat for the rest of the season, while the trimming helps it to form offsets and so make its growth more dense—in much the way that mowing a lawn does. The variegated wood mellic, *M.effusum* 'Variegatum', with its thin, white stripes down the leaves, could be used in a similar way, though its effect when massed is possibly less exciting than that of the golden wood mellic. Indeed, the sight of a patch of golden wood mellic, used boldly to create a broad patch of glowing gold where there is normally darkness under trees, is probably the most dramatic way to plant such an area. But any grass used in this way must be used boldly, as one would use heathers or other ground-cover.

Apart from the grasses proper, the woodrushes are ideal plants to use in place of lawn grasses under trees. Again, they are natives of woodland and so enjoy these conditions. The majority will stand considerable drought, which is usually one of the factors which militates against the success of lawn grasses in shade. The common woodrush, *Luzula sylvatica*, is itself a useful, if drab, plant for such situations. It is a rampant grower, forming an impenetrable ground-cover and needing no attention whatsoever once established. More exciting is the variegated wood rush, *L.sylvatica marginata*, which has a distinct but not very broad white line along each margin. It is a rather more attractive plant than the duller green common plant, but is equally rampant, equally tolerant of drought and total shade. Rather more elegant, but much taller-growing, are the two rather similar woodrushes, *L.luzuloides* and *L.nivea*, both with thin, hairy leaves and attractive heads of white flowers in late spring or early summer. Both are quite tall-growing, up to about 46 cm when in flower, but attractive where this height can be accommodated.

Two other woodrushes are ideal under trees, and both are quite small-growing. The first is *L.pilosa*, a weed in some gardens, but useful because it not only spreads by runners but will seed itself when happy to form really dense carpets. It is low-growing, to about 15 cm, with dark green, hairy leaves and attractive corymbs of flowers in spring. In time it will form impenetrable mats. Far more delicate in idiom is *L.luzulina*, with light green leaves that are densely hairy and only about 4 cm long. In flower, the plant is no more than 10 cm tall. It spreads rapidly by means of offsets, and quickly forms dense mats. A considerable colony can be built up in a short time by dividing the clumps in spring and summer. It will not stand conditions quite so dry as the other woodrushes, and seems happiest in a soil enriched with moss peat to get it started. If the flower-heads are removed as soon as they are over, this little woodrush will remain neat for the rest of the year.

Of course, this is merely a matter of making a virtue out of necessity, but it does illustrate one way in which grasses can be used in quantity with delightful results. Unfortunately, where these grasses are being used as lawn substitutes, they will seldom if ever stand the wear that a conventional lawn would take, and this should be borne in mind when planting them. However, the grasses and woodrushes mentioned so far are all ideal under trees in a part of the garden where there is not much traffic.

Another area of lawn that often presents problems, though this time they are problems of hard wear, is one close to a patio or terrace. There nearly always seems to be some place where most people step off the paving on to the lawn, and the wear is such that, short of returfing the area each year, there seems to be little that can be done to keep such an area from looking patchy. Yet this is only true so long as one continues to think along conventional lines: your problems are somewhat worsened if you have a preconception that, to be a lawn, a lawn must be green.

One very attractive way of overcoming such a problem is to use stepping stones to carry the hard wear, and to put the area down to a blue grass. You could, if you want, have a whole blue lawn, but it probably looks better in most gardens if a boldly curving bed of blue grass is planted adjacent to the patio. The lawn itself can be mown in the conventional way, while the blue grass area need only be trimmed over every spring with garden shears. The blueness of the grass tends to discourage visitors from walking on it, which keeps them to the stepping stones, and since most blue grasses prefer hot, sunny positions, and most patios are put in the hottest, sunniest part of a garden, the combination is an ideal one. Probably the most suitable blue grass for this type of lawn treatment would be one of the forms of *Festuca caesia*. It is also a grass that will stand a certain amount of walking on without suffering too much damage. Even lower-growing is *F.glacialis*, which grows no more than 5 cm tall and has leaves of a fascinating ice-blue colour. It does, however, tend to collect a lot of dead leaves within its slowly spreading mat, and is perhaps too fussy about soil to make a really good lawn substitute. *F.punctoria* is another very blue grass of low-growing habit that delights in hot, dry situations. It is a likely candidate for such a situation, especially if you do not mind its leaves being as sharp and prickly as the spines of a hedgehog. Under some circumstances this might even be a point in its favour, having a deterrent effect on neighbours' pets when they choose their pathways. This grass does, however, need to be planted densely and clipped severely in spring, otherwise it tends to develop bald patches at the centre of each clump.

It takes rather more courage to go the whole hog and put a whole lawn down to bold patterns of coloured grasses. Indeed, to many the very idea of a multi-coloured lawn may seem a contradiction in terms. Yet, in South America, the landscape architect Roberto Burle Marx has done this very successfully, and on a huge scale, in public parks. In one instance he has used alternating squares of a green and a variegated grass, and in another, perhaps even more famous example, the green and the variegated forms of *Stenotaphrum secundatum* in great interlocking S-shapes. The effect is dramatic in the extreme. This grass is, however, a surface-running ground-hugger for which there is no exact equivalent suitable for use in the cool temperate regions of the world, where *S.secundatum* is rather a house or greenhouse plant, though it can be used to good effect in summer bedding schemes. There are, however, grasses which can be used to create multi-coloured lawns in the cool temperate regions of the world, and the fact that Burle Marx regarded Capability Brown as his spiritual master suggests that such an idea is not so alien as it might at first seem.

The important thing to realise when considering the creation of a multi-coloured lawn is that such a lawn is very much more for looking at than for using: it is certainly not ideal for children to play upon. It is also important to aim for a simplicity of design, using perhaps no more than two or three grasses in any one coloured lawn. It may be, for example, that one would use the

6

golden variegated form of pampas grass, *Cortaderia selloana* 'Gold Band', as a feature (very much as one might use a small tree or shrub as a specimen), and take a spur of a dark grass out to this, surrounding the spur with a blue grass. Around this coloured lawn there would then be a border from which grasses and grass-like plants were ruthlessly excluded. Another approach might be to take the curve of an existing border and lay out a series of interrelated curves that would work their way away from the border towards an island specimen plant—perhaps an *Arundo donax*, probably the tallest-growing of all hardy or nearly hardy grasses. The sort of grasses that would be ideal in combinations of this sort are *Festuca caesia*, to provide a dramatic blue; *Hakonechloa macra* 'Albo-aurea', to provide a brilliant but deciduous yellow; *Carex morrowii* 'Aureo-variegata', to provide a dramatic evergreen yellow variegated area; the grass-like *Ophiopogon planiscarpus nigresceus*, to provide a totally unexpected black; *Acorus gramineus* 'Variegatus', to provide a good white variegated area; and *Carex petriei*, to provide a startling contrast by way of rusty red. When plants such as these are used massed, as they can be under these conditions, they take on a drama of contrast one with another that they never achieve when used as individual specimens.

Quieter contrasts can be achieved with plants like *Luzula luzulina*, already mentioned as suitable as a lawn substitute under trees, whose leaves are a delightful soft green; *Acorus pusillus*, whose leaves are a singularly vibrant green; the smallest form of *Ophiopogon japonicus* 'Compactus', whose leaves are an extremely dark green; and *Festuca glacialis*, which, with its ice-blue leaves, is useful to bridge the difference between the true greens and the true blues, providing a gentle gradation from one to the other where too strong a contrast is to be avoided.

Anyone who takes the decision to make a lawn of this type usually goes to some trouble to design it in suitably pleasing curves, bands and whorls. They do not then want to find the grasses growing into each other. This is easily avoided by sinking into the ground at the point where one grass meets another a lawn edging strip, either of aluminium or, preferably, of plastic. Such lawns, once created, need little maintenance beyond an annual trimming over, and can add a whole new dimension to a garden.

An extension or development of this idea is the use of grasses in tightly determined patterns, along the lines of Elizabethan knot gardens or the later parterres or complex Victorian bedding schemes. Patterns for these can be found in most old manuals of horticulture (and, generally, the heavier the tome the better the patterns). They allow more scope for variation in size than do coloured lawns, and it does not matter so much if one uses deciduous species. In schemes of this type you could use, in addition to those plants already mentioned as suitable for coloured lawns, plants such as the marvellous but deciduous golden-striped *Alopecurus pratensis* 'Aureus', the white-variegated *Arrhenatherum elatius* var. *bulbosum* 'Variegatum', the almost evergreen, white-variegated *Dactylis glomerata* 'Variegata', *Holcus mollis* 'Variegatus', an extra-ordinarily dramatic little plant when used in bold patches, and the marvel-lously variegated *Molinia caerulea* 'Variegata', with leaves striped white, cream and yellow in the best forms. One could use slightly taller plants, like Bowles' golden sedge, *Carex elata* 'Aurea', or the brilliant bronze *Carex buchanani* as the 'hedges' in the layout (where box might have been used in a conventional scheme). *Helictotrichon sempervirens* would provide an ideal blue edging to contain the broader splashes of colour. The possible permutations of colour combinations in a planting of this kind are almost endless, especially if in some areas grasses are grown for their flowers rather than their foliage. This would be an ideal way of having what the Victorians would have called a 'reserve garden'—a garden where plants are set aside especially for picking. If the borders were to be used like this, an ideal edging plant would be the grass-like *Lariope platyphylla*, especially the forms 'Majestic', which has particularly rich purple flowers, or 'Monroe White', which has pure white flowers. The bonus of the unexpected flowers in autumn would always be welcome.

Most people, however, prefer to use grasses less formally in their gardens, and there are endless ways and situations in which this can be done. For a start, there is a whole host of low-growing, mainly hummock-forming grasses which are ideal as edgings for a border or for use at the front of a mixed or perennial border. *Festuca amethystina*, *F.scoparia*, *F.caesia* and its variants, together with *Milium effusum* 'Aureum', *Molinia caerulea* 'Variegata', *Carex morrowii* 'Variegata' or 'Aurea Variegata' and *Acorus gramineus* 'Variegatus' are all ideal as plants grown strictly for colour. For flower, *Deschampsia flexuosa* is unsur-passed as a delicate edging, but it seeds excessively freely; while *Bouteloua gracilis* provides something in a totally different idiom; and *Sesleria caerulea* is ideal too, especially for those who enjoy the details of plants, the way the upper surface of the leaf is a different shade of blue from the underside, and the colour of the flowers, which are borne early in the year. *Koeleria cristata* 'Glauca' is another which has attractive flowers, while one of the finest of all is the perennial quaking grass, *Briza media*, whose flower-heads remain decorative for months on end. All these, of course, are grasses for full sun. In shade, the choice of edging or front-of-the-border grasses is more limited. *Luzula sylvatica* 'Marginata' is ideal on the shaded side of a shrubbery, while Bowles' golden sedge *Carex elata* 'Aurea' is excellent where there is some shade, some sun; but it does not give of its best in full shade. Both *Deschampsia caespitosa* and *D.flexuosa* will perform brilliantly in shade at the edge of a shrubbery, while *Hystrix patula*, *Milium effusum* 'Aureum' and *Stipa pennata* all grow well and look good in shade. *Helictotrichon sempervirens* will make a good edging in sun only if you are prepared to put up with the sharpness of its leaves.

For anyone with time to spend gathering seed from one year to the next and resowing, and in some cases pricking out the seedlings and planting them on, there are several annual grasses that make good edging plants. *Briza minor*, annual quaking grass, is one of the loveliest of these, while its miniature form is even more desirable. Another for full sun is the somewhat rambling *Rhynchelytrum repens*, flowering well into autumn with unusual pink flower-heads. *Hordeum jubatum*, *Apera spica-venti*, *Pennisetum setaceum* and *Lagurus ovatus* are others for full sun. *Coix lacryma-jobi* is one of the finest annuals for a semi-shaded position, perhaps a little too tall for an edging plant, but too good to put too far back in a border. Unfortunately, it only shows its paces to perfection during long, hot summers.

There are dozens, possibly hundreds, of grasses which are suitable for the middle of the border. Indeed, almost any of those included in this book which grow between 30 cm and 1 m would be ideal there. Some of the most striking would include *Carex buchanani*, with its reddish leaves, shown to best advantage when grown close to a blue-leaved plant such as *Helictotrichon sempervirens* or a good blue form of *Elymus arenarius*, its spreading rhizomes firmly restrained in a container. If something like the white-variegated *Phalaris arundinacea* 'Picta' can be planted nearby, the contrast will be even greater. Another grass providing a similar contrast would be *Glycera maxima* 'Variegata', while *Dactylis glomerata* 'Variegata' would make a less invasive variegated grass to grow in front of *Carex buchanani*. *Calamagrostis epigejos*, *Stipa gigantea*, *S.calamag-rostis*, *Melica altissima* and *Pennisetum villosum* are ideal middle-order plants where you are after the effect of the flowers rather than that of the foliage. *Deschampsia caespitosa* and *Carex pendula* are two mid-border plants ideal for situations where there is shade for much of the day.

While the great majority of grasses mentioned in this book as growing to more than 1 m are ideal for placing at the backs of borders, there are several different ways in which this can be done. Some look best as specimens, others look better grouped in clumps of three or five, while some make excellent hedges. Others are simply too rampant to grow anywhere without taking the strictest precautions against their spreading in all directions and getting completely out of hand—precisely which are mentioned in the descriptions of the species.

Probably the best way of looking at the larger grasses is to think of them as though they were shrubs, and to use them in the garden in a very similar way. Certainly the only way to use *Arundo donax* is as though it were a shrub. Under ideal conditions, it will grow 3.5 or 4 m tall, and since it spreads by stolons, albeit slowly, it is a plant of giant proportions. In fairness, it should be mentioned that to achieve its maximum proportions it needs good cultivation, a sheltered situation, ample moisture and a rich top-dressing of organic manure every year. Given that treatment it could be used as a small tree in a very small garden. In a very large garden, it could simply be the climax to an ascending border of grasses. But gardening is so much a sense of proportion: an understanding of scale. What looks right in one garden can look absurd in another if the proper sense of scale is lacking. If you want to use a plant as large

9

as *A.donax*, you need to be aware of its size, and to realise that it will be the dominant plant in a small garden—as large as a young *Malus* or flowering cherry. As a specimen, where you might be, in a sense, almost showing off how large a grass you can grow it is ideal; it is also ideal if you want an annual 'tree substitute'. But it is hopeless to try to mix or blend it with anything else: it is a dominant plant and only in the very largest gardens can this fact be disguised. Unfortunately, the variegated form of *A.donax*, known in Britain as *A.donax* 'Variegata' and in the United States as *A.donax* 'Versicolor', is tender through most of both countries. Were it hardier, it would be the most dramatic specimen plant imaginable.

The two other genera that provide superlative specimen plants are *Cortaderia* and *Chionochloa*. In both genera there are plants that, grown on their own, not only look dramatic (as specimen plants should), but are even more so when planted boldly in clumps of threes or fives. *Chionochloa conspicua* and *C.rigida* are two of the best from that genus for specimens, while *Cortaderia richardii* or any of the 13 cultivars of *C.selloana* are just as fine as specimens, which is how they are usually used. Indeed, if one were to look on the plants which make up these two genera as shrubs, and then to plan a shrubbery, possibly to go beside a drive, made up wholly of species and cultivars from them, underplanted with a vigorous running ground-cover like *Carex riparia* 'Variegata', the effect would be stunning. But you do need space to achieve such effects.

In general those species which are ideal as specimens are not really good for hedging purposes, and those which are good for hedging are not much use for specimens. *Cortaderia selloana* 'Gold Band' is obviously a specimen plant; *Miscanthus sinensis* 'Zebrinus' is less obviously a specimen plant. It is, on the other hand, because of the basically erect growth of the stems in its lower half, ideal for hedging—and a very striking hedge it can make. Indeed, the genus *Miscanthus* is full of plants ideal for hedging: *M.sacchariflorus* and its form 'Gigantea' are both ideal, as is *M.sinensis* and its cultivars 'Gracillimus', 'Variegatus' and 'Zebrinus'. *Erianthus ravennae* is another suitable for screening or hedging. Plants that are as invasive as *Phragmites australis* tempt one to use them as hedges: somehow one wants to believe that they will spread only laterally and never simply march off across the garden. But *P.australis*, especially in its very fine white-variegated form, does make an ideal, self-spreading screen or hedge, provided you are prepared to lay two parallel rows of concrete, each at least 45 cm deep and 5 cm wide to contain it.

Many of the grasses mentioned as suitable for screening, for use as specimens or for the middle of a border are also ideal for amenity plantings. It is a curious fact that those who plant public places seem completely blind to the qualities of grasses. Apart from the beauty of these plants, the great majority are undemanding as to soil, tolerant of atmospheric pollution (whether from petroleum fumes or other, usually industrial, pollutants), and singularly undemanding in general cultivation. Many grasses not only look well, but actually do well when grown in what in New Zealand are called pebble gardens, or similar types of gardens. The point about amenity plantings of this sort is that, once the grasses have been planted, all weeds surrounding them can be suppressed by a mulch of pebbles, grit (such as might be used when making up roads) or gravel; in coastal areas, sea-washed pebbles could be used to great advantage. A general-purpose total weedkiller can then be used on the pebbled areas, while the grasses increase in size and beauty year by year. Plantings using *Cortaderia, Chionochloa, Arundo donax, Miscanthus sacchariflorus, M.sinensis* and cultivars, together with phormiums in variety and yuccas could be extremely dramatic. In plantings where more time and attention can be given, some of the plants mentioned as suitable for middle of the border or edging might be used — *Deschampsia, Carex elata* 'Aurea' (especially if planted in very bold groups), *Carex fortunei* 'Variegata' and the blues of *Elymus arenarius* and the self-defensive *Festuca punctoria*, together with the, again fairly self-defensive, *Helictotrichon sempervirens*. The white-variegated *Phalaris arundinacea* 'Picta' could be used wherever it can be contained — and any local council with a spare piece of 1.75 m diameter concrete drainage pipe has the containing materials to hand. It would look even more effective were the drainage pipe to be left sticking up above the ground, adding a new dimension to the planting. Indeed, a whole group of such pipes, arranged sympathetically at different heights, would provide an ideal setting for a planting of invasive grasses that could in this way easily be controlled. Such plantings would be far more attractive and far less labour-intensive than many of the low-maintenance plantings at present made by local authorities.

At the other extreme are the labour-intensive gardens of those gardeners who so love their plants that they never count the hours spent on them. There are many small grasses which are great treasures, and many other grasses which are not too easy to grow and therefore need a constant loving eye kept on them. The majority of these are ideal for rock gardens, screes, peat-beds or other special forms of cultivation. At the same time, such areas of a garden are precious, and it is necessary for the gardener to keep a close eye on any grasses admitted to such areas to make sure that he has not unwittingly planted a grass that has invaded everything in sight by its underground stolons. Mistakes have been made: people have virtually had to rebuild rock gardens when they have admitted stoloniferous grasses and not realised their error in time.

Some of the most treasured of grasses can safely be grown in the confines of a sink. So hard are they to establish, and so slow to spread, that there is little danger of their ever taking over the entire sink. At the same time, a sink provides the ideal mini-garden in which to give such grasses just the sort of loving care they need. Perhaps the most precious of grasses is *Alopecurus lanatus* which comes from the mountains of Spain. It has grey-blue leaves so richly covered in tomentum as to appear woolly, and it is for this combination of blueness and woolliness that this little plant is valued. It is a gem, but it needs

11

really hot, dry conditions in which to thrive. The criterion for its success is that, if the situation is hot enough and dry enough to grow cacti out of doors, then it will thrive. It may well need a pane of glass over it in winter, for it is winter damp rather than cold that kills it; however, given perfect drainage and sun from dawn to dusk, it will survive unharmed without a pane of glass in winter, each year adding about one new culm to its stumpy little form.

As much of a gem, but in a totally different way, is *Poa tasmanica*, a miniature if ever there was one. This is probably most simply described as similar to *Festuca glacialis*, but even smaller and even bluer. The leaf-blades are barely 2.5 cm long when growing in rich soil, a cold, icy blue, and the whole plant very, very slowly forms a tiny little mat. It colours best in a limestone scree sink, but seems equally at home but less blue in a peat-bed. *F.glacialis* itself seems to show its paces best when grown in a sink: only in such a situation can it be fully appreciated and given the care it requires. It seldom seems to run when grown in a sink, but rather tends to grow into a hummock; forever growing taller by rooting into the compost of its dead leaves. Grown in a rock garden, by contrast, it will run quite freely.

Finally, the finest of the carices is definitely a plant for a sink. This is *Carex firma* 'Variegata', a dwarf sedge, no more than 2.5 cm or so high at maturity, with leaves straight, rigid, edged deep green with a broad band of yellow, slowly forming a tiny little hummock that is quite prickly to the touch. It prefers a wetter situation than the other grasses mentioned as suitable for a sink garden, and will tolerate some shade, which the others will not. In its own way, the green-leaved form of *Carex firma* is also an attractive plant.

The rock garden provides not just one but a whole range of possible habitats for grasses. Modern thinking about the construction of rock gardens is that this should be carried out so that the rocks look like a natural outcrop rather than an artificially created mound of stone. If you have managed to achieve the effect of a natural outcrop you will have at least two totally different types of slope: the sharp, almost vertical face of the escarpment, and the slower, more gradual slope up to it. If you have been clever in arranging the rocks, you will probably have succeeded in laying them so as to create a series of tiers of level pavements rather than something that slopes like the overlapping of tiles on a roof. One or other of the slopes of the rock garden probably faces fully into the sun, the other being in shade for much of the year. If you have been even more clever, and have so arranged the rocks that there are folds and crevices in them, with loose screes and moraines as well as open streams running down them, then you will have an even further range of habitats within the rock garden's relatively small area. If you have placed a pool at the bottom of the rocks, with an area of bog garden around it or to one side of it, then you have created in miniature virtually every habitat in which grasses are found in the wild. This does not, however, mean that any grass at all can be grown in the rock garden: far from it. The greatest care must be taken in which grasses to choose, for the wrong ones in the wrong places will look more out of place in the rock garden than elsewhere. Because of the range of possible microhabitats within the rock garden, however, the choice of types of grasses is very wide.

As to the question of precisely which grasses can or cannot be admitted to the rock garden, there is really no absolute answer: so much depends on its scale, on the size of the rocks used and on the background against which the rock garden is set. In the very largest sort of rock garden, such as might be found in a large botanic garden, almost any of the grasses mentioned in this book could be used. In the smaller type of rock garden, usually found in private gardens, the choice is much more limited, though basically any of those grasses mentioned as growing less than 30 cm tall (provided they are not stoloniferous or rhizomatous), as well as most of the smaller sedges, rushes and even the smaller cat-tails, would be suitable.

In general, however, people seem to prefer the more dainty, almost airy-fairy types of grasses on rock gardens, such as the festucas, especially *Festuca scoparia*, which forms rich green hummocks, and *F.caesia*, which is very popular. *F.glacialis* is an ideal plant for most rock gardens, where it can be so planted as to appear to form a small natural lawn or alpine meadow, creeping slowly out across the surface of flat rocks and softening harsh corners. *Poa tasmanica* can be used in a similar way, and will form a larger mat faster here than it would in a trough or sink garden. Another delightful carpeting grass for any rock garden is the little *Holcus mollis* 'Variegatus', which will run happily up and down the crevices between rocks as well as forming mats on any flat areas while not spreading so fast that its growth cannot be controlled quite easily.

Then, again, rock gardens provide perfect settings for little gems that need to be treasured and taken some care of lest they get swamped by stronger-growing neighbours. *Alopecurus lanatus* is one such, though it does need conditions of perfect drainage, like those to be found on a scree slope, if it is to thrive. *A.antarcticus* is another gem for a carefully chosen site where care and attention can be lavished on the plants: it is a very thin, grey-leaved plant of the most delicate yet erect appearance. In complete contrast are the two plants sometimes sold in garden centres as scorpas grass, but which are in fact both sedges: *Scirpus cernuus*, usually with twin flower-heads and a bract extending beyond the head, and *S.setaceus*, with a usually solitary flower-head with no bract to each fertile culm. Both have acicular, undivided culms, completely leafless, or seemingly so, and a weeping habit of growth, with a gentle floppiness as of newly washed hair. Either species, grown in a damp crevice, would provide a complete contrast to the erect growth of the festucas or *Alopecurus alpinus*.

But, apart from the muted tones mentioned so far, the grasses grown for the colour of their leaves also have a place in the rock garden. There is the gold of *Milium effusum* 'Aureum', best in a slightly shaded situation; the richer, more burnished gold of Bowles's golden sedge, *Carex elata* 'Aurea', which needs a damp crevice in full sun, but with the roots fully shaded and able to tap a deep source of moisture. There is *Carex buchanani*, whose erect growth is such a perfect foil for so many of the mat-forming rock plants; the slightly less brilliant *Carex petriei*; and the most marvellous of all the reddish-coloured sedges, *Uncinia unciniata*, which needs a warm, sheltered spot on the rock garden, but again a site where its roots have access to plenty of moisture. Rarities, too, of whose hardiness it is not possible to be too certain, could be grown in such sheltered corners. *Cladium sinclairii* would be a first choice for such a situation, with its leaves as thick as an iris and presented in much the same manner, but with great heads of heavy, chocolate-coloured flowers. Several *Gahnia* species could be tried here, too: all have seeds that look like little nuts hanging at the ends of almost invisible threads.

Peat-beds, now becoming more and more widely accepted as the natural adjunct of a rock garden, could provide a suitable habitat for several interesting grasses, sedges and even rushes. *Scirpus cernuus* and *S.setaceus* are ideal plants for peat-beds, as are *Carex buchanani* and *C.petriei* (though, because of their colouring, these last two need to be grown over a carpet of *Festuca glacialis* or one of the blue-leaved acaenas). One of the gems of the peat-bed is *Cymophyllus fraseri*, with leaves, as broad as those of an iris, which have serrated edges, and which produces in early spring little white puffs of flowers. It is a plant that is hard to get hold of, and none too easy to maintain in cultivation, but worth every effort. It needs a rich, peaty soil and semi-shade to succeed.

Moving down to the bog area, or to a wet part of a peat garden, there are a great many sedges that will grow well under such conditions, as well as the majority of the rushes. One of the most attractive rushes is *Juncus effusus* 'Spiralis', the corkscrew rush, which never fails to fascinate, looking attractive at all seasons of the year, and particularly coming into its own in winter. Many people find it succeeds better in wet peat or a bog garden than planted as a marginal with its feet actually in the water. *J.effusus* 'Aureo-striatus' is another rush that grows well in wet situations, but does not actually need its feet in water. *J.ensifolius* is a gem for a peat-bed or for a position in a bog garden where there is no danger of its getting overrun by its neighbours. It has flattened leaves like an iris, and jet-black flowers like little maces; it is a dwarf, slowly running plant, growing no more than about 7.5 cm in dryish situations and about 15 cm in wet situations.

The pond itself provides the perfect habitat for many sedges, rushes and especially cat-tails. One of the most stunning of the rushes, for those who have room for it, is *Scirpus lacustris* 'Albescens', the white rush, with its rather startling tall, white leaves. Equally attractive but quite different is *S.tabernaemontani* 'Zebrinus', whose leaves bear horizontal bands of yellow across the background green. It is striking not merely because of the curiosity value of any grass in which the variegation runs in bands around the leaf instead of longitudinally along the leaf, but in its own right.

The cat-tails are always attractive, and no pond should ever be without one, however closely it may need confining in a container. The common *Typha latifolia* is far too vigorous for all but the largest gardens, but there are two dwarf forms of cat-tail that could be accommodated in even the smallest pond. One of these is *T.gracilis*, an almost exact miniature replica of the common cat-tail, with tiny tails borne on stems only about 1 m tall. The other is *T.minima*, the smallest of all, even smaller than *T.gracilis*, but with chubby, rounded cat-tails of a rather foxy-red. With these two miniature gems fairly readily available from garden centres and nurserymen, there is no need for a pond ever to have to be without a cat-tail in autumn.

And if this has not exhausted your curiosity as to just where to grow all those grasses, there remain the house and the greenhouse to be exploited. *Arundo donax* 'Variegata' is the most dramatic of the large grasses, but it needs at least a frost-free greenhouse, and preferably one rather warmer. *Stenotaphrum secundatum* 'Variegatum' is beautiful either in the home or in the greenhouse, especially if it is grown on from year to year until it flows and trails over the side of its pot. The basket grass, *Oplismenus imbecillus*, is the sort of plant that one would dearly like to recommend for house or greenhouse, so graceful is it with its long thin trailing culms and finely variegated leaves, green, white and pink, but the truth is that, although it looks like a tradescantia, it is infinitely more difficult to cultivate, needing not only high temperatures but also high humidity to do well. It is hopeless to try to grow it in any house or apartment that has central heating: the atmosphere will simply desiccate the leaves to paper dryness within twenty-four hours. It is also hopeless to try to grow it in a home without central heating: the cold will kill it. It is ideal as an under-staging plant for a greenhouse where the temperature does not drop below 15°C in winter and which has a high relative humidity. There are several carices, however, especially *Carex morrowii* 'Variegata', which make ideal pot plants for home decoration.

Perhaps the most important thing of all to bear in mind, when planning to use grasses in the garden, is that borders made up of grasses and only grasses are for botanic gardens: where it is beauty you are trying to achieve, the grasses will almost invariably gain from being planted in association with other types of plant. Thus, for example, one might use *Miscanthus sinensis* 'Variegatus' in a setting where it stands in front of a hardy palm, with a silver-leaved plant such as an artemisia on one side of it and a golden shrub, perhaps a small holly or a golden yew, on the other. *M.sinensis* 'Zebrinus', with its unusual gold-banded leaves, looks stunning with a little *Thuya occidentalis* 'Rheingold' beside it or planted at its foot, the gold of the conifer seeming to strengthen the gold in the bands on the leaves of the grass. Another dramatic contrast can be achieved by planting Bowles's purple-leaved *Rumex* next to *Helictotrichon sempervirens*, which has rich, silvery-blue leaves. A different effect can be achieved by planting *Stipa gigantea* at the foot of *Phormium tenax* 'Purpureum' where the evening sun shines from behind the group; it will then seem that the delicate flower of the *Stipa* belongs to the *Phormium*, the effect being most dramatic. It is these sorts of contrasts or complements of foliage type and colour that one wants to look for when using grasses in the garden.

So far as is practicable, the outline of each grass should be seen as clearly as possible, either in silhouette or against a definite background. Each grass should be seen as an entity, complete in itself, but gaining from association with other plants.

# 3 *The Cultivation of Grasses*

Few groups of plants are quite so undemanding in their cultural requirements as the grasses and their relatives. Basically, all that the true grasses demand is a fertile, well-drained soil and an open situation. Given that, together with relative freedom from competition from weeds, they will flourish. The bamboos similarly need a rich, moist soil.

The sedges have similar requirements, but need more water available to their roots. This does not mean that they need bog conditions, but it does mean that they need to be grown in a soil with a very high humus content since such a soil is extremely water-retentive. Only the genus *Cyperus* among the sedges seems happy with its feet actually in water.

The rushes in general need even more water than the sedges. There are only two genera cultivated among the rushes, *Juncus*, the true rushes, and *Luzula*, the woodrushes. *Juncus* are marsh-land plants, ideal for growing in bog conditions or even with their feet in water. *Luzula* is a more adaptable genus. As woodland plants, the majority of them are natives of rich, damp woodlands, where they grow with their roots in accumulations of leaf-mould: the sun seldom penetrates the canopy of tree leaves, and when it shines strongly, the leaves of the woodrushes are protected from direct light. They are also found growing on the edges of rivers and streams, under conditions which are extremely wet but in full sun. In cultivation they will not only tolerate these variations of their growing conditions, but, surprisingly, many species will also tolerate extreme drought under trees.

The cat-tails are the most water-demanding group of all. They are all plants that have adapted themselves to growing with their feet in the water, up to the ankles, and are never really happy growing in drier conditions than these. They will usually grow better if you take the trouble to plant them in mud obtained from a local pond or stream rather than in garden soil.

These are obviously only generalisations. Any specific cultural requirements will be found in the descriptions of the species. There are, however, certain other general cultural points that are worth running over briefly.

Many decorative ornamental grasses are either annuals or so-called horticultural annuals (which are, basically, perennials from warm climates grown as annuals in cold climates). People tend to desist from growing these because they think that it will involve them in a lot of fuss and bother. Nothing could

17

be further from the truth. The seeds of most annual grasses can be sown out of doors wherever the plants are to flower. Most will take as little as two to three weeks to germinate if they are sown in early spring. The best guide as to when to sow annual grasses out of doors is to watch your lawn: it starts growing when spring arrives. Indeed, one definition of spring is that it begins when lawn grasses start to grow. You can sow the seed either broadcast or, which is easier to mark, in shallow drills taken out in a criss-cross pattern over the area where you want the annuals to come up. Once the plants have grown, this criss-cross pattern will be lost and the plants will look very much as though they have grown at random. Seed should be sown very shallowly, and barely covered—it is often better to cover the seed with a little sharp sand than with soil, and some sort of protection should be provided to keep birds away, otherwise they will peck and scratch the seeds up. Chicken wire affords protection, or threads of black cotton stretched between short sticks marking the boundaries of the planting area is another. For most annuals, the seedlings should be thinned so that those left are growing about 30 cm apart.

Where plants are started indoors, the seed should be sown three to five weeks earlier than when sown out of doors: the seedlings can then be planted out at about the same time as you would otherwise be sowing seed. It is well worth starting the seeds of horticultural annuals and half-hardy annuals indoors in this way. Again, when planting out, a space of about 30 cm should be left between plants.

All the annuals do best in a hot, sunny situation. They may need a little light and careful watering in spring if the spring is an exceptionally dry one, but otherwise they seldom need watering, making do quite happily with whatever moisture is available to them, provided they are growing in a reasonably fertile soil. The only real problem likely to occur in cultivating annual grasses is that of finding it difficult to distinguish between the seedlings of the grasses sown and the seedlings of normal weed grasses. In general, this should not prove too much of a snag. So long as you mark clearly the area or areas where the seed of annual grasses has been sown, then you can be sure that the majority of grass seedlings coming up within that patch are the grass you sowed. Any grass seedlings different from the majority of seedlings in that patch are almost certainly weed grasses and should be eradicated.

While it is tempting to allow annual grasses to naturalise themselves, as some will quite readily, the practice is one that is, in general, better avoided. Once you have large quantities of naturalised grasses in the garden, you will find it hard to tell which of the seedlings coming up in spring are seedlings of grasses you want and which are seedlings of weed grasses. Hence it is better to weed out any grass seedlings that come up that are not seedlings from grasses you have sown deliberately.

Seed can easily be collected from the plants you grow in your garden and saved from year to year. Very few of the grasses grown as decorative plants in gardens are hybrids, and very few of the annuals hybridise naturally, so the probability is that if you save seed from one year to the next the strain will remain true. If you have something like *Briza minor* and you want a miniature form of it, it is a simple matter to collect seed from only the smallest plants each year. Over the years you will gradually find the smaller strain evolving—not by natural selection but by deliberate selection. Similarly, if you want a strain of an annual grass that has a more than usually vigorous habit of growth, or one that has a larger flower-head, or a flower-head of a richer colour, simply keep selecting plants with the chosen quality and gathering seed from them in preference to other plants each year. The seed should be stored in a dry and cool place where there is plenty of air circulation. With most annual grasses, a germination rate in the region of 80 per cent can be expected if the seed is sown the year after collecting, but with most grasses, the percentage of seed that will germinate will diminish as the years go by between gathering and sowing. In the second year after gathering, only about 60 per cent of the seed will germinate; in the third year only about 30 per cent; while by the fifth year, practically none will germinate.

The only routine maintenance annual grasses require is periodic weeding. The flower-heads of grasses whose self-seeding capabilities make them potential weeds should be picked off before the seeds shed.

The majority of ornamental grasses are perennials, and as such are usually bought from garden centres and nurseries much like other perennials. They can, of course, be grown from seed, but the main disadvantage of growing grasses from seed is that, whereas perennial grasses bought as young plants (which have usually been propagated by division) will look mature in two to three years, it will take grasses grown from seed five to seven years to achieve the same degree of maturity. On the other hand, with some of the rarer perennial grasses, seed is often the only means by which plants can be obtained at all. Where seed is sown it is best sown in small pots: 5 cm pots are quite large enough. The number of grass seeds that will germinate in a pot this size is quite sufficient for the average garden, and will probably yield more plants than you actually want. The technique where you are raising quite a number of grasses at the same time (and if you are keen on grasses and want to have spares to swap with other enthusiasts you will find yourself raising seedlings of your own rarer perennials all the time), is to get a small propagating tray, about 23 cm by 15 cm, put about six little 5 cm pots into it, and then fill the whole thing with a mixture of equal parts of soilless growing mix and coarse sand or grit. The point is that you do not merely fill the pots, you fill all the spaces between them as well. This method has several advantages: you do not have the fiddle of filling each pot individually (though each pot must be sown individually), and you do not have the problem of individual pots drying out; the whole mass is moist and is kept moist, and you can water it from beneath without disturbing any of the seeds. If the propagator has a clear plastic lid that can be fitted over it, you will very often find that the seedlings germinate before the tray needs watering again. Seedlings should be pricked on into larger pots, two or three to a pot, once they are large enough to handle, and then into individual pots once they have made good growth in the second pot. The seedlings will usually be ready for planting out the first spring after sowing, but with plants that might prove tender it is wiser to grow them on in pots for a second year.

Grasses should always be bought from a nurseryman or garden centre you feel you can rely on. If you buy from a source in which you do not have complete faith, you may find that many of the plants are not true to name, which can be infuriating, and you may find that, before being sent out, the divisions were not sufficiently established at the nursery to establish themselves quickly and easily in your garden. If you are buying grasses from a garden centre, always check the plants over carefully yourself. Try to establish, if you can, that the plant has been named correctly, and look for signs of good cultivation. The plant should be free of weeds, it should be well established in its container. If you take all the culms and gather them together in your hand and lift the plant it should not come out of its container; there should be a sufficiently dense mass of roots to prevent this from happening. Always turn the plant upside down in its container: if it is well established there should be a mass of fibrous roots coming out of the bottom.

As a rule of thumb, grasses are best planted in spring. This gives them the best chance of establishing themselves quickly and growing away strongly. Plants put in the ground in winter seldom get away to a good start. When ordering grasses from a nursery, always ask for spring delivery. When dividing grasses in your own garden, always do this in the spring. Generally, early spring is better than late spring, since late spring is often a relatively dry period and therefore unsuitable.

Where you are planting several grasses of the same species as a group, and you want them to grow together in time, a general rule is that the space between each plant should be the same as the ultimate height to which each plant will grow. Where you want the individual shape of each plant to reveal itself, the distance between plants should be roughly twice the height to which that particular species will grow. Where you are making a mixed planting and want the individual shapes to show themselves, the distance between any two plants can be worked out by adding together their combined heights, then adding half as much again. This is only a rough rule to go by, since some grasses have a relatively upright habit, while others have a sprawling, floppy habit. But the better you know your grasses the easier it will be to judge how much space to give each species; the notes on the individual species should always be consulted for this sort of information before planting.

Generally speaking, grasses will do as well for you as the amount of trouble you go to in preparing their planting sites. Much the same principles should be followed as when planting shrubs. A hole should be taken out at least one and a half times the size of the rootball that is to go into it. The sides of the hole should be straight, and the bottom of the hole flat, with the soil at the bottom broken up. Any soil that is going to be returned to the hole should be improved with moss peat, good garden compost or some really well-rotted farmyard manure—this last especially in the case of the larger-growing species. The plant should be lowered on to a cushion of this improved back-fill soil, and then the space between the rootball and the walls of the hole filled with more back-fill soil. This should be made firm with finger tips or a short stick when it is about a quarter full, about half full and about three-quarters full. Finally, it should be firmed with the knuckles (or, in the case of large species, with the heel) once the space has been filled and the back-fill soil is level with the surrounding soil. The grass should never be planted deeper than it was growing in the nursery. It is generally helpful to leave a slight saucer-shaped depression around the newly planted grass so that rainwater will tend to collect in the region of the rootball rather than being shed away from it. This saucer-shaped depression can be created quite easily by placing the left-over back-fill soil from the original excavation in a ring around the plant. Once this ring has been created, the plant should be watered thoroughly. This is important: it is hopeless to leave the plant in the belief that since it is spring it must rain within the next twenty-four hours; it may not rain for a month or more. So water the plant well in. Then cover the region immediately above the roots with a mulch of organic material: moss peat, garden compost, leaf-mould or shredded pine bark.

It cannot be stressed strongly enough that where you are planting any grass of a spreading nature, especially those described as 'aggressively stoloniferous' or 'with vigorously spreading rhizomes', adequate measures should be taken to contain it. A great many spreading grasses can be adequately contained by the simple expedient of knocking the bottom out of a bucket, sinking the remains of the bucket in the ground, and planting the grass inside that. However, even when this has been done, rhizomes and stolons may creep over the top into the world outside, and so the spread of the grass should be checked annually, and any runners that have come over the rim of the sunken bucket should be removed. Where larger patches are wanted, corrugated iron or its rigid plastic equivalent can be sunk into the ground to a depth of about 60 cm. The rhizomes will quickly find the overlap and escape through that, so some sort of marker should be placed where the material does overlap so that escaping rhizomes can be removed. In the case of some bamboos, however, the growing tip of the rhizomes can be sharp enough to pierce even corrugated iron or rigid plastic, and so can really only effectively be contained in a concrete pipe of the type used in drainage work on motorways. The dangers of allowing 'grasses' of a spreading nature into the garden should not be taken lightly: one of the world's most eminent grass experts allowed the delightful scented *Hierochloë odorata* into his rock garden, with the result that after a few years he had to remake his rock garden, literally rock by rock. It may well be that, in smaller gardens, it is wisest not to allow spreading grasses in at all.

The routine cultivation of grasses involves little beyond keeping them watered during dry spells, and free from weeds. Mulching with organic materials will help on both fronts, conserving moisture on the one hand and suppressing weeds on the other. With those grasses which like it really hot and dry, stone chippings make a far better mulch than organic materials. If any staking or other form of support is needed, this should be provided as unobtrusively as possible. Four cans with some garden twine linking them will be sufficient for most grasses. In general, however, if they are floppy grasses, they probably look better allowed to flop, so long as you have room to allow them to behave in this way.

Most grasses should be cut to ground level each year, preferably after the culms have died back to ground level for the winter. Some people prefer to leave the culms standing through the winter and to do their tidying in spring in the belief that dead culms provide a degree of protection to the crowns of the plants through the winter. But, while there may be a little truth in this where tender plants are concerned, it is generally better to do the tidying in the autumn. If the culms are left standing, they are an open invitation to all sorts of pests and diseases to move in and make them their winter habitation. They may then affect the new growths coming through in spring. Most grasses need to be cut to within about 5 cm of soil in winter. Evergreen grasses are the only ones that are better trimmed in spring rather than in autumn, and with these it may not even be desirable to trim them at all: probably all that is needed is to tidy them up and remove dead leaves from the crowns.

It is important to remember that, whenever you remove the dead culms of grass, you are removing materials that came originally from the soil and so must be replaced. If you are using a regimen of mulching with organic materials, this will usually be sufficient, but if you are mulching with pebbles, then the plants need feeding with bonemeal, fishmeal, hoof-and-horn or dried blood each spring. Several of the blue grasses seem to show their colouring best when grown on a starvation diet, but exceptions such as these are mentioned in the specific notes on the species.

These cultural practices are not particularly demanding in terms of either time or effort, but are well worth while. The reason for giving grasses an annual pruning is not simply that they look unattractive with their dead culms left on them, but that, since all grasses initiate new growth from the base, the presence of the old culms can get in the way of the newly emerging new shoots. This is particularly true of some of the blue grasses which will simply die out in the middle if they are not trimmed in this way.

The propagation of grasses is not at all difficult. The great majority can easily be grown from seed as already described (p. 19), but this method does not produce semi-mature plants at once, and it is not a certain method of increase where variegated grasses are concerned. These must be propagated by division. To divide a grass plant, lift it from the soil, keeping as much earth on the roots as possible. Then cut the plant into pieces the size you need with a sharp knife in the case of most of the smaller grasses, or with a spade in the case of strong-growing grasses such as *Cortaderia* or *Chionochloa*. In theory, at least, a grass plant can be divided into as many new plants as there are culms on the old plant. In practice, it is difficult to get every culm off with a root or root initiation point on it, and it is generally more practicable to divide grasses less severely. It is generally better to get four or five semi-mature plants from the original specimen, and divide again a couple of years later, than to try to get a couple of dozen at one time. If you need a particular grass in quantity, divide each plant into four every other year until you have the quantity you require. The best time to lift and divide a plant is just when the new season's growth is beginning to push its way out of the previous year's sheaths.

The majority of grasses that make good house plants are similarly easy to cultivate. Few are true grasses; most are a species of *Carex* or *Acorus*, which, although they seem to prefer semi-shaded positions in the garden, are not in fact low light intensity plants at all, and need to be given conditions of good light when grown indoors. All they need to do well is a fertile growing mix, preferably one of the soilless growing mixes, regular watering and feeding when they are in growth, and freedom from dirt on their leaves. Although they like to be grown in a soil that is moist, they do need good drainage. The time to apply the water is when the soil in the top of the pot feels dry to the touch. You should then apply water until it starts to run out of the bottom of the pot. Let any free water drain through, and then tip away this surplus. Never leave plants standing in water in the belief that they will reabsorb it. They may, but they are more likely to rot. Occasionally grasses grown indoors become infested with insects, usually aphids or whitefly. If they do, first try to get rid of the insects by washing them off with lukewarm soapy water applied under pressure through a spraying device. If this does not solve the problem, apply Malathion strictly according to the manufacturer's instructions. If the plants are growing in the kitchen, move them to another room while applying the Malathion.

The selective breeding and hybridisation of grasses is something which has up till now been little explored, at least so far as the ornamental grasses are concerned. A tremendous amount has been done with the economically important grasses, especially those grown as cereals. Yet there are two lessons to be learned from the experiences of the breeders of cereals. In the first place, the grasses generally do not hybridise freely, and in the second, when they do, the results, far from showing the phenomenon of hybrid vigour, tend rather to show hybrid weakness. The hybrids in general turn out to be smaller, stunted, weaker versions of their parents. The second lesson is that selection within a species can result in far more dramatic results than attempts at hybridisation.

23

The sort of lines of breeding that might be attempted are improvement of flower size or colour, and improvement of variegation. *Molinia caerulea* 'Variegata' often seems to be a variable plant, and sowing of seed will produce seedlings about 90 per cent of which show no variegation; but of those which do show variegation, some will be inferior to the parent, some equal to it and, if you are persistent and lucky, some will be better than the parent. *Holcus mollis* generally has flowers of a muddyish, slightly purplish colour; but sometimes they are definitely green, and at other times definitely quite a bright red. If seed were to be selected from only red-flowered forms, it might in time be possible to fix a strain with only red flowers. In time the size of the flowers might also be increased and the intensity of the red accentuated. *Deschampsia caespitosa* is grown for the delicacy of its huge but airy flower-heads: selective breeding could well increase the size of these until they became veritable clouds of flower. With some of the *Pennisetums*, both the size and colour of the flowers might be improved by selective breeding.

The actual process of selective breeding can be made to sound very complicated. The anthers of the seed parents have to be removed from a number of florets in one or more of the inflorescences of the plants to be used—a job requiring some skill, a steady hand and acute eyesight. The remaining florets are then cut away altogether, and the inflorescences covered with paper or plastic bags to prevent accidental pollination. That is only the easy part. When the anthers are exserted the bags have to be removed temporarily and the pollen applied by hand with the aid of a camel-hair brush to the female organs, and the bags at once replaced. Pollination must be carried out daily for about a week to create a high degree of probability of obtaining seed, for although an enormous quantity of pollen is produced, it retains its viability for only a very short period. A further complication arises during this process since you have to know at what time of day the particular grass you are pollinating flowers. If you want to work with Timothy grass, you will have to rise at dawn; even meadow fescue and cocksfoot will get you out of bed at 6 a.m. if you are to catch them with their anthers exserted. Other grasses will inconvenience you in other ways: you may have to rush back from the office in the middle of the afternoon to catch the vital moment for them. Yet, while there are problems, they can be simplified.

One effective way of simplifying the process, but one which still requires the emasculation of the flowers, is to put the male and female flowers into the same paper or plastic bag and leave them there until flowering is over. This is more easily accomplished if the plants are being grown in pots than if they are in open beds. The percentage success is perhaps not quite so high as with the hand-pollination method, but it is still high enough to make it worthwhile.

The field for the selective breeding of grasses is so little explored that anyone with time and optimism on their side may well achieve some quite spectacular results within a relatively short period.

24

# 4 *Grasses for Arranging*

The popularity of grasses, especially of dried grasses, in floral arrangements seems to be increasing, and certainly there are grasses which are, when dried, suitable for arrangements of almost every size and style, from the tiniest, daintiest home arrangements to the sizeable arrangements seen in churches and department stores. Perhaps the great appeal of grasses for dried arrangements is not so much their delicacy of form as their subtlety of colouring: they dry to shades of green, brown, russet, yellow or white—colours which blend readily with other colours, especially those most often found in arrangements of dried and pressed flowers.

Most grasses are suitable for picking, and almost all are suitable for drying. The only limiting factor on whether you personally decide to pick a grass or use it in a dried arrangement is whether it fits in well with the sort of arrangements you have in mind. Some grasses are not suitable for drying for one reason or another: *Hordeum jubatum*, the squirrel's tail grass, because the flowers shatter at maturity; much the same is true of the golden top, *Lamarckia aurea*; *Rhynchelytrum repens* is unsuitable on two scores—in the first place its beautiful rosy colouring fades completely on drying, and in the second the flower parts quickly drop off the rachis once dry. Apart from those three exceptions, most grasses will dry and dry well.

And they are worth the little trouble it takes to dry them well, because the real appeal of dried grasses is that, in form at least, they look so similar to the grass when in flower—a characteristic they share in common with most of the plants favoured by flower arrangers for dried arrangements. The secret of success in drying grasses is knowing exactly when to pick them.

The magic time at which to pick a grass so that it will dry most closely to resemble the undried grass, and also so that it will last for the longest possible time, is just at the moment when the inflorescence is emerging from the sheathing leaves. This probably sounds far too early to pick it since it has not at this stage even expanded its inflorescence properly. But it is the crucial moment: because it is the only moment at which you can pick the grass and be absolutely sure that the inflorescence will not shatter as it dries. You can leave the flower-heads on the plant until they are fully expanded, but a flower-head picked at that stage is far more likely to shatter early than one picked at the stage recommended. Certainly the very latest at which it is wise to try to pick a grass intended for drying is when the anthers appear, and it will often take very careful observation to be certain when this is happening. In some cases such observations may prove quite useless: if you have a clone of the pampas grass *Cortaderia selloana* that happens to be a female plant (the male flowers being very few or borne predominantly on separate plants) no amount of watching will ever reveal to you the moment at which that particular plant exserts its anthers. The reason why this moment is so critical is that once the anthers have been exserted, pollination can take place, which means, in effect, that the flowers turn into seeds, and once that has happened they will continue to swell and fragment their outer parts until the seeds fall free; at which stage you no longer have a grass fit to decorate the home. The rule, to summarise, is therefore that the earlier the stage at which you pick a grass, the longer it will last in a dried arrangement.

Another reason for the popularity of dried grasses in arrangements is that they are so little trouble to arrange. They certainly do not require any special equipment, nor do they demand any time-consuming processing. All they need is to be picked and hung upside down in a room that is cool and dark, but in which there is also plenty of air circulation. A draughty, windowless garage is an ideal place. High temperatures are undesirable because they are likely to cause the grasses to shatter in the drying process, while sunlight, especially strong sunlight, will cause the natural colour of the grasses to fade. There may, on the other hand, be occasions when you want the grasses to fade in the sun; in which case, go ahead and put them in sunlight, provided you do not let them get too hot. Where you have grasses much of whose natural elegance comes from the way in which the head curves or bends at an angle to the stem, and where you want to retain this characteristic curvature in the drying process, then rather than hang the cut grasses, simply stand them in a wide-mouthed vase without water, where the heads can hang at their natural angle until dry. Stood in a vase in this way, they will need the same dark, cool conditions and free air circulation that they would need if they were hanging. Most grasses will be dry and ready for use between one and two weeks from the time of picking. If you do not want to use them at once, simply put a large plastic bag loosely over their heads to keep dust off them. The way to tell when grass is dry and ready for using in a flower arrangement is to feel the culms: when these are dry and brittle, then the grass is ready.

A little trick worth knowing is that, since many grasses change colour as they go through the process of flowering and setting seed, it is sometimes possible, by picking them at different stages of their development, to have the same grass dried in two different colours, or at least in two different shades. *Briza media*, for example, has pale green flowers to begin with, which, if picked at this stage, dry a very pale green: later in the season they turn first golden and then reddish-brown, and if picked now will dry to a pale brown: the contrast can be most charming.

26

As to whether the leaves of the grasses should be left on the culms or stripped off, this is partly a matter for the arranger's personal taste, partly a matter of the particular arrangement for which the grasses are intended, and partly a matter of the personality of the grass itself. In some grasses the leaves add such character that it would be a shame to strip them off; in others, the dried leaves look so wretched that it is wisest to strip them completely.

There is another aspect of using dried grasses which is also entirely a matter for personal taste, and that is whether you use them in their natural colours or dyed. Left to their own devices, dried grasses will assume rather muted, autumnal hues, russets, golds, creams, beiges and so on. But if they are dyed they can take on much brighter colours: vivid greens, peacock blues or others according to choice. These brighter colours are often more easily accommodated in modern room settings than are the quieter natural tones.

While several different dyeing techniques can be used with most dried flowers, only one works really well with dried grasses, and this is the hot-dip method. It consists quite simply of dipping the flowers into a boiling solution of a dye of the wished-for colour and a mordant (see below) until the flowers take on the intensity of colour required. Then they can be left to drip dry.

Easy as this process may sound, the main problem most people encounter is finding dyes sufficiently strong to create the desired colour intensities. Normal fabric dyes are certainly not strong enough, and even stronger dyes, like those used on carpets, are seldom effective. The ideal dyes are the aniline dyes, widely used in commercial dyeing practice but not so readily obtainable through normal retail channels. These aniline dyes come in a range of colours through purple, blue, green, yellow and orange. They are usually sold in powdered form, and the colours are much brighter than those of fabric dyes, which tend to produce rather heavy, dull colours.

The dyes, if used on their own, would not be sufficient, however, to produce the desired colour changes in the grasses. The grasses, when dry, contain chemicals which naturally tend to repel wetting and so would reject the dyes. Thus a wetting agent, or mordant, has to be included in the dyeing mix. What the mordant actually does is to allow the dye to penetrate the tissues of the grasses, and so effect the colouring. Readily available mordants are vinegar (acetic acid), stannous chloride and alum (preferably potassium alum rather than ammonium alum). Alum is readily available from chemists and drugstores, and comes in powdered form.

It is difficult to give precise 'recipes' for dyeing solutions, since there are a number of variables: some grasses dye more readily than others; soft water is more effective than hard water; different colours vary in their power of staining the tissues of the grasses; and so on. Only practice and experience can teach you how strong a solution of which dyes to make up for which grasses. Vessels used for mixing these dyes should not subsequently be used for cooking. The following is simply a basic starting recipe:

Take 3.5 litres (1 quart) of water; add 8 teaspoons alum powder; add ½ teaspoonful aniline dye. Bring the water to the boil, add first the alum powder and stir well in, then add the aniline dye, stirring until the liquid is of even colour throughout.

The grasses that are going to be dyed should be clean and firm. There should be no loose fragments on them, and no signs that they are beginning to shatter. If they have reached that stage, plunging them into boiling dye will shatter them at once. If you have a number of culms of the same species to dye, use those that are palest; the paler they are before they are dyed the more intense the resulting colour will be.

The actual dyeing of the grasses is best done in a deep, narrow vessel, so that not only the flower-heads but also the stems can be fully submerged in the dyeing mix. You can either use tongs to hold the stems while submerging them, or else tie a group of culms together with wire and hold the wire while submerging the grasses. Ideally the water should have been brought to the boil, but should be just below boiling point during the actual dyeing.

Different grasses take different lengths of time to take up the dye, and, again, only experience can really teach you which grasses need how long and in which mixture. Some grasses will take up all the colour they need if merely dipped into the dye and taken out again at once; others need to be held under for some time. Unfortunately, there are no golden rules, such as that annuals take only a minute or perennials ten minutes. Even a single species will vary according to the soil on which it has been grown, or the stage of development at which it was picked.

Apart from using dried grasses in floral arrangements, there is another way in which they can be used to charming effect. This is when they are pressed, and made into pictures or used under a sheet of toughened glass at the bottom of a tray or for a table-top. The art probably reached its highest perfection in Edwardian times, and seems now to be little practised, but with the growing interest in ornamental grasses it is a craft that could well be revived.

Grasses to be pressed should be picked at exactly the same moment as grasses for drying. However, some equipment and a little skill is required in pressing them well. Grasses are far too delicate to be dried by the crude methods that are often quite effective for laurel, beech or bracken leaves. They cannot simply be put between sheets of newspaper and placed under the corner of a carpet that is much walked on. A proper press is needed. It is possible to buy herbarium presses, for that is essentially what these are, but they are so simple to make that it scarcely seems worth the bother of finding a store that stocks them.

To make your own press, all you need are two sheets of plywood, either six-ply or eight-ply (which will not warp), and four pairs of nuts and bolts to put through the holes that you will drill in each corner of both pieces of plywood. You then need six pieces of corrugated cardboard and ten sheets of white blotting paper, all the same size as the plywood pieces, but with the squared corners cut off to allow for the bolts. Having acquired these materials, lay first a piece of plywood, then a piece of cardboard, then a sheet of blotting paper, then the grasses, then another sheet of blotting paper, then another sheet of cardboard, then blotting paper, then grasses, and so on until you come to the top piece of plywood, which you tighten down on to the grasses by the wing nuts on the four corners. The press can be made to any size that is convenient: a press 30 cm square is probably suitable to begin with, but larger presses may be needed for more ambitious projects.

Perhaps the most important point to bear in mind when pressing any type of flower is that you should only press one type of plant between any two sheets of blotting paper: the sap from different species could discolour a neighbouring pressing. Great care must be taken in arranging the grasses on the sheets of blotting paper. They should be laid out in such a way that no part of any grass overlaps part of another grass. Anywhere where there is an overlap there will be unwanted indentations in both of the grasses involved. The actual arranging of the grasses on the sheet, in such a way as to get as many pieces into one sheet as possible, twisting and turning here and there, can become as intriguing an exercise as arranging the pressed grasses themselves. People who are very dextrous with their fingers can do most of this arranging by hand, but it is generally easier to move the grasses into position using tweezers.

Once the grasses have been arranged between their sheets of blotting paper, the press should be screwed down firmly. It should then be left well alone for a minimum of four weeks, preferably for six weeks. The longer the grasses are left in the press the better. Some people leave them for as long as six months.

Once the grasses have been pressed they will be completely dry, and that means that they readily absorb moisture from the atmosphere. If you have a lot of material to store, it is best to store it in transparent plastic bags, which can be bought from photographic shops. These, if sealed with a piece of clear sticky tape, will preserve the pressed flowers until you are ready to use them.

Exactly how you use your pressed grasses must remain very much a matter of personal taste. You can use them to make pictures, using a clear adhesive to mount them on artist's mounting board, which comes in a wide range of colours; or you can use smaller pieces on seasonal gift cards. Perhaps the most satisfying way of using them is in the old, traditional ways: under glass on trays, tables or the tops of dressing tables. If you prefer things in a more modern idiom, they could be used on the top of a vanity unit, or laid in acrylic blocks to be used as paperweights or simply for their own decorative qualities. It is really very much a matter of your own taste and inventiveness.

Any grass that can be dried satisfactorily can be pressed satisfactorily, and that in practice means the great majority of ornamental grasses, as well as many of the wild ones.

# 5 Grasses

## STRUCTURE AND IDENTIFICATION

Grasses are the most advanced plants in the world. They have abandoned the meretricious showy floral organs so necessary for survival in insect-pollinated plants and favour economy and wind pollination. The floral parts are reduced to their barest minimum. Indeed in some grasses floral parts are present which are vestigial and on the evolutionary road to disappearing. But such economy of structure means that grasses cannot be described in the usual terms. A special vocabulary has been developed to describe grasses and it is necessary to have some acquaintance with this terminology if one is to identify grasses.

The simplest introduction to the terminology of grasses is to take a fairly common grass and examine its various parts, and then so see how these parts may vary in other types of grasses. The simplest way of telling a true grass from any other sort of plant is that the true grasses always have lance-shaped leaves, arranged in two ranks, alternately on a jointed stem; the leaves always have the veins parallel, and have two distinct parts, the sheath (which sheaths the stem) and the blade (the part that is free from the stem).

The best grass upon which to demonstrate the parts of a grass plant is the oat, *Avena sativa*, partly because it is so widespread, and partly because it is a relatively simple grass in which all the parts are reasonably large, so there is little need to use a hand lens to look at details. If you gather a plant of *Avena sativa* to examine while reading this identification procedure, make sure that it is a complete plant, with roots, stem and flowers intact.

The oat is an annual and therefore within its life cycle has only one growth initiation point: from this the roots will grow downwards, and the stem upwards. The roots of the common oat, as with most annual grasses, are rather fibrous in nature, with no tap root. Above the roots is the stem, haulm or, more properly for grasses, the *culm*, which bears the leaves, flowers and later the fruits. In the oat there is usually only a single culm growing from the roots; in other grasses there may be many culms. The culm itself is formed of several interlocking cylindrical tubes of differing lengths, those nearest the ground usually being longer than those nearer the top of the plant. Each segment of the culm is closed at each end and is entire in itself: in most grasses, if you take hold of one section of the culm and pull the one above it upwards, it will break cleanly away from the segment below, slipping gently out of the furled leaf sheath enclosing it. The point at which one segment of the culm will break away from the next is called the *node*. The position of this node or joint is marked externally on the stem by a slight swelling encircling the culm, and also usually by a slight deepening of the colouring at the node. The hollow portions between the nodes are called *internodes*.

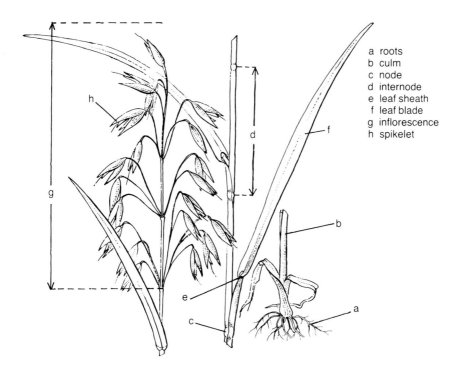

a roots
b culm
c node
d internode
e leaf sheath
f leaf blade
g inflorescence
h spikelet

1 Structure of a grass: *Avena sativa*

The leaves of the oat, as of other grasses, are arranged alternately in two rows on opposite sides of the stem or culm. Each leaf of grass is made up of two parts; the *sheath*, which closely embraces the culm, and the flattened, pointed part which leans away from the culm, which is called the *blade*. Each leaf of grass is initiated at a node. At the point closest to the node (if you break the culm at the node) you will find it very difficult to see which is culm and which is leaf. However, as you move on up the internodal section, the sheath will begin to become apparent, closely embracing the culm but always open on one side. Still further up the internodal section, the sheath will have the appearance of having split open. Sometimes, instead of the appearance of being split open on one side, the sheath appears to have been rolled round the internodal section of the culm. The sheath does not simply continue upwards until it flops

31

away from the culm under its own weight. The blade is clearly differentiated from the sheath by a distinctive structure called a *ligule*. This, in effect, is an extension of the inner surface of the sheath, often forming a small, whitish, shield-like frill. The ligule (which means 'little tongue') is something unique to the grasses: it is possessed only by the true grasses (including bamboos) and by some sedge. It can play an important part in the identification of grasses since it is substantially the same for any given species. The size, shape, colour and position of the ligule in relation to the node enables many grasses to be identified when not in seed or flower.

The growth of grass continues for some time in the internodes, and the manner of growth is interesting. Whereas in most dicots extension growth is added to the growing tip of the plant, it is quite otherwise in the grasses. The part of the culm that makes the extension growth is the part inside the sheath immediately above the node. This is one reason why this part of the culm is so well protected. Not only is it protected from external damage by the sheath, but also by the ligule, which diverts water so that it does not run straight down inside the culm and prevents internal damage such as might be caused by water collecting near the node.

The culm of the oat is highly polished, and again this is typical of most grasses (but not all). This higher polish is acquired because the culms are rich in silica.

At the apex of the culm is the flower of the grass. In the oat this consists of a central axis, itself jointed like the culm, but less noticeably so. Where these almost imperceptible joints occur, the head branches: each stalk of these branches is known as a *pedicel*; at the end of each pedicel is a *spikelet*. A branched flower head of this type is called a *panicle*, but there are several other arrangements of the parts within the heads of the flowers of grasses.

If you now examine the spikelets closely (see Figure 2), you will note that each is made up of two rows of modified leaves or scales on opposite sides of an extremely short, thread-like axis known as a *rachilla* (b). The outermost of these two scales on each spikelet are called *glumes* (c). When they are fresh they are plump and green, but as the flower ripens the glumes become dried, somewhat yellowish and leathery. They are usually rather narrow and pointed. Through much of the development of the spikelet the glumes envelop it and protect it; towards ripening they open. The outer or first to open is the lower glume, and this is followed by the upper glume. These glumes are empty; theirs is a purely protective function.

To examine the spikelet further you need either to push or cut away the glumes: this will reveal two or three slender, tapering structures very similar to the glumes, but smaller, and each composed of two scales. The outer scale of each pair is known as a flowering glume or *lemma* (d). It frequently has a long, shiny projection at its tips, or a bristle on its rounded back: both are known as *awns* (e). The lemma tightly embraces a smaller, narrower, inner scale known as the *palea* (f). This is flattened on its back and is arranged next to the axis of the spikelet. Both structures are, like the glumes, modified leaves, and their prime function is to protect the flower.

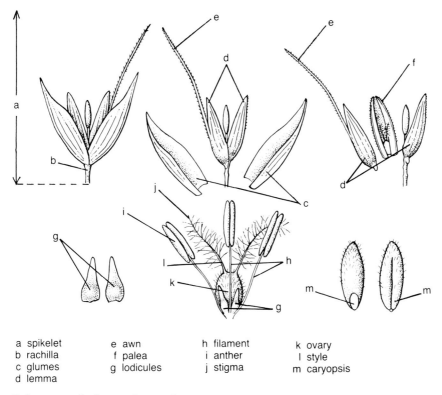

| | | | |
|---|---|---|---|
| a spikelet | e awn | h filament | k ovary |
| b rachilla | f palea | i anther | l style |
| c glumes | g lodicules | j stigma | m caryopsis |
| d lemma | | | |

2 Structure of a flower: *Avena sativa*

To see the flower of the oat you need to prise open the lemma and the palea with a scalpel or needle point. Grass flowers, and the oat is no exception, are usually perfect; that is, they bear both male and female parts, stamens and pistils. They also usually bear greatly reduced calyces and petals, though you will usually need a hand lens to see these: they are tiny, and usually almost translucent—a far cry from the showy flowers of their lily forebears. The floral parts are reduced, but very seldom absent. In the oat the petals are present. They are the two small, narrow scales called *lodicules* (g) which are found inside the lemma and the palea. As flowering time approaches, the lodicules fill with sap, forcing the lemma and palea apart and allowing the flower to emerge. There are then the male stamens: each stamen is made up of a stalk or *filament* (h) at the tip of whcih is a two-celled organ called the *anther* (i) which produces pollen. It has been estimated that a single anther of rye can produce about 20,000 pollen grains. At the centre of this cluster of three filaments is a rounded, hairy body called the *ovary* (k)—the womb, as it were, of the grass flower. At the apex of the ovary are two feathery whitish organs called *stigmas* (j), whose function it is to collect pollen, borne on very short stalks called *styles* (l); the whole female part of the flower is called collectively the *pistil*. Inside the ovary is a single *ovule* which, when fertilised with male pollen, develops into the grain. Properly, the seed of any grass is called a *caryopsis* (m), but most people call them grains or seeds, the term 'grain' being used mainly of those grasses whose seeds are used as cereals.

At maturity, the grain or seed bears on its rounded side at the base a shield-shaped body called the *embryo*. The other side of the grain is grooved, with a dark line in the groove called the *hilum*: this marks the point where the seed was attached to the ovary. The flower or, later in the season, the seed, together with the lemma and palea, make up that part of the spikelet which is properly called the *floret*.

Once the grain or seed is fully ripened, it is shed by dehiscence, and since the parent plant is, in the case of the oat, an annual, it then dies, relying on its progeny to carry on the race.

The diversity of grasses has already been stressed, and this is as true of their structure as of anything else about them. While the basic structure of all grasses remains very much as has been described for the oat, the variations on the theme are many, and it is these variations that give grasses such a wide range of uses in the garden.

While it might seem logical to examine the different parts of the plant over which variation can occur quite literally from the ground upwards by starting with the roots, it is, in fact, quite impossible to separate the type of root growth from the general habit of growth of the plant itself.

Grasses may be annual, biennial or perennial. There are two main areas of difference between the three categories. In the annual and biennial grasses, there is a remarkable consistency of root type. There is no tap root (there never is in grasses), but there is a mass of usually fine, rarely coarse, roots. The top growth is also consistent in that all or nearly all of the culms bear flower-heads, whereas in perennial grasses a greater or smaller proportion of the culms may be purely vegetative, without flowers.

While annuals and biennials are generally tufted in plant form, sometimes densely tufted, more commonly loosely tufted, and rarely approaching a form with a solitary culm, the plant form of perennial grasses varies much more widely. Probably the commonest perennial plant form is the loosely tufted type, though the densely tufted type seems almost as common. There are interesting differences, however, in the mode of growth of each. Both have fibrous root systems, usually finely fibrous, only occasionally coarsely fibrous, and the root fibres are produced at the base of each of the basal nodes of the culms. Both increase the size of their tufts by a type of internal division of the number of culms growing from any one rooting point, but in the case of densely tufted perennials the young shoots, called *innovations*, are produced inside the basal enveloping sheath: this is called an *intravaginal* mode of growth. Once the innovations have achieved some size they simply split open the old sheath, and new roots are formed from the basal nodes of the new shoots. In the case of loosely tufted perennials, the innovations grow through the sides of the enveloping sheath, and this is therefore known as an *extravaginal* mode of growth. The new roots are then initiated through the sides of the old leaf sheaths. The *intravaginal* mode of growth is typical of all densely tufted perennials, for example *Festuca ovina*, while the extravaginal mode of growth is typical of all loosely tufted perennials, for example *Holcus lanatus*.

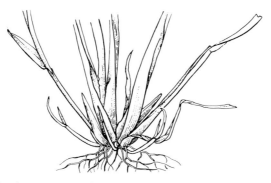

3  Grass multiplying by extravaginal innovations: *Holcus lanatus*

Many perennial grasses have a spreading mode of growth, some like *Agrostis stolonifera* being mat-forming, others like *Phragmites australis* forming large stands. There are several different mechanisms by which grasses can spread vegetatively, but the two commonest are by rhizomes or by stolons. The two should not be confused. A rhizome is properly an underground stem, and as such is very much an extension of any existing root system; a stolon is an over-ground creeping stem which roots at the nodes, and as such is very much a part of the top-growth of the plant and not a part of its root system. Stolons are probably the commoner of the two modes of growth, being an ideal vegetative method of colonising ground. Rhizomes seem to be pretty well confined to those grasses which inhabit wet places, especially bogs, fens and the like, the rhizomes pushing easily through the soft growing medium. *Agrostis stolonifera* is a typical stoloniferous grass. Only a relatively small proportion of its culms bear flower-heads, the rest being vegetative. The great majority of these vegetative culms will either keel over under their own weight, rooting from node to node as this logging process goes on along the length of the stems, or else send out culms virtually horizontally, the sole intention of these culms being to root at their nodes wherever they touch the ground. Each node which roots will then produce a new plant which can be detached and grown as a separate individual.

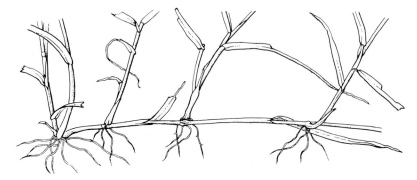

4 Grass multiplying by stolons: *Agrostis stolonifera*

Rhizomes originate from the root system of the plants, and are definitely root-like structures rather than culm-like structures. If you are in any doubt at all as to whether a horizontal vegetative extension growth is a stolon or a rhizome, the differences to look for are these: stolons bear complete, green leaves complete with sheath and blade at each node; rhizomes develop only scale-like vestigial leaves at the nodes. There are, in fact, two distinct types of rhizomes found among grasses (as well as in sedges): those which are known as *sympodial* and those which are known as *monopodial*. A sympodial rhizome is one in which the growth of the rhizome terminates in a flowering culm; further growth of the rhizome then begins anew from a lateral bud on the node from where the flowing culm arose from the rhizome. A monopodial rhizome is one in which growth continues to be made year after year from the same apical growing-point regardless of how many nodes may be formed along the length of the rhizome or how many of these nodes give rise to either a vegetative or flowering culm. Clearly the monopodial rhizome is potentially more likely to spread far and fast than the sympodial type. *Poa pratensis* is a typical example of a grass spreading by means of sympodial rhizomes, while *Carex arenaria* is typical of a sedge spreading by means of a monopodial rhizome. It is, in passing, just because so many of the carices do have this monopodial type of rhizome that some are such notorious land-grabbers. Many bamboos and grasses spread with similar vigour.

There are four other modes of vegetative increase worth mentioning, one because it is something of a misnomer, the other three because they are intrinsically interesting or curious. The first is what is loosely called a 'runner'. A runner is basically a culm which happens to have a more or less horizontal mode of growth and which also happens to produce roots and culms at the

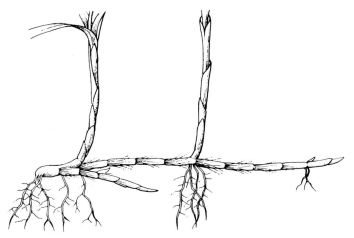

5  Grass structure, monopodial rhizome: *Carex arenaria*

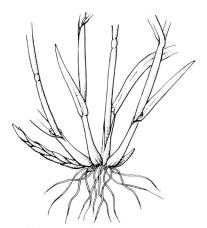

6  Grass structure, sympodial rhizome: *Poa pratensis*

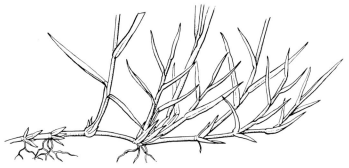

7  Grass multiplying by runners: *Cynodon dactylon*

nodes: it very often tends to produce these roots at the nodes whether or not they are in contact with the ground. A runner is thus an organ that has never quite evolved itself into either a stolon or a rhizome, but something between the two. However, since the majority of its characteristics are those of a stolon, it is probably better included within that definition. *Cynodon dactylon* is typical of a plant that produces runners, which are, as even a quick glance will show, not strictly stolons.

A curious mode of vegetative reproduction is found in *Phleum bertolonii*, in which a proportion of the basal internodes become so swollen that they closely resemble bulbs. If detached from the parent plant they will grow on into mature plants and themselves produce these curious bulb-like swollen internodes.

A far more rapid method of vegetative reproduction is found in onion couch, *Arrhenatherum elatius* var. *bulbosum*, in which it is not merely the basal internodes but virtually every node on the plant which are capable of forming a bulb-like organ from which a young plant will grow. The method is a curious but effective one, especially when it is borne in mind that, with very few exceptions, the culms of perennial grasses are of merely annual duration: at the end of the growing season the withered culm falls to the ground, the leaves decay, but the nodal bulbs overwinter to produce new plants in spring. This mode of reproduction appears to have been adopted mainly by plants in which the fertility of the flowers seems to have been lost or to be poor.

Perhaps the most curious of all modes of vegetative reproduction found among grasses is the viviparous habit. In this the flowers are replaced by young plants, or at least seem to be. What, in fact, would appear to happen is that in these grasses the spikelet axis continues to grow from the tip, bearing a succession of small leaves and in effect forming a miniature plant; the spikelet axis tip grows right through this miniature plant and then flowers, the flowers being much reduced and usually overlooked. The weight of these miniature plants causes the culms to bend under their weight till they touch the ground. Occasionally the miniature plants detach themselves under their own weight from the culm and fall to the ground. In either event, in true viviparousness these miniature plants should then root and grow on to form new, mature plants. In fact, only a very small proportion of those which touch the ground root and grow on, and this lends support to the idea that these plants are merely proliferous growths rather than truly viviparous. The phenomenon is curious, and such plants are avidly sought by grass buffs. The condition is found in *Deschampsia alpina, D.caespitosa, Festuca vivipara, Poa bulbosa, P.alpina* and others.

The culms seem to be about the least variable part of the grasses. They may be erect or prostrate, or they may ascend from a curved or prostrate base. The thickness of the culms can vary from thread-like narrowness to the thickness of a man's thumb or more. They can also vary in their rigidity, some being quite unbending and almost stiff while others are flexible and bend gracefully in the wind. The number of nodes may vary not only from species to species but from plant to plant within a species or even on a single plant. The culms are almost invariably cylindrical and hollow (though in *Poa compressa* they are somewhat flattened, and in the bamboo *Chusquea culeou* they are solid, not hollow). In general the culms are single and undivided, but occasionally, as in the bamboos, they branch, the branches developing from buds in the axils of the leaf sheaths.

A far greater diversity is found in the leaves of grasses. As has already been explained, the leaves of grass are made up of two, or more properly, three parts, the sheath, the ligule and the blade, each of which can vary in several ways. The purpose of the sheaths is to protect the growing points of the young shoots. There are two basic types of sheath, those which are rolled and have free margins and those which are cylindrical. The way to find out which any type of grass has — and it can be important in identifying certain species — is to take a basal shoot and strip it of all but the innermost leaf sheath, and then to pull the young leaf blade gently from side to side. If the sheath is of the rolled type (that is, if it has free margins), the movement of the blade will cause the free margin to move over the rolled part of the sheath: if the sheath is cylindrical, this movement will simply tear the sheath, usually near the top. All species of *Bromus*, *Glycera* and *Melica* have cylindrical sheaths. The sheaths are often, but not invariably, provided at the base with a swollen ring of soft tissue called the *sheath-node*.

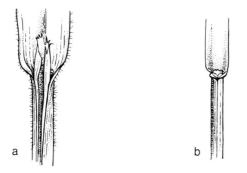

8 Two sorts of leaf sheath: (a) cylindrical, (b) rolled

The way in which the young leaf is folded inside the sheath is interesting, and there is a curious correlation between the type of sheath and the manner of folding. In some grasses the blade is folded within the sheath longitudinally along its middle nerve: in others it is rolled longitudinally with one margin innermost. In grasses where the leaf blade is rolled within the sheath, the sheath is of the cylindrical type; in grasses where the blade is folded along the middle nerve, the sheath is of the free-margin type, with the sheath frequently keeled on the back.

The ligules are fascinating structures found on almost all grasses (including bamboos) and on many sedges. The ligule is basically a shield-shaped membrane growing on the upper edge of the point where the blade and the sheath meet. In many grasses it is very small, almost transparent, while in others it is much more substantial and clearly green or white in colour. Its degree of rigidity can vary considerably, being at least a flimsy structure, at most an almost horny structure capable of inflicting a cut. Frequently the ligules are strengthened by fibres, but quite often they are merely hairy on the back. In some cases they are completely hairless. In a few genera the ligules seem to be absent except for a small fringe of hairs. Only in one grass, the cockspur grass *Echinochloa crus-galli*, is the ligule completely absent.

The blade of the grass is what is usually referred to as its leaf. In general, the blades of grasses are long, narrow, with the sides parallel for much of their length, tapering towards the end, and with either a pointed or a blunt tip. Occasionally the blade merges imperceptibly into the sheath, but more usually they are clearly differentiated at the ligule. There is often a change of colour, albeit a slight one, at the junction, and frequently there is a slight constriction of the blade. In many species there is a distinct collar, usually of a different colour, at the junction of blade and sheath. The blade can vary in several other ways, chiefly in its shape and in its degree of hairiness. It may be completely smooth, as in rye grass or bent grass: it may be softly hairy as in the soft brome, and densely but softly hairy as in the Yorkshire fog. In *Alopecurus lanatus*, the hairiness of the blade has become a virtual woolliness. In some grasses the hairiness is of a more bristly nature, the hairs being sharp enough and rigid enough to cut the hand if drawn the wrong way along the edge of the blade: this is especially true of pampas grass. The blade itself may be obtuse, linear-lanceolate, lanceolate, linear, setaceous or terete. The tip may be obtuse, obtuse-hooded (as in *Sesleria albicans*), acute or acuminate. Still other leaf forms will be found when we discuss the sedges and the rushes.

The part of grass plants that most people refer to as the flowers are in fact inflorescences, which are groupings of flowers. The actual flowers themselves are really tiny and, except at flowering time, completely hidden within the scales of the spikelets. The arrangement of the flowers within the inflorescence can vary enormously, not only in the general structure of the influorescence, but also its density. There are, however, only three basic forms of flower-head in grasses, though the degree of variation which occurs within these three forms can make the underlying simplicity of the structures difficult to determine. In those grass flower-heads in which the spikelets are borne on stalks on branches from the main stem or axis, the flower-head is called a *panicle*. If the spikelets grow on stalks directly attached to the main axis, then the flower-head is called a *raceme*. Where the spikelets grow actually on the main axis without any intervening stalk, the flower-head is known as a *spike*. The inflorescence of *Briza media* is a typical panicle; that of *Brachypodium sylvaticum* a typical raceme; and that of *Lolium perenne* a typical spike.

9 Two sorts of inflorescence: (a) panicle, *Brizia media*, (b) spike, *Lolium perenne*

However, the story does not end there, since a panicle may be loose or contracted, narrow or dense: it may also be one-sided, carry the spikelets in two distinct rows, or have branches wandering off in all directions from the axis. Narrowly contracted spikelets are said to be spike-like, as in *Phleum pratense*; the inflorescence of *Lagurus ovatus* is said to be dense, spike-like; while the multi-fingered inflorescence of *Cynodon dactylon* is said to be composed of digitate spikes.

The spikelets themselves are of great interest to agrostologists in the identification of species and genera, but of rather less interest to anyone growing grasses for purely decorative purposes. The spikelet of the oat as described earlier is fairly typical of the great majority of garden grasses. The spikelets of these grasses normally possess two glumes at the base, with one or more florets above, each with a lemma and palea enclosing a bisexual flower (that is, a flower made up of both stamens and pistil). There are exceptions, and some of the spikelets of *Holcus*, *Hierochloë* and *Arrhenatherum* will be found to contain only male flowers, while the lower two florets of the spikelets of *Anthoxanthum* are normally found to be barren. In the pampas grass *Cortaderia selloana* this character is very pronounced, any one plant bearing predominantly male or predominantly female spikelets, it being exceptional to find a genuinely bisexual plant. An extreme variation on the theme occurs in *Zea mays*, where each sex is borne in a distinct flower-head, the male spikelets being borne in the terminal panicle, the female spikelets in thick spikes in the axils of the leaves.

The flowering of grasses is in itself something of a curious phenomenon, few other plants being quite so rigidly set in their habits. The great majority of grasses flower through May, June and July, though there are front runners in flower as early as January, while species of *Molinia*, *Phragmites* and *Spartina* extend the flowering season into November. Most species of grasses have their own particular hour of the day for flowering—though the timing may be advanced or retarded by daily variations in weather conditions. Many species flower only in the morning (usually between 4 and 9 a.m.). Others flower only in the evening (usually between 3 and 7 p.m.). A few flower at midday. In any event, the actual period in any one day during which the flowers of a particular species are open is surprisingly short. If a morning-flowering grass misses its flowering 'slot' because, say, of a thunderstorm, it will wait till the same time the following day to open its flowers rather than flower in the afternoon instead. There are only one or two species which flower twice in the same day, *Holcus lanatus* being one of these: its flowering times are 5 till 10 a.m., then 5 till 7 p.m. It all sounds rather like feeding time at the zoo, and, indeed, the reasons why grasses have adopted the strictly regulated mechanisms for their flowering may well be connected with the times of day most propitious for pollination. The grasses, with only a very few exceptions, are wind-pollinated, and there is a statistical probability that there will be more wind in early morning or at dusk than at midday. It may be as simple as that; it may be infinitely more complex. The reasons for the rhythms of flowering in grasses are not yet well understood.

While the great majority of grasses are what is called *chasmogamous*, that is, they open their florets for the exsertion of the stigmas and anthers, there are quite a number of species which are *cleistogamous*, that is, they do not open their flowers at all, self-pollination taking place within the closed flower. This phenomenon is normally found only in the annual grasses, since it is usually only the annual grasses which are self-fertile; even then, they are usually only self-fertile when they have to be, this facility being merely a fail-safe device to ensure continuation of the species when cross-fertilisation has failed to take place. Most perennial grasses are self-sterile: they would rather not produce seed at all in a year when they do not get cross-pollinated than resort to self-fertilisation: but then, being perennials, there is always another year, another chance, which is not the case with the annual grasses.

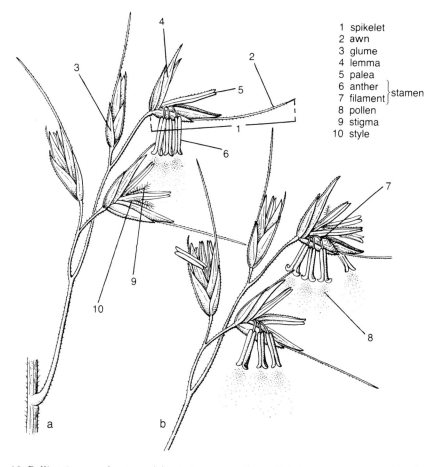

1 spikelet
2 awn
3 glume
4 lemma
5 palea
6 anther  } stamen
7 filament }
8 pollen
9 stigma
10 style

10 Pollination mechanism: (a) at stage one, the spikelets are open, exposing the stamens of one and the stigmas of another; (b) only when the stamens of the first spikelet have shed all their pollen will the stigmas of the same spikelet become receptive

## A-Z of Grasses

### AEGILOPS L.

A genus of about 20 species of annual grasses from dry, stony places in the Mediterranean and Middle East to Pakistan, grown for the typically bristly inflorescence, which is excellent for drying and dyeing. Leaves usually flat; inflorescence a slenderly linear raceme bearing single spikelets at the nodes of the axis, all bisexual, usually falling entire but sometimes shattering from the top. Spikelets 2–8-flowered; glumes equal oblong to ovate, truncate, toothed, with 7–13 parallel nerves, rounded on the back, 1–5 awned; lemmas rounded on the back, usually 1–3 awned. The species show considerable variation and the genus has been divided by some authors into 6 sections. Sow seed in spring out of doors in a sunny position where plants are to grow.

### *A.ovata* L.: Annual goat grass

Compact, tufted annual up to 30 cm in the wild, usually about half that in cultivation in the UK. Culms usually several, erect, sometimes decumbent at the base becoming erect; rather slender, the nodes conspicuous. Leaf sheaths rounded at the back, sometimes slightly inflated, loose-fitting, especially near the base. Leaf blades up to 10 cm long, 6 mm across, flat in section, narrowing to an obtuse point; hairy. Inflorescence, produced April to June, a compact spike up to 2.5 cm long, composed of from 2–4 spikelets, of which only the lower two are fertile, the other or others being rudimentary. The inflorescence has extremely long, rough awns (up to 38 mm) and nut-like spikelets.

### AGROPYRON Gaertn.

A genus here understood in the narrow sense and embracing only species with keeled glumes and more or less pectinate racemes. The blue-leaved ornamental species are here treated in *Elymus* q.v.

### *A.repens* (L.) Beauv.: Couch, twitch, quick, scutch, quack grass

Perennial rapidly spreading by means of invasive, wiry rhizomes. A ubiquitous and noxious weed. H1.

### AGROSTIS L.

A genus of about 220 species of annual and perennial grasses, many from open grassland habitats but occasionally from lightly wooded places throughout the temperate regions and high mountains in the tropics. It is nearly related to *Calamagrostis*, the boundary with which is fairly arbitrary. The genus contains many species of importance in pasturelands, while several of the fine-leaved species (*A.capillaris*, for example) are important ingredients of good turf. One or two of the annual species are ornamental, grown for their delicate, open panicles: these are also excellent for drying. Seed should be sown sparingly in spring out of doors in a sunny position.

Panicle diffuse or sometimes contracted; spikelets without rachilla extension, laterally compressed, with floret; glumes equal or unequal as long or longer than floret, shiny, 1-nerved; lemma cartilaginous, with 3–5 nerves, truncate, with the nerves running out at the edges and forming lateral awns, and sometimes with a sharply bent dorsal awn; palea shorter or much shorter than lemma; rachilla elongate.

### *A.nebulosa* Boiss & Rent.: Cloud grass

Loosely tufted annual to 38 cm when in flower. Culms extremely slender, wiry, dark green, shiny, the nodes markedly swollen, brownish-purple in colour. Leaf sheaths rough; mid-green. Leaf blades up to 10 cm long, 1.3 cm wide; rough; mid-green. Inflorescence, produced July to August, a very loose, diffuse, wide-spreading panicle with 10 or more very long basal branches, up to 15 cm long, about two-thirds as much across. Grown for its light, airy inflorescences, which are huge in comparison with the foliage. Flower-heads last well. Not suitable for dyeing.

## AIRA L.

A genus of about 8 species of annual grasses from Europe and the Mediterranean through to Iran, natives of open places on dry, sandy soils. They are closely allied to *Deschampsia*, but differ in being annuals not perennials. They are cultivated for their open, airy panicles which are also often picked for drying and are much used in bouquets. Sow seed in spring in an open or partly shaded position.

Leaves sometimes rolled. Panicles open or sometimes contracted; spikelets laterally compressed, 2-flowered, the lower flower stalked, the upper stalkless; glumes equal or nearly so, longer than the florets which they enclose, lemmas lanceolate, with 5 nerves, rounded, bilobed at the tip, with a geniculate, dorsal awn arising from the lower half. Grain fusiform, with longitudinal grooves.

### *A.caryophyllea* L.: Silvery hair grass

Tufted annual or biennial to 30 cm with slender stems. Inflorescence, produced May to June, a large, loose panicle with widely spreading branches. Spikelets silvery or purplish.

### *A.elegantissima* Schur.: Hair grass

Tufted annual to 30 cm with slender stems. Panicles very diffuse, the branches loosely divided, the branchlets very slender. Flowers May to June. Creates a most delicate effect.

## ALOPECURUS L.: Fox-tail grasses

A genus of about 35 species of annual or perennial grasses from the north temperate zone and South America, natives of damp meadows and stony slopes, popularly known as fox-tail grasses from the similarity of the inflorescence to a brush. The meadow fox-tail, *A.pratensis*, is a good pasture grass, while a black grass, *A.myosuroides*, is a *common* weed: in some species the spikes are good for picking but only one or two are really good ornamentals. *A.bulbosus* is a curiosity in that the lowest internode swells into a bulb-like, perennating organ.

Leaves usually hairless. Panicle spike-like, cylindrical or capitate; spikelets laterally compressed; glumes equal, the lower part united at the margin, longer than and enclosing the floret; strongly keeled; lemma translucent, running together at the lower margins, with a straight or geniculate, dorsal awn; palea small or absent.

### *A.antarcticus* L.

Enchanting dwarf blue grass, rare both in the wild and in cultivation. Pieces of this grass have been found among the stomach contents of mammoths many millennia old preserved in ice. A dwarf perennial, with slowly creeping rhizomes, to 30 cm, occasionally taller. Culms erect, somewhat stiff; slender, smooth blue. Sheaths smooth, blue, somewhat inflated in the upper part. Blades to 23 cm long, flat in section; rough above, smooth beneath. Inflorescence, produced July to October, a dense, spike-like panicle.

Grown for its erect blue foliage. Difficult to cultivate. Scree or moraine; full sun; propagate by division. H1.

### *A.lanatus* Sm.: Woolly fox-tail grass

One of the gems of the grass world. As difficult to maintain in cultivation as it is to obtain at all. A densely tufted perennial to about 10 cm. Culms erect, rather stout; blue, densely covered in white, woolly hair. Leaf sheaths rounded, blue, densely covered in white, woolly hair. Leaf blades up to 5 cm long, 6 mm wide, U-shaped in section; extraordinarily thick, narrowing to an abrupt point; blue, densely covered in white, woolly hair. Inflorescence, produced March to June, a very dense, spike-like panicle, erect, ovoid, thickly beset with silky hairs.

A native of dry scree slopes in Spain, it needs an extremely gritty soil—at least equal parts of grit to soil, and a layer of chippings around the collar to prevent collar-rot. Keep winter wet off the crown by covering with a pane of glass. Best in a trough or alpine house. Extremely slow to increase. Divide established plants very carefully. H3.

### *A.pratensis* L.: Common fox-tail grass, Fox-tail grass, Lamb's-tail grass, Meadow fox-tail grass

The typical plant is of little garden merit, but the 2 yellow-variegated forms are among the brightest and showiest of grasses.

A densely tufted perennial with slowly but persistently creeping rhizomes.

46

Culms erect, or at first decumbent becoming erect; fairly slender with relatively few nodes; smooth; green or green becoming whitish higher up. Leaf sheaths smooth, cylindrical, split, somewhat inflated, the basal part turning brown, the upper part becoming green or greenish-white. Leaf blades flat in section, evenly narrowing to a fine point, varying from rough to smooth. Inflorescence, produced April to May, a very dense, cylindrical, blunt-topped panicle, soft to the touch, green or purplish.

One of the easiest grasses to accommodate. Grows well in sun or partial shade, in any fertile, well-drained soil, but dislikes extremely poor, dry soils. The coloured leaf forms are best clipped over in early summer to prevent them from flowering and to keep them low: this clipping seems to keep the colour strong throughout the growing season. Clipped plants will spread to form dense, attractive ground-cover. On heavier soils, they are better divided and replanted every 2–3 years. If planted closely, the division will quickly cover the ground. Increase by division in spring. H1.

### A.p. 'Aureo-variegatus'
By far the brightest gold-striped grass in cultivation, the leaves being faintly striped yellow with broad margins of deep, rich gold, this golden edging continuing the same width all along the leaf so that the narrower part of the leaf, towards the tip, is entirely gold.

### A.p. 'Aureus'
Believed to have arisen as a sport of *A.p.* 'Aureo-variegatus'. Leaves entirely gold with just a hint of a green mid-nerve. Even more dramatic than the variety of which it is a sport, but hard to obtain.

### A.p. glaucus
The leaves have a distinctly glaucous bloom to them. Superior to the type plant from a garden point of view.

## ANDROPOGON L.
A genus of 100 or so species of annuals and perennials, mainly from the tropics, where they are one of the dominant savanna genera. They tend to have coarse, unattractive foliage, and so are not particularly ornamental. One or two species are sometimes grown, and these need a sheltered position in full sun, and a good, fertile soil.

Leaves never aromatic. Inflorescence usually a pair of racemes or sometimes the racemes palmately arranged. Spikelets dissimilar, the sessile spikelet laterally or dorsally compressed, with 2 florets; the lower floret reduced to a transparent lemma; the upper floret bisexual; the pedicelled spikelet male or sterile, large or vestigial, awnless or with a long, fine hair.

47

### *A.gerardii* Vitman

A large, coarse grass grown for its bold glaucous foliage. Robust perennial up to 2 m forming tufts, sometimes with stolons. Culms erect, sparingly branched. Blades flat, up to 1 cm wide, the margins rough and both sheaths and blades bearing shaggy hairs. Inflorescence, produced May to July, racemose, on a long stalk, purplish. H5.

### *A.scoparius* Michx.: Little bluestem

A North American bunch grass grown partly for its rather glaucous foliage and its good foxy-red autumn colouring, but also for its rather curious inflorescences which can look attractive in dried arrangements. In its native country, it forms one of the wild hays of the Great Plains and is cultivated as a forage grass.

A rather erect, densely tufted perennial with slowly spreading, rhizomatous roots, growing up to 1.2 m in its native North America, rather less in the UK. Culms erect, or at first decumbent, becoming erect; smooth; blue-green. Leaf sheaths rigid; hairy. Leaf blades up to 50 cm long, 1 cm wide, flat in section, somewhat hairy, tending to be erect or slightly curled, seldom arching; blue-green. Inflorescence, produced August to October, a sparse panicle, the branches of which bear racemes singly, blue-green at first becoming foxy-red. Grows best in light, sandy, well-drained soil in full sun. Increase by seed or division. H2.

## ANTHOXANTHUM L.

A genus of 10 or 15 annual or perennial grasses widespread through temperate Eurasia and Africa including the tropical mountains, and central America, natives of meadows and dry grasslands. It is close to *Hierochloë* (q.v.) and like it has sweetly scented coumarin. One annual species is sometimes grown. Seed should be sown in spring out of doors in an open, sunny position.

Panicle dense; spikelets, lanceolate, laterally compressed; the 2 lower florets replaced by empty lemmas; glumes unequal, the upper enclosing the florets; sterile lemmas longer than fertile, bilobed; with a short awn, the upper one with a bent awn arising from below the middle.

### *A.gracile* Bivon

A slender, tufted annual to 30 cm with short, linear leaves drawing to a slender point, more or less hairy above, the ligules much-torn and ragged. Panicle, produced in April, spike-like, ovate, few-flowered. Not in the first rank of ornamental grass but useful for its scent.

## APERA Adans.

A genus of 3 species of annuals from Europe and Asia, generally plants of dry, sandy soils but also common as weeds in cultivation. They are ornamental because of their open, airy panicles, and are easily grown in ordinary soil in a sunny place. Seed should be sown in the open in spring.

Panicle open; spikelets laterally compressed, with one floret; glumes unequal, the upper about equal or a little more than the floret, 3-nerved, shortly awned; lemma papery, 5-nerved, with a long, flexible awn arising near the apex.

### *A.interrupta* (L.) Beauv.: Dense silky-bent
Annual to 60 cm, culms slender, erect; leaves smooth, narrow, evenly tapering. Panicle produced June–July, spikelets green or purple with fine awns.

### *A.spica-venti* (L.) Beauv.: Loose silky-bent, Silky bent, Wind grass
A delicate-looking grass of reasonably robust habit, cultivated as much for its flowers which are remarkable for the whorled arrangement of the spikelets, as its autumn colour, the whole plant turning a glowing foxy-red.

A loosely tufted annual of rather upright growth. Culms several or solitary, usually erect, sometimes at first decumbent and becoming erect; rather slender; nodes well-defined, smooth. Leaf sheaths green or purplish, usually smooth, sometimes becoming rough in the upper portion. Ligules conspicuous, up to 8 mm long. Leaf blades up to 25 cm long, 8 mm wide, usually rough above, smooth below, sometimes entirely rough; green. Inflorescence, produced June to August, a much-branched, rather diffuse panicle, the branches presented in whorls around the axis; green or purplish.

## ARRHENATHERUM P.Beauv.
A genus of some 6 species of perennial grasses from Europe, North Africa and Asia, natives mainly of dry grasslands. Very close to *Helictotrichon*, from which it differs in its theoretically dimorphic florets. In practice the dimorphism varies so greatly that two genera could well be one. A white-variegated form of one species is sometimes cultivated and is most ornamental. It needs no particular conditions.

Leaves rolled when young, opening flat, scarcely ribbed. Basal internodes often swollen into more or less spherical forms. Panicle dense; spikelets somewhat laterally compressed, 2-flowered, the lower floret male with a strong, sharply bent awn arising from the lower part of the back of the lemma, or with only a rudimentary awn: sometimes both florets bisexual and awned; glumes unequal, the upper as long as the spikelet; lemmas leathery, rounded, doubly toothed, the lower one bearing a sharply bent dorsal awn.

### *A.elatius* (L.) J. & C. Presl.: Bulbous oat grass, False oat grass, Onion couch, Tall oat grass
The typical form of this European native, apart from being among the dullest of grasses, is exceedingly invasive, as is the variety or subspecies *Arrhenatherum*

*elatius* var. *bulbosum*, sometimes known as onion couch from its habit of forming bulbs at the base of the stems, which, when they fall, root readily. The variegated form of the bulbous subspecies makes an attractive plant.

Loosely tufted perennial with slowly spreading rhizomes, 1 m when in flower. Culms erect or somewhat spreading, rather stout; usually smooth, but sometimes hairy at the nodes. Leaf sheaths rounded on the back, smooth. Leaf blades up to 40 cm long, 1 cm wide, flat in section; slightly hairy above, smooth beneath. Inflorescence, produced June to September, a narrow panicle, erect or nodding, and when nodding tending to be somewhat but never entirely 1-sided. H2.

### *A.e.* var. *bulbosum*

Differs from the type in the swollen bulbous bases of its stems. If the plant is cut to ground level immediately after flowering this will reveal a mass of old and new bulbils on and in the soil around it. H2.

### *A.e.* var. *bulbosum* 'Variegatum'

Leaves striped and conspicuously margined clean white, holding the variegation well throughout the year. Far less vigorous than the type, growing to no more than 30 cm tall, and with much narrower leaves. Needs frequent division to remain robust. H2.

## ARUNDO L.

A genus of perhaps 3 species of tall, robust perennial, reed-like grasses, widespread in river margins and wet places from the Mediterranean to China. Though similar in general appearance to *Phragmites* the two genera are not especially closely related. Some species make striking foliage plants. They need to be grown in rich, preferably damp, soil in a warm, sheltered place.

Growth reed-like; roots coarse and knotted; leaves always cauline, flat. Panicle large, loose, plumose; spikelets laterally compressed with few, usually bisexual, florets (1-flowered in *A.plinii*); glumes nearly equal, as long as the florets, 3–7 nerved; lemmas 3–5 nerves, with long, soft hairs on the backs.

### *A.donax* L.: Giant reed, Provence reed, Indian grass

Probably the largest grass hardy in the cool temperate regions, only exceeded in size by some of the bamboos. It is always impressive and contributes a unique visual element to any planting. It can help create a tropical effect when used with suitable companions. In its native haunts along the riversides of southern Europe, it often forms monospecific stands, as *Phragmite australis* does in cooler climates. The tough, hollow stems are a source of reeds for musical instruments.

Robust perennial with a stout, knotty rootstock, vigorously stoloniferous in the wild, usually slow-spreading in cultivation in the UK. Culms stout, up to

3 cm across, up to 4 m tall. Leaf blades up to 5 cm across, and as long as 3.3 m, almost smooth; glaucous green; arching in habit, regularly alternate on the stems. Autumn-produced inflorescence a much-branched panicle up to 60 cm long, erect or somewhat drooping; at first reddish, later becoming white. The largest leaves and most vigorous shoots are produced on plants that are cut to ground level at the end of each season. The flowers, when produced, provide excellent material for floral arrangements. In cool regions culms will not achieve flowering size. H5.

### A.d. 'Macrophylla'
Leaves even broader than the type, up to 9 cm wide, and even more glaucous. As vigorous and hardy as the type, and even more dramatic on account of its larger leaves. H5.

### A.d. 'Variegata'
Known in the USA as *A.d.* 'Versicolor'. Leaves striped white, usually with broad white bands at the margins. Generally smaller in all its parts than the type, and also very much more frost-tender, needing at least conservatory treatment in the UK, and thriving when grown in a border in a warm greenhouse. Typically, the leaves are no more than 30 cm long, 5 cm wide, and the stems seldom above 2 m.

### A.d. 'Variegata Superba'
A name of doubtful authenticity, but used to distinguish a superior variegated form in which the leaves are much broader than in *A.d.* 'Variegata', and normally as much as 6.5 cm across, about 30 cm long, borne on stems only about 1 m tall. The leaves grow much closer together on the culms than in *A.d.* 'Variegata', which adds to the effectiveness of the plant, and it also seems to be much hardier, though it is not as hardy as the type. G1.

### *A.plinii* Turra
A plant of curious aspect—spiky—almost prickly. Close to *A.donax* but differing in that the culms are never more than 2 m tall and are always slender, and in the leaves, which are rigid and which stick out stiffly from the culm at a right angle or rather less, the tips sharply pointed, up to 3 cm × 0.7 cm. H4.

### *A.phragmites* var. *pseudodonax*
See under *Phragmites australis*.

## AVENA L.
A genus of about 25 species of annual grasses, mainly natives of the Mediterranean and the Middle East, inhabiting disturbed ground. It is an important genus economically as 6 or 7 species are grown as grain crops, including

*A.sativa* (oats). *A.fatua* (wild oats) is one of the world's major cornfield weeds. Most species make attractive ornamentals and possess well-formed, open panicles with large, showy spikelets. They are easily grown in any reasonable garden soil: seed may be sown spring or autumn. The genus is very close to *Helictotrichon* from which it differs mainly in its annual habit.

Leaves flat; panicle loose and nodding; spikelets large, 2-several-flowered; glumes membranous, about equal, thin and papery, as long as the spikelet, rounded on the back, smooth; lemmas leathery, doubly toothed, with a bent awn on the back (the awn often reduced or absent in cultivated species): palea shorter than lemma, with a translucent margin.

### *A.sterilis* L.: Wild oat, Animated oat
The wild oat is much-loved by flower arrangers. In country districts there is usually no problem in collecting wild oats for drying from the edges of cornfields, but in urban and suburban areas it is worth growing a clump or two each year partly to grace the garden, but also to dry for arranging. The panicle is most attractive in the garden, especially if the plant is grown where light can strike it against a dark background, revealing the full beauty of the dangling, hairy-mouthed spikelets. Good for drying and dyeing.

Loosely tufted annual. Culms solitary or usually several, erect, or decumbent becoming erect; rather stout, the nodes clearly pronounced. Leaf sheaths smooth. Leaf blades up to 46 cm long, 1 cm wide, flat or slightly U-shaped. Inflorescence, produced April to June, a widely spaced, open panicle, erect or slightly nodding, symmetrical or slightly 1-sided; green becoming corn yellow.

## BECKMANNIA Host
A genus of 2 species of annual or perennial grasses from damp meadows in the north temperate zone. It is closely related to *Phleum*, though its inflorescence is anomalous in Aveneae. One species is sometimes grown as an ornamental. It has no particular cultural requirements.

Annuals or, when perennials, with the lowest culm internode tuberous. Inflorescence composed of 1-sided racemes from a central axis; spikelets orbicular, 1-flowered with or without an additional male floret; glumes inflated, surrounding all but the very tip of the floret; lemmas rounded at the back, tapering to an awn-point, or merely pointed.

### *B.syzigachne* (Steud.) Fern.: Slough grass
A hardy marsh grass, native to both North America and eastern Asia, of wide distribution and tolerant of great temperature variation, being indigenous as far south as California and as far north as Alaska. It is locally abundant, makes a moderately good forage grass and is sometimes grown for this purpose or for hay-making. In gardens it is cultivated for its beauty of flower, the flowers being ridiculously large for the size of the plant.

A loosely tufted annual. Culms several, usually erect, sometimes becoming decumbent at maturity; smooth, the nodes scarcely swollen. Leaf sheaths smooth. Leaf blades up to 25 cm long, 8 mm wide; flat, smooth, arching. Inflorescence, produced July to August, a spear-shaped, 1-sided panicle, up to 5 cm long, the lower branches well-spaced, the upper ones becoming confluent, the spikelets 1-flowered, rarely 2-flowered, awnless; greenish-white becoming tawny at maturity.

## BOTHRIOCHLOA Kuntze

A genus of some 35 species of annual or perennial grasses from open, grassy places throughout the tropics and warm temperate regions of both hemispheres. Two species are sometimes grown as ornamentals. They should be treated as annuals and the seed sown in spring where it is to grow in a warm, sunny position.

Leaves sometimes aromatic: inflorescence digitate or nearly so, with paired, dissimilar spikelets, one stalked, one stalkless; spikelet stalks, internodes and raceme axes with a clear median line; stalkless spikelet with 2 florets, vertically compressed; lower floret reduced to a transparent lemma; upper floret bisexual, the lemma running into a sharply bent awn. The stalked spikelet similar but smaller.

### *B.caucasica* Kuntze: Purple beard grass

This is a really outstanding ornamental, grown for its showy purple panicles. The intensity of the colouring compares favourably with the flowers of many dicots. Its somewhat sprawling habit may be a disadvantage in tidy gardens. Unfortunately seldom seen outside botanic gardens, it ought to be far more widely grown.

Loosely tufted perennial with slowly spreading rhizomes, growing up to 1 m when in flower. Culm more or less erect, often decumbent becoming erect, frequently weakly branching, the nodes not conspicuously swollen; smooth. Leaf sheaths smooth in the lower portion, becoming hairy. Leaf blades up to 60 cm long, 1 cm wide, flat, arching or curling; smooth. Inflorescence, produced July to August, a much-branched panicle up to 10 cm long and almost as much across, the branches all spreading upwards and outwards away from the axis, and all at the same angle to the axis, all of similar length, so that the top of the inflorescence appears to have been removed; deep pink or purple. H2.

### *B.ischaemum* Kuntze

Tufted perennial to 1 m; stems ascending. Panicle, produced during July to September, is composed of up to 15 racemes each 3–6 cm long all arising very close together near the apex of the stem. Spikelets are narrowly elliptic and papery. H2.

### *B.saccharoides*: Silver beard grass

Tufted perennial to 1 m. Grown for its overall silvery-grey appearance. Leaves grey, smooth, up to 5 mm wide. Panicles, produced August to September, dense, silvery-white, silkily hairy, up to 15 cm long, composed of numerous erect racemes 5 cm long. H2.

## BOUTELOUA Lag.

A genus of 24 or 25 species of annual or perennial grasses from the open grasslands of the Americas from Canada to Argentina with a centre of distribution in Mexico. The genus contains many important forage grasses, and several species make attractive ornamentals, grown for their curious, 1-sided spikes. Easily cultivated in ordinary garden soil: they may be raised from seed sown in spring or propagated by division of the roots.

Leaves always narrow, flat or rolled; plants tufted or with stolons. Inflorescence of up to 80 dense, 1-sided spikes or racemes arising from a common axis; the axis ending in a straight or sometimes forked point; spikelets 1–20, stalkless or nearly stalkless, arranged in 2 rows on one side of the axis, usually with 1 fertile floret below and 1 sterile floret above; lower glume lanceolate with a setaceous tip; lemmas 3-nerved, the fertile lemma shortly awned, the rudimentary lemmas with 3-nerves elongated into awns.

### *B.curtipendula* (Michx.)Torr.: Side-oats grama

Differs from the more familiar *B.gracilis* in its larger size and coarser growth, and in that its spike is erect, the spikelets well-spaced not dense, but still 1-sided as in *B.gracilis*. H5.

### *B.gracilis* Lag.: Mosquito grass, Blue grama grass

A grass perhaps more valued as a curiosity than for its beauty. It gets its name from the form of inflorescence, the main axis of which is set at an oblique angle to the culm, the spikelets hanging down on the lower side of the axis, with the florets subtended below them, these last looking like many mosquitoes hanging on to the flower. The flowers dry well and afford some delicacy in contrast to bolder grasses. Its natural habitat extends from the Great Plains southwards into Mexico and through Central America to South America. One of the main short grasses of the Great Plains. It seems more at home in acid soils than alkaline ones.

Densely tufted, deciduous perennial with very slowly spreading rhizomes, growing up to 50 cm when in flower. Culms erect, occasionally decumbent at the base and becoming erect; very leafy at the base, bearing few, short leaves higher up; nodes not conspicuous; smooth; green. Leaf sheaths shorter than the internodes; green, becoming brown on the basal leaves early in the season. Leaf blades mainly basal, up to 13 cm long, 6 mm wide, flat or somewhat U-shaped, the basal leaves curly or arching, the upper leaves more or less straight; smooth; green. Inflorescence, produced June to September, a 1-sided spike up to 5 cm long, 1, 2 or rarely 3 to a culm, each bearing numerous dependent spikelets, sometimes as many as 80, densely packed on the rachis, the exserted florets hanging below the spikelets, brown or grey. H5.

## BRACHYPODIUM Beauv.

A genus of about 15 perennial grasses with one annual, sometimes with spreading rhizomes, natives of woodland and open grassland in temperate Eurasia and also Mexico and Bolivia. It is a curious genus for while its loose raceme and elongated spikelets give it a superficial homogeneity, it is cyto-logically a complete mess. On the one hand it intergrades morphologically with *Elymus*, and on the other it seems quite isolated. *B.sylvaticum* is sometimes grown as an ornamental.

11  *Brachypodium sylvaticum*

Inflorescence a loose, linear raceme of alternate, shortly stalked spikelets; spikelets 5–20-flowered, laterally compressed; florets numerous; glumes oppo-site, unequal lanceolate, shorter than the lowest lemma, 3–9-nerved, rounded on the back, usually short-awned; palea a little shorter than the lemma, notched, with short hairs.

### *B.distachyon* (L.) Beauv.: False brome

A stiff, rather dull, dwarf grass grown for its spike-like inflorescence. Tufted annual, leaves linear, up to 10 cm long up to 20 mm wide. Panicle, produced June to August, a spike-like raceme up to 3 cm long, 6–12-flowered, the lemma terminating in a stiff awn to 2 cm long. H1.

### *B.sylvaticum* L.: Slender or Wood false-brome

A grass of generally similar aspect to *B.distachyon* but differing in its perennial not annual character and in its greater stature. Tufted perennial to 1 m tall, stems erect or spreading. Leaves linear-lanceolate, hairy, yellowish-green up to 4.5 cm long with up to 16 flowers, produced July to August, the lemmas terminating in a fine awn up to 1.2 cm long. H1.

### BRIZA L.

A genus of about 20 species of hairless perennials and annuals from open grasslands in temperate Eurasia and South America. The genus although close to *Poa* is very distinct with its very broad almost overlapping lemmas, whose margins seem to press on the flanks of the floret below creating a slight, dry rattling sound when shaken by the wind. Three or four species are grown as ornamentals and they need rich soil in full sun. They provide excellent material for drying and dyeing, and should be culled and dried as soon as they are fully developed.

    Panicle open, much-branched; spikelets many-flowered, broadly triangular, flattened; florets 4–20; glumes nearly circular, heart-shaped at the base with wide, papery margins; lemmas again nearly circular, heart-shaped at the base; palea shorter than lemma, ovate.

### *B.humilis* M.Bieb.

Tufted annual up to 30 cm tall, the stems slender, rarely solitary. Panicle, produced April to June, narrow, spike-like, erect, the spikelets ovate on short pedicels. The least ornamental of the cultivated species.

### *B.maxima* L.: Big quaking grass, Large quaking grass, Puffed wheat

Mediterranean, occasionally naturalised in Britain. Possibly one of the earliest grasses grown for other than edible purposes. Loosely tufted annual up to 30 cm. Culms several, erect, round, smooth. Sheaths smooth, blades to 20 cm long, tapering to a fine point; the vegetative parts starting light green, becoming mid green, maturing light straw-yellow. Inflorescence, produced May to July, a many-flowered loose panicle, sparingly branched, to 10 cm long, bearing 1–12 densely packed, ovate or oblong, plump spikelets; pale green or silvery, sometimes suffused reddish-brown or purple, the glumes bright red. A generally coarser plant than *B.media*.

*B.m.* var. *rubra*
Has glumes margined white.

***B.media*** L.: Common quaking grass, Cow quakes, Didder, Dillies, Doddering dickies, Lady's-hair grass, Maidenhair grass, Pearl grass, Perennial quaking grass, Quaker grass, Quakers, Quaking grass, Rattle grass, Shivering grass, Totter grass, Trembling grass
Its popularity, as well as the length of time it has been cultivated, may be judged from the enormous number of common names which have been given to it. (As a general rule, the longer a plant is in cultivation the more common names it has.) Mentioned as an ornamental in some of the earliest herbals.

Loosely tufted perennial with short, creeping rhizomes to 45 cm. Culms erect, occasionally decumbent becoming erect; very slender, stiff, smooth; somewhat arched at the tip. Leaf sheaths entire, splitting very early in the season; smooth. Leaf blades up to 15 cm long, 3 mm across; flat in section, minutely rough on the margins, narrowing to a blunt tip. Inflorescence, produced June to August, a very loose, more or less pyramidal panicle up to 18 cm long, about the same across; the branches wide-spreading, seldom branching; the spikelets loosely scattered, rather fat; shining, green, becoming purplish then light beige. H1.

*B.m.* var. *flore albo*
Flowers white.

*B.m.* var. *flore viride*
Flowers green, becoming beige.

***B.minor*** L.: Lesser quaking grass
Mediterranean, also Britain. The smallest-flowered of the quaking grasses, a plant of great charm. A loosely tufted annual to 20 cm. Culms several, very slender, round, smooth. Blades to 25 cm, flat in section, tapering to a narrow point, slightly undulate; finely nerved and minutely rough on the upper surface and margins. Inflorescence, produced June to September, a very loose, open, roughly pyramidal panicle; spikelets small, nodding; shining green or tinged purple. Comes into flower just as *B.maxima* is over. Readily distinguished from that plant by its wider, weaker blades, and the more numerous and smaller spikelets. Sow seeds spring or autumn where plants are to flower; fertile soil, sun.

*B.m.* var. *minima*
Grows to 15 cm, proportionately small in all its parts.

### *B.subaristata* Lam.

Tufted perennial with slender, erect stems. 30 to 60 cm tall. Leaves flat or rolled, linear up to 22 cm long; ligule truncate, short; panicle, produced June to September, lanceolate, erect or nodding; spikelets oblong, plump with up to 12 flowers, purple or green. H1.

## BROMUS L.

A genus of about 150 annual, biennial or perennial grasses from the temperate zones of both hemispheres, though mainly from the northern one, natives of woodlands and meadows. It is easily confused with *Festuca* from which it can only be distinguished with certainty by examining the ovaries, and less easily with *Helictrichon* which however has awns that are plainly dorsal and usually bent. Several perennial species are grown as forage grasses in the mountains of the western USA and one, *B.mango*, is or was grown as a cereal in South America. Several species are grown for ornament, and have panicles suitable for drying. They grow well in ordinary garden soil. Seed may be sown outdoors in spring or autumn.

Leaves flat or somewhat rolled, hairy with leaf margins connate for most of their length. Panicle often showy; spikelets wedge-shaped, with 1–many florets; glumes herbaceous with 1–9 nerves, the upper usually longer; lemmas somewhat leathery, the awns short or long but always straight and nearly terminal; the ovary crowned by a hairy, fleshy cap from beneath which the styles emerge.

### *B.arvensis* L.: Field brome

An attractive little native grass with stiff panicles, useful for dried decoration. Loosely tufted annual with slender stems; leaves flat or rolled, hairy. Panicles, produced June to August, up to 25 cm long and 20 cm wide, erect or nodding, loose and open with wide-spreading branches. Spikelets lanceolate to oblong, 4–10-flowered, with a fine, straight awn.

### *B.brizaeformis* Fisch. & Mey.

One of the most beautiful of the bromes, with large, ornamental panicles rather in the manner of *Briza maxima* but perhaps even lovelier with their huge, drooping, hairy heads.

Loosely tufted annual or biennial up to 1 m in flower. Culms usually several, rarely single, erect or decumbent at the base becoming erect; round, hairy. Leaf sheaths round, hairy. Leaf blades up to 25 cm long, 8 mm wide, gradually tapering to a fine point; hairy on both surfaces; slightly toothed, flat in section. Inflorescence, produced June to September, a very sparsely and loosely branched panicle up to 20 cm long, the individual branches as much as 10 cm long, the spikelets about 2 cm long; ovate, not awned. H4.

## B.carinatus
See under *B.unioloides*.

## B.danthoniae Trin.
A most attractive, small, usually rather rigid grass with highly ornamental panicles. Low, tufted annual with slender stems up to 45 cm tall. Leaves narrowly linear, up to 10 cm long, softly hairy: sheaths softly hairy. Panicle, produced June and July, with sometimes only 1 spikelet; spikelets oblong or oblong-lanceolate, up to 5 cm long, green or purplish; 3-awned just below the tip, the central awn flattened at first becoming recurved and twisted at maturity, reddish-purple to purple. H4.

## B.diandrus Roth.: Great brome
A rather coarse brome but useful for its dried panicles. Annual, usually tufted, with slender or stout hairy stems up to nearly 1 m. Leaves loosely hairy. Panicle, produced June and July, nodding, very loose, up to 23 cm long and wide, with few to many spikelets. Spikelets oblong becoming wedge-shaped and gaping, up to 9.5 cm long; lemmas linear-lanceolate with a fine, stiff awn up to 6 cm long arising from just below the bifid tip.

## B.erectus Huds.: Upright brome
When in flower this is one of the most striking bromes, with its showy, bright, reddish-orange anthers. It is a coarse but very ornamental grass, often dominant on the chalk downs of southern England. The panicles are lovely when dried. Densely tufted perennial up to 1.24 m tall, stems erect, slender or stout. Leaves loosely hairy. Panicles erect or nodding, loose or dense, up to 25 cm long, reddish, purplish or green. Spikelets narrowly oblong, 4–14-flowered, June and July; lemmas narrowly lanceolate terminating in a fine stiff or flexuous awn. H2.

## B.macrostachys Desf.: Brome grass
Very different from the preceding species in its densely tufted habit and its erect, rather spiky inflorescences. A densely tufted annual to 60 cm, culms solitary, nodes conspicuous, reddish or purplish. Sheaths round, hairy; blades to 5 cm long, hairy, flat, light green. Panicle, produced June and July, compact even dense with few, large spikelets each up to 2.5 cm long, spikelets compact with long, spreading rather stout awns. It is these which give the flower-head its prickly charm. Conspicuous in the garden.

## B.m. var. *lanuginosus* (Poir.) Dinsmore
Has almost white-woolly spikelets and is more often grown for ornament than the typical plant.

### *B.madritensis* L.: Compact brome, Stiff brome, Wall brome

Differs from *B.macrostachys* most noticeably in the colour of the inflorescence and in being feathery rather than spiky. Loosely tufted annual to 60 cm. Culms several, sheaths tubular, splitting early, blades to 20 cm long, light green, lower blades hairy. Inflorescence, produced May and June, a panicle to 15 cm long, 7.5 cm across, usually somewhat drooping, rather loose, spikelets oblong, becoming wedge-shaped and gaping, awns very long and fine; overall tinged red, rich purplish-red or wine-coloured; quickly shattering. Distinctive in its flower colour and form. Beautiful in the garden, useless for drying.

### *B.ramosus* Huds.: Hairy or Wood brome

The tallest, stateliest and most graceful of the British native grasses, this is certainly one of the most decorative. It is a woodland grass which may be confused with the somewhat similar *Festuca altissima*, from which it differs in its generally larger size.

Loosely tufted perennial without rhizomes, growing up to 3 m under optimum conditions, more usually under 1.25 m. Culms erect, unbranched; rather stout, hairy. Leaf sheaths tubular, splitting, rounded on the back, generally hairy, but sometimes with the upper part lacking hairs. Leaf blades up to 60 cm long, 2 cm wide, flat in section, arching or drooping; generally hairy, rarely hairless; somewhat blue-green. Inflorescence, produced July to August, a loose, open, nodding panicle up to 45 cm long, the branches usually occurring in pairs, spreading and drooping, dividing more than once, the spikelets pendulous, narrowly oblong up to 2.5 cm long; purplish, bearing fine, straight awns. H2.

### *B.r. benekenii*

Has been accorded the accolade of a species, but its status remains in some doubt. It differs from the typical plant only in its generally slender as opposed to stout culms, and in its rather thinner panicles. It is never found growing in isolation, but only in association with the type plant, which rather suggests that it is an unfixed mutant or hybrid, and sowings of the seed of the subspecies might well produce a proportion of the type plant. Of academic rather than horticultural interest.

### *B.secalinus* L.: Rye, Brome, Chess, Cheat

Used to be a common cornfield weed in Britain, but is now seldom seen as a weed. Occasionally grown as an ornamental because its heads are less fragile than those of other bromes. Loosely tufted annual or biennial growing to 1.2 m. Culms erect, slender, stiff. Sheaths smooth. Leaves loosely hairy. Panicle, produced June–July, erect, open and loose or dense, ultimately nodding, 5–15 cm long, the spikelets oblong, up to 1.5 cm long, 4–11-flowered;

lemmas elliptic, the margins ultimately tightly incurved, with a fine, straight awn up to 12 mm long.

12  *Bromus secalinus*

## *B.tectorum* L.: Dropping brome

Ornamental mainly for its rather glistening green or purplish panicles. Annual, usually tufted, with stems up to 60 cm. Leaves softly hairy. Panicle, produced May to June, usually loose and drooping to one side, up to 18 cm long, the spikelets 4–8-flowered, becoming wedge-shaped and gaping, the lemmas lanceolate tipped with fine, straight awns.

## *B.unioloides* H.B.K.: Rescue grass, Schrader's bromegrass

Tufted annual or biennial grown for its large, decorative spikelets. Stems slender or stout. Leaves hairless or only sparsely hairy. Panicle, produced July to September, large, loose, open, occasionally narrow and contracted, with branches up to 7.5 cm long, the spikelets much compressed, up to 12-flowered, the lemmas awnless or with a short awn. *B.carinatus* is similar but has the lemmas with longer awns.

# CALAMAGROSTIS Adans.

A genus of some 270 species of perennial, usually moderately tall, robust grasses from the temperate regions of the world, natives of damp places in open woods and heaths. One or two are very ornamental, both growing and dried. They are suited to wet places in the garden, in otherwise ordinary soil. They are easily propagated by division in spring.

Leaves flat or rolled. Panicle open, usually narrow and spike-like; spikelets narrow, 1-flowered; glumes equal or unequal, as long or longer than the floret; lemmas shorter and firmer than the glumes, with a tuft of hairs arising from the callus, these hairs often copious and sometimes longer than the lemmas; the lemmas with inconspicuous dorsal awns, sometimes twice as long as the lemma but lost in the hairs.

### C. × acutiflora 'Karl Foerster'
Formerly thought to be a form of *C.arundinacea*, this is in fact a hybrid between *C.arundinacea* and *C.epigejos*. Has narrow, showy brown flower heads. 1.5–2 m. Mid–late summer.

### C.canescens (Weber) Roth.: Purple small reed
A delightful grass that grows 60 cm or 1.2 m and produces, in midsummer, elegant loose panicles of usually pale flowers. Slender but strong-growing perennial with slender rhizomes slowly forming large clumps. Culms slender, erect. Leaf blades up to 45 cm long, up to 6 mm wide, bearing short hairs on the upper surface, rather rough to the touch. Inflorescence, produced June to July, a panicle, lanceolate to oblong, usually of loose, open structure; erect, up to 25 cm long, 10 cm across; purplish, greenish or yellowish. The whole inflorescence moves gently in the breeze on its slender culms. A native of bogs, fens and wet woodlands it needs similar conditions in the garden. H3.

### C.c. 'Variegata'
A form with leaves variegated white. Variegation poor and of little garden merit. H3.

### C.epigejos (L.) Roth.: Wood small reed, Bush grass, Reed grass
An elegant tall grass to 2 m and worthy of a place in most large gardens, grown purely for its open, airy flower-heads, which are a joy on the plant, picked or dried. The general habit of the plant is not attractive, the foliage being sparse. Best grown where this aspect can be hidden by surrounding plants. It spreads

by rhizomes and so needs room to grow: best divided every five years to keep it to size.

Coarse, stout perennial with creeping rhizomes. Culms erect or very slightly spreading, strong but usually slender, becoming rough close to the inflorescence. Leaves dull green, hairless; sheaths smooth, blades finely pointed, up to 69 cm long and 1 cm wide, coarsely textured and rough to the touch. Inflorescence, produced June to July, a narrowly erect panicle up to 30 cm long and 6 cm wide, purplish, brownish or green, spreading with age. H1.

### C.e. 'Hortorum'
A garden form far superior to the type plant for garden decoration and flower arranging. It has a much more narrowly erect habit of growth, is far slower to spread, and bears inflorescences of a rich, foxy-red. The inflorescence remains more tightly erect than that of the type plant, which tends to spread with age. H1.

## CATAPODIUM Link
A genus of 2 species of annual grasses from open, dry places in Eurasia and North Africa. It differs from *Desmazeria* in its glabrous lemmas, and from *Puccinella* in the texture of the lemmas.

Panicle 1-sided with short, stiff side-branches; spikelets several, many-flowered, borne on stout pedicels: glumes nearly equal, leathery, 3–5-nerved; lemmas leathery, 5-nerved.

### C.rigidum (L.) C.E. Hubbard: Fern grass
Tufted perennial to 15 cm, erect or spreading, occasionally grown for its 1-sided panicles. Leaves up to 10 cm long, hairless; panicles more or less linear, dense or fairly loose, up to 7.5 cm long; spikelets 10-flowered, green or purplish: flowers May–July. H4.

### C.r. var. *major* (J.B. Presl.)
A bright green grass about twice the height (i.e. 30 cm), of equal garden merit.

## CENCHRUS L.
A genus of about 25 species of annual and perennial grasses from the drier parts of the tropics, usually readily recognisable by its prickly burs, but anatomically closely related to *Pennisetum*. Some species are quite ornamental in the garden on account of their unusual burs, but these soon fall when the spikes are picked. Increase by seed sown in frost-free conditions, or by division in spring. They need a sunny position in the garden, in ordinary soil but will rot below ground unless the drainage is good.

Tufted, low-branching plants with flat leaf blades. Panicle spike-like; spikelets solitary or few together, surrounded and enclosed in a spiny bur or whorl of bristles made up of sterile branchlets; glumes shorter than the spikelet, the lower glume sometimes suppressed; lower floret male or sterile, with lemma as long as spikelet; upper floret bisexual.

### C.ciliaris L.: Buffell grass

A frost-tender perennial grown for its curious spike-like inflorescences with bun-like spikelets. Stems slender, rigid, up to 90 cm ascending from a sharply bent base. Rhizome thick, tough. Leaves hairy or hairless, up to 30 cm long, 4 mm wide; ligule merely a row of hairs. Inflorescence, produced August and September, cylindric, fairly dense, up to 15 cm long, pale or purplish; spikelets solitary or in clusters of 2s or 3s, surrounded by numerous bristles, the inner bristles densely ciliate, thickened and united at the base. H5–G1.

### C.echinatus L.

Widespread in the tropics; may be grown as an annual. It is similar to *C.ciliaris*, but the bur is less prickly and has a ring of slender bristles at the base of the stout prickles.

### C.tubuloides L.

A tropical American dune grass, similar to the above, with large, showy, villous burs.

## CHASMANTHIUM Link

A genus of about 6 species of perennial grasses from the semi-arid woodlands of the eastern USA extending north to the Canadian border, and Mexico. The species of *Chasmanthium* used to be included in *Uniola* from which they differ in small and variable taxonomic details. Highly ornamental, after the style of *Uniola*, both in the garden and when dried. Increase by division or by seed sown spring or autumn. Needs good soil in a semi-shaded position, and will not tolerate waterlogged conditions.

Leaf blades flat, linear to narrowly lanceolate. Inflorescence a panicle or with the primary branches reduced to racemes; spikelets few-to-many-flowered, shattering at maturity, the rachilla extension bearing a rudimentary floret, the lowest 1–2 florets sterile; glumes shorter than lemmas; lemmas with up to 15 nerves.

### C.latifolium (Michaux) Yates

A North American grass grown for its beautiful drooping panicles of large green spikelets. The spikelets bear a superficial resemblance to *Briza maxima*. It is a native of rich woodlands, and needs good cultivation in semi-shade to give of its best.

Loosely tufted, deciduous with stout, slowly spreading rhizomes, growing up to 1.2 m in its native woodlands, rather less in cultivation in the UK. Culms erect becoming arching, smooth. Leaf sheaths rounded on the back, rather loose, slightly inflated, especially the lower ones. Leaf blades up to 20 cm long, 19 mm wide; flat in section, smooth, the margins slightly rough; somewhat stiff but very slightly arching. Inflorescence, produced in August, an open, drooping, 1-sided panicle up to 20 cm long, sparsely branched, the branches bearing few, very large, flattened spikelets, each up to 13 mm long; at first green becoming tawny. H2.

# CHIONOCHLOA Zotov.

A genus of about 20 species of coarse, tussock-forming perennial grasses from the alpine grasslands of New Zealand, with one species in south-eastern Australia. The species form a generally cohesive genus but intergrade with *Cortaderia* and *Rytidosperma*. Several species are in the first rank of ornamental grasses. Increase by seed or by division in spring. Ordinary garden soil but *C.toetoe* grows as a marginal on lakes in the wild.

Densely tufted tussocks packed with old leaf sheaths; blades often pungent, clearly ribbed and harsh to the touch. Panicle usually nodding and 1-sided; spikelets with several florets; glumes shorter than spikelet, and often shorter than lemma, with up to 5 nerves; lemmas membranous, 7–9-nerved, hairy overall or only at the margins, distinctly bilobed, each lobe awned, the awn an elongation of the central nerve, straight or bent.

## *C.conspicua* (Forst.f.) Zotov.: Hunangamolio grass

A highly decorative New Zealand grass, much in the manner of the pampas grasses, but more open and refined in all its parts, and of particular value for its early flowering. The flowers are exceptionally elegant when dried.

A vigorous perennial forming large tussocks 2 m tall in flower. Roots coarse and fibrous, not stoloniferous. Leaves mid or light green with a distinct orange midrib; mainly basal, narrow, linear, up to 3.6 m long and 1 cm wide; flat, strongly nerved and usually softly hairy along the margins. Leaf sheaths basal, very rigid, hairy and tightly compressed. Inflorescence, produced May to August, a much-branched, very open panicle, up to 45 cm long and about half that in width; pale green to yellowish; flowers hermaphroditic. The panicles are heavy often pulling the stems down to nearly horizontal. It is not happy on heavy soils. H4.

## *C.c.* var. *cunninghamii*

Differs from the type only in minor botanical details: the basal leaf sheaths are glaborous, not hairy; only moderately rigid instead of extremely rigid; and on drying become flat rather than compressed. Both are of equal garden merit. H4.

### C.flavescens (Hook.f.) Zotov

One of the most decorative of the New Zealand tussock grasses, forming mounds of an overall brownish-green, the colour being unique among the cultivated large grasses. Particularly valued because it flowers very early in the year, and because the large, lax panicle not only lasts for months on the plant, but is also ideal dried for floral arrangements. Differs from *C.conspicua* in its smaller stature, leaf colour and earlier flowering.

Tussock-forming, growing 1–1.7 m. Leaves green, tinged reddish-brown. Leaf sheaths yellow to orange, not green. Inflorescence a much-branched panicle up to 60 cm long, about half as wide, of very loose, open structure; pale green or whitish; produced May–August. Probably the hardiest of the tussock grasses, it needs good cultivation in rich, damp soil, perfect drainage and shelter from cold winds. Intolerant of heavy clay soils. H4.

### C.flavicans Auct.

A native of rock outcrops at high altitudes in New Zealand. Generally similar in appearance and performance to *C.flavescens*, it differs from that species in that the basal leaf sheaths are green, not orange or yellow; that its overall appearance is green, not reddish-brown; and that the branches of the flower-head bear spikelets all along their length, which they do not in *C.flavescens*. It differs from *C.conspicua* in its smaller stature.

Leaves green, flat, up to 1.6 m long. Inflorescence, produced June and July, a much-branched panicle bearing spikelets along the length of each branchlet. Probably the most tender of the cultivated tussock grasses, taking many years to reach flowering size from seed, and needing a dry, arid position where it can get a good summer baking. H3.

### C.rigida (Raoul) Zotov: Snow grass

Native of the alpine and cold temperate regions of New Zealand, this is the hardiest of the cultivated tussock grasses. Differs from the other cultivated species in forming a loose rather than a compact tussock, and is notable for the way in which the basal leaf sheaths tend to persist on the plant, gradually building up into an untidy mess of shattered sheaths at the centre. Grows to about 1 m. Leaves semi-erect, U-shaped in section. Inflorescence, produced July and August, a much-branched panicle up to 25 cm long, rather less than half as much across; pale green, whitish, sometimes buff. H2.

### C.rubra (Hook.f.) Zotov

A dingy little grass forming tussocks to about 30 cm tall. Leaves narrow, dull reddish-brown. Panicles small, not ornamental, July and August. H4.

## CHLORIS Swartz

A genus of about 50 species of annual or perennial grasses from the tropical and warm temperate regions of both hemispheres. They are natives of short grasslands, generally on poor soils, or pioneers of disturbed soil. One species, *C.gayana*, is a major tropical forage grass. Chloris is the goddess of flowers, and one would expect the species to be exceptionally showy. They are only reasonably so; several species are ornamental for their many-fingered panicles. They can be grown out of doors in summer in a sunny position from seed sown outdoors after May or in a greenhouse from early April.

Tufted or sometimes stoloniferous; leaf blades linear to filiform, flat or folded with distinct midrib. Inflorescence a digitate raceme; spikelets with 1 perfect floret and 1 or several sterile florets above usually reduced to empty lemmas, sessile, arranged in 2 rows along 1 side of the rachis; glumes unequal, the lower shorter; lemmas broad, keeled, 1–5-nerved, conspicuously awned from the tip.

### *C.barbata* Swartz: Annual finger grass
Loosely tufted annual, stems often horizontal at first becoming erect, up to 75 cm tall. Leaves flat, linear, up to 25.5 cm long; panicle with 5–15 fingers, each up to 75 cm long, purplish or brownish; spikelets white-bearded. Flowers August to September.

### *C.truncata* R.Br.
A showy, stoloniferous perennial treated as an annual in the UK. Stems to 30 cm. Leaves flat or folded. Panicles, produced August and September, with 6–10 fingers, each up to 15 cm long, these soon becoming horizontally spread or even deflexed. Spikelets not bearded. H4.

### *C.virgata* Swartz
Tufted annual, stems erect or spreading, at most 60 cm tall. Leaf sheaths somewhat inflated; blades flat, up to 6 mm wide. Panicles, produced August and September, 5- to 12-fingered, silky or feathery, each up to 7.5 cm long, green or purplish.

## CHRYSOPOGON Trinius
A genus of some 26 species of perennial and 1 annual, usually tufted, grasses from the tropical and warm temperate regions of both Asia and Australia, with 1 species in Florida and the West Indies, varying in habitat from semi-desert to rain forest. *C.aciculatus* is an excellent lawn grass in warm, humid regions. One or two species are decorative and should be treated as tender annuals.

Leaf blades linear, somewhat glaucous, harsh to the touch. Inflorescence a terminal panicle with whorls of slender branches bearing terminal racemes, the racemes reduced to a triad of 2 stalked and 1 stalkless spikelets, the latter laterally compressed, its lower glume leathery, its upper glume usually awned, the upper lemma prominently awned.

### *C.fulvus* (Sprengel) Chiovenda

Grown for its strange, open, slender-branched panicles. Perennial, growing to 150 cm. Panicle, produced July to September, broadly ovate, up to 15 cm long, the branches fine and delicate, brown-bearded at the tip. Stalkless spikelet oblong, 1–1.5 mm long, the upper glume awned and the upper lemma with an awn up to 3 cm long: stalked spikelet with the lower glume awned. H5.

## COIX L.: Job's tears

A genus of about 5 species of annual grasses from forest margins and marshes in tropical East Asia, but introduced to and now naturalised throughout the tropics, all known as Job's tears. The genus is unique in the curious hard, flask-like shells which encase and protect the lower, pistillate portion of the flower. These structures are involucres (much modified sheathing bracts). These can vary in shape from round to almost spindle-shaped, and in colour from white through bluish-grey and browns to nearly black. They are much used as ornamental beads. In temperate regions they are grown as a curiosity. Seeds should be sown in a greenhouse in February or March, or outdoors in May where the plants are to grow. They need a sunny position in ordinary garden soil.

Plants moderately tall, branched, with broad, flat leaves. Inflorescence compound, composed of 2 racemes separated by a prophyll, 1 raceme female and stalkless, the other male and stalked, the inflorescences arising from the leaf axils and enclosed in a conspicuous, bony flask-like structure, with usually a terminal spike of male spikelets. Female raceme entirely enclosed within the flask-like utricle and consisting of 1 stalkless spikelet and 2 spikelets with stalks, the stalkless spikelet female, glumes membranous, the lower floret reduced to a lemma; the male raceme projecting beyond the mouth of the utricle, the spikelets in 2s or 3s, the lower glume with lateral wings, both florets male.

### *C.lacryma-jobi* L.: Job's tears, Christ's tears, Adlay

Believed to be one of the first grasses brought into cultivation as an ornamental. In spite of its large grains, which are the 'tears' of its common names, it is rarely grown as a grain crop. The grains are used for a variety of purposes such as making bead necklaces, bead dresses and bead rosaries. It is essentially a plant of the tropics, and in cold climates needs to be treated as a half-hardy annual.

Loosely tufted annual growing up to about 1 m under ideal conditions, usually rather smaller. Culms usually several, rarely solitary, frequently branched, rarely unbranched; smooth; bright green. Leaf sheaths smooth; bright green. Leaf blades up to 46 cm long, usually rather less, and 1.5 cm wide; flat or slightly U-shaped, somewhat undulate along the margins; arching, with a pronounced mid-vein, especially on the underside, flared near the sheath then gradually tapering to a fine point; light to mid green, the lower leaves browning early. Inflorescence, produced September to October, a loosely branched panicle, the terminal one staminate, the axillary ones pistillate, the grains being borne on long, thread-like stalks, each grain up to 1.5 cm long, about half as much across; white to bluish-grey, becoming dark grey or black at maturity.

## *C.l-j.* 'Aurea-zebrina' hort.
Has the leaf blades striped yellow.

## *C.l-j.* var. *stenocarpa* Stapf.
Has cylindrical fruits and it is this form that produces the seeds used for ornament.

## CORTADERIA Stapf.
A genus of about 24 species of generally robust, tussock-forming perennials from scrubland and rough grassland in South America with 4 species in New Zealand and 1 in New Guinea. Separate plants either male and female in some species, or female and bisexual in others. One or two of the large species are highly ornamental and are widely grown for their showy, feathery panicles, the female plumes being showier than the male ones. These are excellent for indoor decoration, but should be picked as soon as the panicles have emerged. If left any longer the spikelets are soon shed and the plumes shatter early. Generally easily grown in good, fertile soil in a sunny, open position. Best increased by division in late spring (April). The planting site should be thoroughly prepared in advance as for a shrub or tree. Seed-raised plants exhibit appreciable variation.

Leaves flat. Inflorescence a large, plumiose panicle; spikelets with the glumes longer than the lowest lemma up to as long as the spikelet, 1-nerved. Lemma membranous with shaggy hairs and a terminal awn; rachilla with shaggy hairs.

## *C.fulvida* (Buchanan) Zotov: Kakaho, Erect-plumed tussock grass
Sometimes included in *C.richardii* (*C.conspicua* Auct.), but quite distinct in its erect 1-sided plume. The New Zealand *Cortaderia* spp. of which this is typical are intermediate in character between the true pampas grasses and the tussock grasses. The flowering culms of this species are widely used for thatching in New Zealand, and the Maoris make beautiful plaited artifacts from the split culms. Differs from *C.selloana* most noticeably in having lighter green leaves, the narrowness of the leaves, the vestigial ligules, being reduced to a mere wavy line of short hairs; and in its tussock-like inflorescence.

Grows to about 2 m when in flower, leaves mainly basal, the blades involute, sparsely covered with soft hairs, margins toothed; leaf tips ending in a long, attenuated curling point. Inflorescence, produced May to July, a much-branched panicle up to 45 cm long, about one-third as wide, the weight of the spikelets causing the culms to bend over, making the inflorescence look 1-sided, though it is not; flowers pale golden-brown. Native of open grassland, it makes an ideal lawn specimen.

### *C.jubata* (Lemoine) Stapf.: Purple pampas

Broadly similar in vegetative characters to *C.selloana*, this species differs from *C.selloana* chiefly in its more loosely constructed panicles with nodding branches, smaller spikelets and in the different colouring, the plumes of this species tinged pink, red, mauve or purple. Flowering stems to 3 m: plumes 60 cm or more long, September and October. Generally not so satisfactory as *C.selloana*, the flowering culms often broken by high winds and rather more frost-tender and liable to be killed in cold districts. H5.

### *C.richardii* (Endl.) Zotov.: Toetoe, Plumed tussock

The largest of all the New Zealand grasses, it differs notably from *C.fulvida* chiefly in its greater size, its more showy inflorescence and most of all in its outward-arching flowering culms. Grows to 2.4 m. Leaves serrated rather than toothed. Inflorescence a much-branched panicle up to 60 cm long, about one-third as much across, bearing spikelets on all its branches, the weight of these causing the branchlets to droop to one side, giving the inflorescence a 1-sided appearance. The flower-head is very much more dense and a more nearly white than that of *C.fulvida*. Makes a magnificent lawn specimen. Grows in the wild often in boggy ground, at the edges of lakes, sometimes as a marginal, the crown covered by 5–10 cm of water. H5.

### *C.selloana* (Schult.) Aschers & Graebn.: Pampas grass

The true pampas grass from the pampa prairies of South America. Without doubt one of the finest of all grasses, both for garden and home decoration. An imposing plant at all seasons, even when not in flower, the tussock of arching leaves giving it a worthwhile architectural quality. The flowers are impressive by any standards: not only for their size, but because of their gracefulness; extremely long-lasting on the plant, they come into flower in late summer and remain unshattered well into winter. Can be used either as single specimens in the lawn, in groups among shrubs or in massed plantings. They contrast well with such broad-leaved plants as *Bergenia*, and blend harmoniously with the yuccas. Such combinations would be well suited to amenity plantings as well as to private gardens. The flowers show to best effect when grown against a dark background, especially if the afternoon or evening sun can shine through them. The female is to be preferred to the male, having more showy and longer-lasting inflorescences.

Large, densely tufted, tussock-forming perennial growing to 3 m. Roots coarse and fibrous, not stoloniferous. Leaf sheaths less rigid than in other species, the ligules vestigial, replaced by a fringe of coarse hairs. Leaves mid to glaucous green, up to 3 m long, and as wide as 2 cm at the base, evenly tapering to an attenuated point; more or less arching, flat or slightly U-shaped in section, the margins very scabrid. Flowering season late summer to autumn. Inflorescence a more or less loosely formed panicle. The plant is dioecious: the male inflorescence is a narrow, oblong panicle up to 1 m long, about one-quarter as much across, the spikelets very glabrous. The female panicle is broadly pyramidal in form, up to 1 m long, about half as much at its widest point across; hairy, silky, opens creamy-white, usually matures to silvery-white, sometimes slightly tinted rose.

The pampas grasses grow best in fertile, well-drained soil in sun. Inclined to be intolerant of cold clay soils. The best colouring of the foliage is achieved on sandy soils where the plants are growing rather drier than is ideal. Can look stunning grown by the side of a pond or pool, where the reflection can double the appeal of the plant; but they will not grow well if their roots are actually in water. The white-flowered forms are gems for brightening up a dark corner in the garden, but the plant itself, however dark its background, must have good light, preferably full sun. Plants tend to gather a lot of dead material at the centre of the tussock, and this should be removed by cutting the plants down in earliest spring just before new growth appears, and carefully removing the dead material by hand. If done annually, the task will never become daunt-ingly difficult. However, tough gloves must be worn. The leaf margins are serrated like a finely honed saw, and can inflict severe cuts—as deep as the bone. Some people recommend setting fire to the dead material in spring: but this method could, at the least, burn the incipient shoots, or, at the worst, so damage the rootstock that the plant itself is killed. A quick singe with a flame gun can achieve the degree of cleaning up required. In those parts of the USA where the plant is not winter-hardy (it will not stand temperatures below 7°C for prolonged periods), specimens can be lifted and moved to a cool, frost-free place, their roots covered with damp peat through the winter, and then replaced outside in spring once the danger of frosts is over. The cultivars can be increased by division in earliest spring, just as the new growth is about to emerge: late February in southern Britain, early March in colder areas. Where plants of both sexes are being grown, fertile seed may be produced after long, hot summers, and this is worth sowing. The cultivar 'Silver Stripe' is female, and sowing of fertile seed will produce a small proportion of seedlings with a greater or lesser degree of white variegation on the leaves. It will also produce albino seedlings which will not grow. H4.

### C.s. 'Bertini'

A dwarf cultivar, a perfect miniature of the type, with narrow, grassy foliage and perfectly formed female panicles, rather broader in proportion to their length than in the type plant. Grows no more than 60–100 cm when in flower. H4.

### C.s. 'Carminea Rendatleri'
Sometimes incorrectly referred to *C.jubata*, a more tender species with some-times pinkish plumes. *C.s.* 'Carmina Rendatleri' can be made to sound enchanting in catalogues, but all too frequently is a disaster in the garden. Differs from the type in having distinctive pinkish-purplish plumes borne on 2.4 m culms high above the foliage. Culms weak, frequently broken by the wind. H4.

### C.s. 'Carnea'
An outstanding cultivar in which the plumes are delicate pink. Otherwise, similar to the type. H4.

### C.s. 'Elegans'
Differs from the type in that its panicles are distinctly silvery-white instead of the rather rich creamy-white of the type. H4.

### C.s. 'Gold Band'
Formerly known as 'Aureo-lineata'. In this cultivar, the leaves are broadly margined with rich golden-yellow, turning completely old gold as they age. Smaller than the type, growing to about the same proportions as 'Silver Stripe'. Probably the better of the two golden-variegated pampas grasses, seemingly as hardy as the type, and as effective in flower as the cultivar 'Pumila'. H4.

### C.s. 'Marabout'
Reputedly the finest of all the white-flowered cultivars, bearing huge plumes of the purest white on strong, erect culms. The panicles are more dense than in the type, and also slightly larger. H4.

### C.s. 'Montrosa'
The largest-growing of all the cultivars, forming a huge mound of foliage—as tall as 2 m—and bearing gigantic panicles, well over 60 cm in length on the heads of stems that can, with good cultivation, top 3 m. More usually, the plumes are not carried high enough above the foliage to be as effective as other white-flowered cultivars. H4.

### C.s. 'Pumila'
The dwarf pampas grass. A perfect small form of the type, growing to about 1.2 m when in flower. Probably the most floriferous of all the cultivars. Certainly the best choice for smaller gardens. H4.

### C.s. 'Rosea'
The pink pampas grass. Perhaps less exciting than its name might lead one to

72

hope. Panicles tinged pink: certainly not true pink. Interesting where several cultivars are grown together. H4.

### C.s. 'Silver Beacon'
Similar to 'Silver Stripe' but differing in its more rigid, less arching leaves, and in the purple colouring of its flowering culms. H4.

### C.s. 'Silver Stripe'
Formerly known as 'Albo-lineata'. Leaves edged with white, the brilliance of whiteness increasing as the season advances. Smaller-growing than the type, possibly slightly less hardy though not yet sufficiently widely grown for this to be fully assessed. The flower is female, borne on stems up to 1.6 m tall, not so effective as those of the type. H4.

### C.s. 'Sunningdale Silver'
By far the best of the larger-growing, white-flowered forms with elegant panicles borne on stems up to 3.5 m tall, well clear of the foliage. The stems are strong enough to withstand all but the fiercest storm winds. In all respects, an outstanding form. H4.

### C.s. 'Violacea'
A fascinating cultivar in which the panicles are distinctly violet. The strength of the colouring is good enough to make this worth growing. In other respects it is similar to the type. H4.

## CORYNEPHORUS Beauv.
A genus of 5 or 6 species of annual and perennial grasses from Europe and the Mediterranean through to Iran. They are natives of sandy places, including littoral dunes. They are very similar to *Aira* but differ in having club-shaped awns. One species is cultivated for ornament. It is an annual, easily grown in good or light soil, from seed sown in late spring.

Panicle contracted; spikelets 2-flowered with rachilla extension; glumes equal; as long as spikelet; lemmas membranous, with a basal club-shaped awn.

### C.canescens (L.) Beauv.: Grey hair grass
Low, tufted annual grown for its very fine, almost hair-like leaves of a distinct blue-grey colouring.

## CYMBOPOGON Sprengel
A genus of about 40 species of robust usually perennial savannah grasses from the Old World tropics and subtropics. They are widely cultivated for the essential oils which can be distilled from their leaves and which are sometimes used as perfume. One species, *C.citratus*, is also used both as a medicinal and

as a culinary herb, and is grown as an ornamental in America though scarcely used as one in Europe. Another species, *C.nardus*, is the source of oil of citronella. They are best grown as perennials in a pot in a greenhouse to be stood out in summer, as plants grown from seed do not reach sufficient size in a single season to be of any account.

Large, strong-growing, tufted grasses with linear to lanceolate leaf blades and large, much-branched inflorescences bearing curious spathe-like bracts at the axils of which arise a pair of slender, spike-like racemes: spikelets in pairs on the raceme axis, each pair consisting of 1 stalkless, bisexual spikelet and 1 stalked and male spikelet always without awns.

### *C.citratus* (DC. ex Nees) Stapf.
Densely tufted perennial, stems stout or slender, smooth, up to nearly 2 m. Leaves to nearly 1 m long, 2 cm wide, with stout midrib. Late summer, panicle nodding, loose, much-branched, up to 60 cm long, the racemes spreading. Spikelets without awns. Grown for its lemon-scented leaves: the source of lemon-grass oil. G2.

### *C.nardus* (L.) Rendle: Citronella grass
Densely tufted perennial; stems smooth, stout, erect, up to 2.3 m. Leaves to 1 m long, 2 cm wide. Panicles much-branched, congested, up to 60 cm long; spikelets awnless, late summer. The source of citronella oil. G2.

### *C.schoenanthus* (L.) Spreng.
Densely tufted perennial, with erect, slender stems to 45 cm tall. Leaves filiform, flexuous, up to 30 cm long. Panicle, produced in late summer, up to 30 cm long, racemes to 2.5 cm long, densely hairy, becoming spreading. The source of camel-grass oil. G2.

## CYNODON Rich.
A genus of some 8 to 10 species of perennial, sward-forming grasses from grazed areas in the Old World tropics, with one pantropical species reaching into the warm temperate regions. *C.dactylon*, the commonest lawn grass in the tropics, is sometimes grown as an ornamental in cool temperate regions. It should be grown in an open, sunny position and is easily increased by its stolons.

Low-growing; with creeping rhizomes or stolons, the leaf blades short and narrow; the inflorescence digitate at the tops of the slender, erect culms; spikelets laterally compressed, 1-flowered, with sometimes a rachilla extension on which a vestigial floret is sometimes borne; glumes narrow, acute; lemmas keeled, awnless.

**C.dactylon** (L.) Pers.: Bermuda grass, Couch, Creeping dog's tooth grass, Creeping finger grass, Doob, Kweek, St Lucie's grass
An interesting low grass with purple fingers. Probably not native to the UK but introduced long ago and now naturalised in some, especially mild, coastal, areas. It has endured in a lawn at Kew for over 100 years, surviving extremes both of frost and drought.

Mat-forming perennial with profusely branching runners rooting at the nodes to form new leafy shoots and flowering culms, growing up to 15 cm rarely more. Culms erect or decumbent at the base becoming erect; very slender, smooth. Leaf sheaths rounded, short, becoming whitish on the older stems. Leaf blades up to 15 cm long, 3 mm across, flat in section, minutely rough, stiff, invariably produced at 45° to the culm, evenly tapering to a point; greyish-green; short-haired or almost hairless. Inflorescence, produced July to September, a cluster of 2 or 3 spikes produced at the tips of the flowering culms, each up to 5 cm long; digitate, the fingers at first compressed, soon spreading; straight, stiff, dark purple. Its densely creeping habit can make it a useful binding grass on warm, sandy soils and on banks, but otherwise its spreading habit needs controlling. H4.

## CYNOSURUS L.
A genus of 5 species of annual or perennial grasses from meadowlands around the Mediterranean. Two species are sometimes grown as ornamentals, for their 1-sided panicles, but have nothing much to commend them. They prefer light, sandy soil.

Tufted grasses. Leaves flat. Inflorescence a 1-sided spike; spikelets of 2 kinds, the 2 kinds paired sterile and fertile together, the outer sterile covering the fertile which is stalkless; sterile spikelets made up to 2 glumes and several narrow lemmas on a continuous rachis; the fertile spikelets 2- or 3-flowered, glumes narrow, lemmas broader and with a terminal awn.

**C.cristatus** L.: Crested dog's tail grass
Low, compactly tufted perennial with slender, erect stems up to 60 cm tall. Leaves up to 15 cm long. Panicles, produced June to August, dense, 1-sided, spike-like, stiff and erect, up to 12.5 cm long, green or tinged purplish. Spikelets in dense clusters, 2–5-flowered. H5.

**C.echinatus** L.: Rough dog's tail grass
Tufted annual, stems erect or ascending to nearly 1 m. Leaves to 20 cm long. Panicles, produced June and July, 1-sided, dense, erect, bristly, up to 7.5 cm long, green or tinged purplish, shining. Spikelets in dense clusters the fertile ones 1–5-flowered, the lemmas tipped with a fine straight awn. *C.elegans* Desf. is similar.

13  *Cynosurus echinatus*

### *C.elegans* Desf.
See under *C.echinatus*.

## DACTYLIS L.
A genus of a single species of tufted perennial from Eurasia found in a variety
of habitats including woods, meadows and waste land. It is of value as a forage
grass but scarcely ornamental except in its variegated forms. It is easily grown
in any fertile soil and is readily increased by seed or by division in spring.

A coarse, erect, tufted perennial soon forming large tussocks; leaf blades flat.
Inflorescence a panicle with few spreading branches and the spikelets crowded
in dense clusters at the ends of the branches; spikelets 1–5-flowered, laterally
compressed; glumes about equal, keeled; lemmas papery, shortly awned at the
tip.

### *D.glomerata* L.
The typical plant is a common and unattractive weed, but important as fodder
and pasture grass. The variegated forms cultivated in gardens, being much
less strong-growing, are, at their best, very desirable garden grasses.

Densely tufted perennial with compressed shoots, growing up to 1 m when in flower. Culms erect or spreading, sometimes somewhat decumbent at the base and becoming erect; the nodes well defined but not greatly swollen, variable in thickness from slender to rather stout, smooth or rough. Leaf sheaths clearly keeled, at first entire; rough; usually hairless, occasionally somewhat hairy. Leaf blades up to 46 cm long, 1.5 cm wide, somewhat V-shaped in section, at first folded but then opening, firm, somewhat arched, becoming straight on the upper part of the culms; rough; mid-green to bluish-green. Inflorescence, produced June to September, a 1-sided panicle up to 18 cm long, the spikelets dense, 1-sided. H1.

### D.g. 'Aurea' hort.
Leaves yellow instead of green. There is some doubt as to whether this variety is still in cultivation. H1.

### D.g. 'Elegantissima'
A slender dwarf with green-and-white-striped leaves, tending to form small hummocks to about 15 cm tall, and excellent as an edging plant or for rock gardens. Seldom flowers. H1.

### D.g. 'Variegata'
Slightly more vigorous than D.g. 'Elegantissima', growing to about 25 cm, leaves brightly striped with green and white. There seems to be some confusion in the trade as to which variety is which, this one probably being the more common on the market. H1.

The variegated forms do badly on heavy clay or poorly drained soils but are most attractive in spring and early summer, though they tend to lose their brightness as the summer wears on, and to look rather untidy through winter. They can look dramatic when thickly planted as ground-cover.

## DANTHONIA Lam. & DC.
A genus of about 20 species of perennial tussock grasses from the grasslands of Europe and North and South America. The name is sometimes used in a wider sense to embrace *Chionochloea*, *Rytidosperma* and some other nearly related genera. The distinctions between these genera can only be maintained by splitting botanical hairs; but if the genera are lumped together the species so overlap that distinctions fail. Not particularly ornamental and easily grown in fertile garden soil.

## DESCHAMPSIA Beauv.
A genus of about 40 species of generally tufted perennials (annual species in America) from the temperate regions of both hemispheres. They are natives of woods, meadows and moorlands. A few species are highly ornamental and

make good showy garden plants. They can be grown in most fertile soils and will tolerate some shade (as in light woodland) as well as rather dry conditions. Easily increased by seed sown outdoors in autumn or by division in the spring.

Small or tall, tufted plants with flat leaves and showy spikelets in large, open panicles. Rachilla hairy; spikelets laterally compressed, 2-flowered with rachilla extension, this sometimes bearing a reduced floret; glumes about equal, and equal to or longer than the florets; lemmas thin, truncate, 2–4-toothed at the apex, with short hairs at the base, and with a slender awn arising on the back from the middle or below the middle, the awn straight, bent or twisted.

### *D.caespitosa* (L.) Beauv.: Hassocks, Tufted hair grass, Tussock grass

An outstanding grass at all seasons, grown for its huge panicle—among the most graceful of all grasses. There is probably no other grass that looks quite so delicate when in flower, the inflorescence dwarfing the basal leaf tuft. The stems are very stiff and carry their heads well into winter. Flower colour variable, and in localities where this grass is abundant, it is worth seeking out forms with differently coloured flowers for the garden. The shiny, deep green, rather spiky leaves are attractive in winter and earliest spring.

Densely tufted, evergreen perennial, without stolons, growing to 1 m, usually more than half that height. Culms erect in warm climates, rather slender, stiff and smooth; deep green. Leaf sheaths usually rounded on the back, sometimes keeled, usually smoothly, sometimes somewhat rough; deep green. Leaf blades up to 60 cm long, 5 mm wide, flat or rolled, tapering to a point, or sometimes rather blunt at the tip; the upper surface ribbed, with the ribs and margins very rough, the underside smooth; deep green. Inflorescence, produced June to August, a huge, loose panicle, usually erect, sometimes slightly nodding, up to 50 cm long and 20 cm across, the slender branches produced in whorls along the main axis, very spreading, the spikelets loosely arranged along the branches; very variable in colour, green, silver, golden, purple, sometimes with several of these colours occurring together in the same panicle.

A grass of wet, ill-drained places and heavy soils, needing semi-shade to do really well. Mixes well with ferns, hostas and other woodland plants. Seeds freely in some gardens, and seed provides a ready means of increase. H1.

### *D.c.* 'Bronze Veil' ('Bronzeschleier')
A form with large, bronzy-yellow panicles.

### *D.c.* 'Dew Carrier' ('Tautraeger')
A small, compact form with bluish heads.

### *D.c.* 'Gold Dust' ('Goldstaub')
Golden-yellow spikelets.

*D.c.* 'Golden Showers' ('Goldhaenge')
Flower-heads golden-yellow. Similar to *D.c.* 'Gold Veil' but flowers later.
Good for cutting.

*D.c.* 'Gold Veil' ('Goldschleier')
Large plumes of silvery flowers in summer. Heads in autumn excellent for
cutting.

*D.c. parviflora* (Thuill.) Coss. & Germ.
Differs from the typical plant in its smaller panicles, its smaller leaves and its
generally shorter stature. H1.

*D.c.* 'Scotland' ('Schottland')
A variant found in Scotland. Seems to differ little from the typical plant.

*D.c. tardiflora*
A low-growing (20–80 cm), late-flowering form with light green spikelets.

*D.c. vivipara*
One of the few viviparous ornamental grasses. The young plants which occur
in place of seed are freely produced, their weight bowing the wiry stems to the
ground. To be fully appreciated, needs to be grown in a raised bed. H1.

*D.c. vivipara* 'Fairy's Joke'
Apparently a fancy name for the typical *D.c. vivipara*.

**D.flexuosa** (L.) Trin.: Wavy hair grass
A smaller, more refined version of the preceding species. A densely tufted
perennial to 60 cm. Culms stiff, wiry, smooth, very slender. Sheaths rounded
on the back, slightly rough. Blades to 30 cm long, tightly incurved in section;
stiff, dark green, the tip hairy. Inflorescence, produced June and July, a very
loose, open panicle to 15 cm long, 10 cm across; branches hair-like, spikelets
borne in pairs; varing in colour, silvery, brownish or purplish, always glistening. Acid soil, sun or shade; seed or division. H1.

*D.f.* 'Fly Swarm' ('Mueckenschwarm')
Myriads of small, dark spikelets.

## DIGITARIA Haller
A genus of about 230 species of mainly perennial grasses from the tropics and
warm temperate regions. They come from a wide variety of habitats, one
species being a minor cereal in West Africa, another an important pasture
grass, while one, *D.didactyla*, known as blue couch, is used in lawns. Some are

serious weeds. One annual species is grown as an ornamental annual. It needs a warm sunny position and is easily raised from seed sown outdoors in spring where the plants are to grow.

Plants erect or prostrate. Leaves flat. Inflorescence digitate composed of up to 5 1-sided racemes at the top of a short central axis. Spikelets in groups of 1–5; shortly stalked or nearly sessile, alternate in 2 rows on one side of a 3-angled rachis; the spikelets lanceolate; the lower glume reduced to a minute scale or absent; upper glume much reduced; lower floret sterile and replaced by a lemma; fertile lemma with transparent margin embracing most of the palea.

### *D.sanguinalis* (L.) Scop.: Crab grass, Hairy finger grass

Small, loosely tufted annual to 30 cm, rarely more. Culms erect, sometimes branching low down, occasionally rooting at the lower nodes; thickish, somewhat hairy at the nodes; generally hairless. Leaf sheaths loose, sparsely hairy. Leaf blades up to 10 cm long, 8 mm across, rounded at the base; slightly undulate along the margins, especially in the lower part; broad, then narrowing to an abrupt point; hairy, rarely hairless; rough along the margins. Inflorescence, produced August to October, a digitate raceme with 4–6 spikes each up to 18 cm long, becoming spreading, the spikelets in pairs along one side of the axis; brownish-purplish.

Grown for its digitate inflorescence, in complete contrast to the more usual grass flower-heads.

### ECHINARIA Desf.

A genus of a single species of annual grass from dry, open habitats in the Mediterranean and Middle East. It is sometimes grown for ornament for its showy heads which are huge in proportion to the plant. Easily grown in fertile garden soil in a sunny place. Sow seed in April in drifts or patches where the plants are to grow.

Small annual with usually flat leaves. Inflorescence a dense, spherical, prickly head; spikelets 3–4-flowered (rarely 1-flowered). Glumes about equal, 2-nerved; lemmas leathery with 5–7 strong nerves prolonged into flattened, spine-like awns; palea with 2 strong veins similarly prolonged into awns.

### *E.capitata* (L.) Desf.

A delightful dwarf with heads that are huge in proportion to the plant, and fearsome in the manner of a miniature, medieval war mace.

Dwarf, tufted annual to 20 cm. Culms several, rarely solitary, erect or spreading; stiff, smooth. Leaf sheaths rounded at the back; green; soon splitting. Leaf blades up to 5 cm long, 2 mm wide, flat in section; hairy, bright green. Inflorescence, produced June to July, a densely packed, round panicle up to 19 mm long and the same across; becoming hard and spiny (*echinaria*), the spikelets stalkless, short-awned.

# ECHINOCHLOA Beauv.

A genus of 30 or perhaps more species of annual and perennial grasses from the tropics and the warm temperate regions. They grow in water or damp places. One species mimics rice and has become a serious rice-field weed: other species provide minor cereal crops. Two species are sometimes grown as ornamentals. They should be raised from seed sown in a warm greenhouse and the plants returned under glass for the winters.

Coarse, sometimes succulent, plants with narrow, flat leaves and lacking ligules. Inflorescence a compact panicle composed of several to many short, densely flowered racemes arranged along a main axis. Spikelets 1 or several in clusters along one side of the branches; glumes unequal, the first about half as long as the spikelet; the second equal to the sterile lemma, the glume short-awned, the lemma long-awned; the fertile lemma hard, smooth, clasping the margins of the palea.

## *E.crus-galli* (L.) Beauv.: Cockspur grass, Barnyard millet

Tufted annual to 1.2 m, usually grown for ornament in its long-awned forms, when it is most decorative and excellent for drying if the heads are picked as soon as they develop. Stems stout, usually branched, erect or spreading; leaves hairless, the blades up to 20 cm long. Panicles produced August, September, erect or nodding, up to 20 cm long, 7.5 cm wide, the racemes very dense, green or purplish, up to 5 cm long; the spikelets awned or awnless, the awns up to 5 cm long.

## *E.polystachya* (H.B.K.) Hitchc.

Coarse perennial to nearly 2 m. Stems stout, stem joints densely covered with stiff, hair-like bristles and yellowish hairs. Panicle up to 30 cm long, dense, late summer. Occasionally grown, but not as ornamental as the preceding. G1.

# EHRHARTA Thunb.

A genus of about 35 species of annual and perennial grasses of which 25 are endemic to South Africa, the others coming from Indonesia and New Zealand. They vary greatly in habitat. One perennial species is grown as an ornamental. It succeeds in any fertile soil in sun. Seed should be sown in April.

Generally tufted plants, rarely with a tuberous, basal internode. Leaves flat or rolled, ligule membranous. Inflorescence a panicle or raceme; spikelets stalked, 3-flowered, the lowest 2 reduced to the lemma, the upper fertile; glumes persistent, shorter than florets; sterile lemmas transversely wrinkled, narrowing to a hook at the base; fertile lemma smaller.

## *E.erecta* Lam.: Veldt grass

Loosely tufted perennial. Stems branched, ascending, up to nearly 1 m. Leaves to 15 cm long. Panicles, produced August and September, loose, up to 20 cm

81

long, pale green. Spikelets awnless, the second lemma transversely wrinkled. H5–G1.

## ELEUSINE Gaertn.

A genus of 9 or 10 species of annual and perennial savannah grasses, mainly from east and north-east tropical Africa, but 1 species is cosmopolitan and 1 occurs only in South America. *E.coracana* is the finger millet of Africa, China and India where its grain is used for making beer. They make attractive ornamentals with their unusual, digitate panicles. They should be treated as tender annuals.

### *E.coracana* (L.) Gaertn.: Finger millet

Annual with robust stems up to 1.5 m, solitary or tufted. Panicles, produced July and August, with 2–5 digitate spikes at the apex of the stem. Spikelets persistent; grain foxy-red, small.

14 *Eleusine coracana*

### *E.indica* (L.) Gaertn.: Goose grass

Similar to *E.coracana*, but smaller in stature with larger digitate spikes.

## ELYMUS L.

A genus of about 150 species of erect, rather tall, tufted or rhizomatous, mainly perennial grasses from the temperate regions of both hemispheres but particularly concentrated in Asia. They come from a wide range of habitats including meadows, woodlands and sand dunes. A couple of species are excellent forage grasses, and another is a notable sand dune binder. Several species are ornamental for their blue leaves, though *E.arenarius* is very rampant. They can be grown in ordinary garden soil, preferably a sunny position and may be increased by division at any time other than winter or by seed sown out of doors in April.

Tufted or rhizomatous perennials with generally flat leaf blades and terminal spikes; spikelets solitary or in pairs or 3s at each node, usually crowded, almost stalkless, often overlapping, 1–11-flowered; the rachilla articulating above the glumes but between the florets; glumes equal, rigid, 1–11-nerved, asymmetric, awnless or shortly awned and often positioned just in front of the spikelets; lemmas round on the back, usually with awns.

## *E.arenarius* L.: Blue lyme grass, Bunch grass, Lyme grass, Sand wild rye

This aggressive grass is a native of coastal sand dunes, which it can colonise. It has the ability to bind sand, and is sometimes deliberately cultivated to stabilise shifting dunes. In spite of its potential aggressiveness, it is a highly desirable garden grass, grown for its distinctive blue-grey foliage.

Vigorously stoloniferous, deciduous perennial, forming extensive tufts or colonies. Root system extensive, composed both of fine feeding roots and long, stout and extremely tough stolons. Leaf sheaths smooth, with 2 spreading auricles at the apex; ligules minutely hairy. Leaf blades up to 60 cm long, 1.75 cm wide, flat or inrolled, rigid, sharply pointed, rough on the upper surface, smooth beneath; minutely hairy above and on the margins; metallic blue-grey in colour. Inflorescence, produced June to August, a stiff, stout but compact spike up to 35 cm long, 2.5 cm wide; metallic blue, becoming buff or brown with age. H4.

A particular favourite of Gertrude Jekyll, who recommended planting it among seakale. She suggested cutting back almost to ground level once the flowering culms start to rise, to obtain a second crop of fresh foliage in midsummer. It would also look good grown, as Bowles has suggested, in front of a dark shrubbery.

## *E.a.* subsp. *mollis* (Trin.) Hult.

Differs in its wider glumes and pubescence beneath the spikes. H4.

## *E.canadensis* L.: Canadian wild rye

Very variable species, 60–180 cm tall, stems erect, slender or stout, green or blue, sharply pointed, up to 45 cm long, rough and hispid above; panicles dense, bristly, nodding or dropping, up to 25 cm long, July to September. An interesting grass in its smallest, green-leafed forms. H1.

## *E.c.* var. *glaucofolius*
A subtle metallic bluish-grey throughout. H1.

## *E.giganteus* Vahl.
A very striking grass grown for the colour of its foliage, which is an even better blue than that of *E.arenarius*. Grows to 1.2 m. Culms stout, sheaths blue, blades to 60 cm long, erect, tapering to a fine point, smooth above, prominently ribbed below, giving a spiky appearance. Inflorescence, produced June to August, a dense spike to 25 cm long; white. Grows best in full sun in fertile, well-drained soil. H4.

## *E.g.* 'Vahl Glaucus'
Appears to be a fancy name for the typical plant.

## *E.hispidus* (Opiz) Melderis
Ssp. *hispidus*. Tufted perennial without stolons. Stems up to 100 cm. Leaves held upright prominently veined, the margins conspicuously hardened, rough to the touch, usually with long sparse hairs on the upper surface, hairless beneath. Spikes fairly dense, up to 20 cm long. Spikelets up to 15 mm, hairless. Glumes up to 8 × 3 mm. Lemmas up to 11 mm, sometimes mucronately awned. The whole plant is intensely blue, though the seed heads fade to a parchment colour. Of easy cultivation. H2.

## *E. magellanicus* (Desv.) A.Löve
One of the most brilliantly blue of all grasses all above-ground parts of the plant being of an intense electric blue. A laxly tufted perennial, sometimes with rhizomes. Leaves flat or folded, smooth or minutely hairy above, up to 3.5 cm × 7 mm: ligule 0.3–2 mm, truncate, sheath smooth or minutely hairy. Culms up to 100 cm, smooth, round in section. Spikes up to 19 cm long, dense, the spikelets longer than the internodes the rachis smooth or rough on the margins. Spikelets up to 29 mm, with 2–7 florets. Glumes equal or the upper slightly longer, up to 16 mm. H4.

There has been much confusion over the naming and identities of the two blue grasses grown in gardens as *Agropyron glaucum*, *A.magellanicum* or *A.pubiflorum*. The plant described here has leaves that lie almost flat on the ground. I have encountered it variously as *A.magellanicum* and *A.pubiflorum*, but these two names are synonymous since *A.magellanicum* was distinguished from *A.pubiflorum* solely on the grounds of its possessing rhizomes, which *A.pubiflorum* lacks. However, this is a habitat-induced phenomenon and is not therefore sufficient to distinguish species. The blue 'Agropyron' with erect leaves rather like a dwarf *Elymus arenarius*, which for long has been known as *A.glaucum*, is now referred to *Elymus hispidus*.

### *E.paboanus* Claus.
A blue grass forming small, dense tufts. Rhizomes shortly creeping. Stems erect, 30 to 90 cm tall. Leaves up to 30 cm long, flat or rolled, stiff, prominently veined above. Panicles, produced June to August, spike-like, erect, whitish to greyish-green, up to 12.5 cm long. Decorative with its densely woolly, whitish spikes in combination with the steely blue leaves. H1.

### *E.sibiricus* L.
A tufted perennial, to 1 m, differing from the other ornamental species in its nodding not erect spikes which are attractive cut and dried. Stems slender, erect, with black nodes. Leaves green, finely pointed 25 cm long, thin, rough. June to August, spikes nodding, up to 25.6 cm long, curved or flexuous, quite dense. Spikelets in pairs, 3–7-flowered, green or purplish; glumes linear, awn-tipped; lemmas lanceolate, rough, tipped with a curved awn, 2.5 cm long. H1.

### *E.virginicus* L.: Virginia wild rye
This is a far cry from the blue-leaved *E.arenarius*, not only in that, instead of growing on sun-baked sand dunes it comes from shaded woodland and low, damp ground, but also in that, whereas Gertrude Jekyll thought the flowers of *E.arenarius* so insignificant that she recommended cutting them off, it is for the glory of its inflorescence that this species is grown. Grows to about 30 cm. Leaf blades to 15 cm long; flat, scabrous, dark green. Inflorescence, produced July to August, a narrowly compact spike to 15 cm long, relatively thick; at first erect, later nodding or drooping. The flowering culms are exceptionally strong and seldom broken even in gales, though they may bend towards the soil under the weight of the inflorescence. The whole plant takes on an interesting brownish colour if grown in full sun. H4.

### *E.v.* var. *submuticus* Hook.
Differs in having awnless glumes. H4.

## ERAGROSTIS Wolf.: Love grass
A very varied genus of some 350 species of annual and perennial grasses from a great variety of habitats in the tropics and subtropics. *E.tef* (teff) is the stable cereal in Ethiopia. A few species are worth growing for their showy panicles. They can be grown in ordinary garden soil in sun. The annual species should be raised from seed sown in April where the plants are to be grown or under glass earlier. The perennials can be increased by seed or division.

Tufted plants with leaves mostly flat, the sheaths usually glandular, the ligule usually reduced to a ring of hairs. Inflorescence a panicle—open or contracted; spikelets 2–many-flowered, the florets intricate, the rachilla disarticulating above the glumes and between the florets; glumes equal or unequal, shorter than the florets. Lemmas acuminate, 3-nerved, membranous, round on the back, without awns: the grain free, falling with the lemmas, the palie remaining on the rachilla.

### *E.aspera* (Jacq.) Nees

An elegant, beautiful grass grown for its decorative, erect, much-branched panicle. A tufted annual with erect stems to about 1 m. Leaves flat, finely pointed, up to 30 cm long. Panicles, produced August and September, very open, loose, often nearly half the height of the plant. Spikelets long-stalked, linear, 4–16-flowered, purplish or pale.

### *E.capillaris* (L.) Nees: Lace grass

Grown for its elegant, much-branched and delicately divided panicles. A tufted annual with erect, slender stems to 60 cm. Leaf blades erect, flat; sheaths hairy, bearded at the top. Panicles, produced July to September, large, loose, open, about two-thirds the height of the plant, very finely branched. Spikelets ovate, 2–5-flowered, long-stalked, lead-coloured.

### *E.chloromelas* Steud.: Boer love grass

Grown for its almost grey foliage and bright purple panicles. Densely tufted perennial to 1 m. Culms erect, usually rather stout. Sheaths green, rounded, smooth, persistent. Blades to 46 cm long, filiform, bluish, curling. Inflorescence, produced August to September, a lax, open panicle to 20 cm long; branches fine, filiform, flexible, purplish, tending to fall to one side of the head; spikelets dark olive-green. Drought-tolerant. Full sun, any fertile soil; seed or division. H4.

### *E.cilianensis* (All.) Lutati.: Strong scented love grass

Grown for its large, showy, almost lead-coloured panicles. Loosely tufted annual; stems erect or ascending to about 1 m, freely branched. Leaves up to 25 cm, finely pointed, glandular at the margins, the sheaths bearded at the top. Panicles produced July to October, often large, sometimes small, open or contracted, up to 20 cm long, about 10 cm wide, the spikelets short-stalked, up to 50-flowered, light to dark greenish-grey.

### *E.curvula* (Schrad.) Nees: African love grass

Sometimes grown as an ornamental for its strangely coloured panicles. Probably the most widely cultivated of the love grasses. Forms a densely tufted perennial to 1.2 m. Culms erect, stout, dark green. Sheaths rolled, hairy at the base, dark green. Blades to 30 cm long, U-shaped in section, rough on the upper surface, dark green. Inflorescence, produced August to September, a lax, open panicle to 30 cm long, 23 cm across, the spikelets dark olive-grey.

15 *Eragrostis curvula*

These large, loose, somewhat weeping panicles of a curious greyish colour are in perfect contrast to the dark green, persistent foliage. Looks best as a specimen. Hot, dry position in full sun, sandy soil; seed or division. H5.

### *E.japonica* (Thunb.) Trin.: Japanese love grass
Grown for its delicate plumes with dainty spikelets. Tufted annual to 60 cm. Stems slender; leaves flat, pointed, up to 20 cm long, hairless. Panicles, produced August to September, up to 25.5 cm long, bearing branches in whorls, the branches very fine, widely spreading; the spikelets short-stalked, pale or purplish.

### *E.obtusa* Munro ex Stapf.
Grown for its lovely open panicles decked with spikelets resembling those of *Briza media*. Densely tufted perennial with slender, erect stems to 60 cm. Leaves usually rolled, finely pointed, up to 15 cm long. Panicles, produced August to September, open or contracted, up to 13 cm long, 8 cm wide with finely stalked spikelets, the spikelets ovate, strongly compressed, 8–20-flowered, the glumes and lemmas navicular. H4.

### *E.spectabilis* (Pursh) Steud.: Purple love grass, Tumble grass
Well worth growing for its relatively huge, showy panicles. It is one of the tumble grasses, and at maturity the panicles break off and blow about in the wind. Densely tufted, deciduous, perennial grass with slowly spreading rhizomes growing up to 76 cm when in flower. Culms erect or slightly spreading, slender. Leaf sheaths bearded at the top, rolled. Leaf blades up to 30 cm long, 8 mm wide, usually flat in section, straight or slightly undulate, narrowing to an attenuated point; usually hairless, rarely bearing a few hairs. Inflorescence, produced August to September, a lax, open, much-branched panicle up to 23 cm long, almost as much across; the branches hairy at the axils, deep green or purple, the spikelets dark purple or light purple. H4.

### *E.tef* (Zuccagni) Trotter.: Teff
An important food plant grown as an ornamental for its variously coloured spikelets. Annual with slender, erect or spreading stems up to 1.5 m tall. Leaves flat, green, pointed, up to 45 cm long. Panicles, produced August to September, loose, open or contracted, up to 60 cm long with long, slender branches, the spikelets lanceolate on long, slender stalks, 3–18-flowered, green, greyish, white, pink, red, purple or violet.

### *E.trichodes* (Nutt.) Wood.: Sand love grass
An easily grown species with open, ornamental panicles. Frost-hardy at Kew. Densely tufted perennial with slow-spreading rhizomes, to 1.2 m. Culms erect, stiff, slender. Sheaths rolled, hairy in the upper half. Blades to 1 m, flat or

inversely U-shaped, arching, dark green, shiny. Inflorescence, produced August to September, a loose, open panicle to 46 cm long, 30 cm across; branches at first erect, gradually spreading, much forked, with few hairs in the axils; spikelets purplish.

Although this plant has the largest flower-head of the cultivated love grasses, it is a less lovely plant because the heads are not held clear of the foliage. H4.

## ERIOCHLOA Kunth

A notably uniform genus of about 30 species of annual or perennial grasses from the tropics, mainly inhabitants of damp soils. The genus is quite distinct in the way in which the lowest rachilla internode becomes swollen and fused with the lower glume, forming a curious bead-like structure at the base of each spikelet. One annual species is sometimes grown for ornament. It needs a warm, sunny position in good soil and seed should be sown where the plants are to grow.

Generally tufted, often branching, grasses with terminal panicles consisting of several 1-sided racemes arranged (usually closely) along a central axis. Spikelets compressed from top to bottom, single, paired or clustered, with 2 florets, the lower glume reduced to a scale attached to the swollen, bead-like lowest rachilla internode; upper glume as long as the spikelet; lower floret empty, the lemma similar to the upper glume; upper floret fertile, the lemma leathery, enclosing the margins of the palea.

### *E.villosa* (Thunb.) Kunth

Occasionally grown for its substantial terminal spikes which are especially effective in winter decorations. Tufted annual to 60 cm, the panicle composed of 3–15 racemes each up to 2 cm long, the stalks beset with long hairs, summer.

## FESTUCA L.

A genus of about 400 species of usually tufted perennials from the grasslands of the temperate regions of the world and from mountains in the tropics. They vary from small to tall, from tufted to rhizomatous, and in having the spikelets in narrow or open panicles. Some authors divide the genus into 8 sub-genera. Most of the species are good pasture grasses: *F.rubra* is an essential grass in fine lawns. Many species are grown as ornamentals; some are valued for the intense blue of their leaves. The species are all frost-hardy and can mostly be grown in ordinary garden soil in sun. They are easily raised from seed sown out of doors in spring, or by division also in spring.

Low to tall grasses of diverse habit. Leaves mostly rolled to filiform, rarely flat. Panicle open or contracted; spikelets stalked, 2–several-flowered; glumes narrow, unequal, the lower sometimes very small, the upper wider, usually

3-nerved; lemmas rounded on the back, with or without an awn, the awn if present terminal or nearly so.

### *F.altissima* All.: Feed fescue, Wood fescue

An attractive grass, which though not in the first rank of ornamentals, is quite decorative in damp woodlands and by streamsides. Densely tufted perennial with slender or quite stout stems to 1.2 m. Leaves flat, finely pointed, hairless, up to 60 cm long, rough on both surfaces or sometimes only at the margins. Panicles produced May to July loose, open, up to 18 cm long and 13 cm wide; the spikelets 2–5-flowered, oblong to wedge-shaped; lemmas finely pointed. H3.

### *F.amethystina* L.: Large blue fescue

Superficially similar to *F.glauca* var. *caesia* (q.v.), generally of larger, looser habit, a less glaucous blue with a relatively larger and more spectacular inflorescence. A densely tufted perennial to 45 cm with short rhizomes, culms erect. Sheaths rolled, marked with a distinct groove the greater part of their length. Blades glaucous, inrolled, filiform and angular to 15 cm long. Inflorescence, produced May to July, a panicle to 15 cm long; branches in pairs, except the apical one which is single; spikelets green and violet, sometimes only green. A heavier blue than *F.glauca* var. *caesia*. H3.

### *F.a.* 'April Green' ('April Gruen')

Fresh, grey-green leaves.

### *F.a.* 'Bronze Glazed' ('Bronzeglanz')

Has the typical blue-green leaves overlaid a rich bronzy colour. More curious than lovely.

### *F.a.* 'Klose'

Named for German perennial nurseryman Heinz Klose. Leaves olive-green. Unexpectedly attractive and useful.

### *F.arundinacea* Schreb.: Tall fescue

A robust fescue with large, showy panicles suitable for ponds, streams and lakesides. Tufted perennial with stout, erect stems to nearly 2 m tall. Leaves finely pointed, up to 60 cm long; sheaths with ciliate auricles at the apex. Panicles produced June to August large, usually somewhat nodding, open and loose or contracted, up to 53 cm long, green or purplish; the spikelets oblong, up to 10-flowered; lemmas awnless or shortly awned. H3.

### *F.eskia* Ram.

Unlike most of the small fescues, which are grown for their blue or bluish foliage, this is grown for its brilliant green, soft foliage and for its ability to form carpets—useful in rock gardens or among small-growing conifers. A very dense mound or carpet-forming perennial with short but persistently spreading rhizomes, to 15 cm. Culms erect, very slender. Sheaths dark green, slightly rough. Blades to 15 cm inrolled, somewhat U-shaped in section, stiff, ending in a sharp point (hence *eskia*); dark green. Inflorescence, produced June to July, a narrow panicle to 10 cm long, branches narrowly ascending; spikelets at first green, becoming reddish-brown. Does best on light soils. H3.

### F.flavescens Bell
Scarcely differs from *F.eskia* (q.v.) except in that the panicle is strongly yellowish. H3.

### F.gigantea (L.) Vill.: Giant fescue, Giant brome
One of the relatively few ornamental grasses that will thrive in shade, where it should be used. There are better grasses for sunnier situations.

Loosely tufted perennial with both fibrous and coarse roots, not stoloniferous, up to 1.2 m high when in flower. Culms erect, unbranched, smooth, the nodes noticeably purple, sometimes deep purple. Leaf sheaths smooth, rounded, with auricles at the apex. Leaf blade to 60 cm long, 2 cm wide, usually flat in section, sometimes shallowly V-shaped; tapering evenly to a fine tip; deep green, smooth and glossy beneath, rough at the margins and on the upper surface, often twisting in a manner unusual in grass leaves so that both the rough upper surface and the shiny lower surface, can be seen simultaneously. Inflorescence, produced July to August, a loosely formed panicle up to 45 cm long, about two-thirds as much across; nodding, the branches well spaced, spreading and flexuous, usually produced in pairs; green becoming buff. H3.

### F.g. var. *striatus*
Has some leaves feebly striped white. H3.

### F.glacialis Miegev
Essentially a small *F.glauca* var. *caesia*, but of a rather icy blue-green. A densely tufted perennial to 15 cm. Culms erect. Sheaths rolled, blue-green. Blades blue-green, filiform, smooth. Inflorescence a short, thick, clustered panicle; spikelets violet, July–August. Possesses an air of delicacy matched by few other grasses. Full sun, sandy soil. H3.

### F.glauca Lam.
Perhaps the most brilliantly blue of all the cultivated grasses, and probably one of the bluest of all garden plants. Over the years a number of different plants have been sold as this, the confusion arising partly from muddles over nomenclature, partly through misunderstanding of the diagnostic characteristics of the grasses. It is quite often sold as *Festuca ovina glauca*. It could

superficially also be confused with *F.amethystina* (q.v.) or *F.glacialis* (q.v.). It is most commonly confused with *F.rubra*, especially var. *pruinosa*, and it is not uncommon for *F.rubra* to be sold in its stead. The most obvious differences between the two are in the flowering: *F.rubra* flowers May–June, the inflorescence being very narrow; *F.glauca* flowers June–July, the inflorescence being relatively tubby. The only reliable morphological diagnostic characteristic is the sheath: in *rubra* these are entire; in *glauca* split. Further, *glauca* is a densely tufted plant without runners; *rubra* forms a looser tuft, with quite long tillers (underground stems). *F.glauca* is the more attractive garden plant, being a better blue and of a more desirable habit.

Densely tufted perennial to 30 cm with numerous vegetative shoots. Culms erect, slender, stiff. Leaf sheaths split, blue. Leaf blades to 23 cm long, glaucous blue, smooth, hairless, rigid, tightly infolded and sharply pointed. Inflorescence, produced May to July, a compact panicle, lemmas awned. H3.

### *F.g.* var. *caesia* (Sm.)
Even more brilliantly blue. A clone called 'Silver Seas' ('Silbersee') is of a similar colour, but of smaller stature. H3.

All grow best in light soils in full sun. They need regular grooming to remove dead leaves and flowering stems. Some people clip them over with shears in early summer. Lifting and dividing is usually necessary every 2 or 3 years to clear dead sheaths and to maintain vigour.

Planted very densely they can be mown somewhat like a lawn.

### *F.ovina* L.: Sheep's fescue
A densely tufted small grass with very fine green or greyish-white leaves much used as a lawn grass. Included here because the blue fescues now included in *F.glauca* and *F.rubra* were formerly included here—as *F.ovina glauca*, for example. Not the finest of the fescues, but sometimes grown as an edging plant. Has frequently been confused with *F.glauca* var. *caesia* and *F.rubra*. Differs from *F.rubra* in its larger awns, its lack of flat upper-stem leaves or creeping runners; also in its split not entire sheaths on non-flowering shoots. And from *F.glauca* var. *caesia* in its sheaths, which are rounded on the back, smooth and tufted with rounded auricles; also in the way in which the leaves tend to curl in the leaf tips, which are blunt not pointed.

A densely tufted perennial to 30 cm. Culms erect or spreading, very slender, stiff, becoming angular and rough near the inflorescence. Sheaths rounded on the back, smooth, tufted with rounded auricles. Blades tightly infolded, U-shaped in section, blunt-tipped; slightly bluish-green. Inflorescence, produced May to July, a loose panicle.

*F.o.* subsp. *coxii*
Some 70 subspecies have been named. The only one of particular ornamental interest is subspecies *coxii*, a plant of unknown origin, of particularly good blue colouring, and valuable among blue grasses in that it does not flower. Full sun; well-drained, fertile soil. H3.

*F.o.* 'Azurit'
A new, strong-growing (30 cm) clone with brilliantly blue leaves.

*F.o.* 'Blue Finch' ('Blaufink')
A small clone (15 cm), of a rather leaden blue.

*F.o.* 'Blue Fox' ('Blaufuchs')
Good, but undistinguished blue leaves. 30 cm.

*F.o.* 'Blue Glow' ('Blauglut')
Another blue-leaved form.

*F.o.* 'Harz'
Collected on the Harz mountains. Leaves olive-green. 15 cm.

*F.o.* 'Palatinate' ('Palatinat')
A variety found near Heidelberg. Blue-green leaves. 15 cm.

*F.o.* 'Sea-blue' ('Meerblau')
Leaves sea-green. 15 cm.

*F.o.* 'Sea Urchin' ('Seeigel')
Spikey blue-green leaves in a tight bun. 15 cm.

*F.o.* 'Silver Blue' ('Blausilber')
More silvery and less blue than most. 15 cm.

*F.o.* 'Silvery Egret' ('Silberreiher')
Silvery-blue leaves. 15 cm.

*F.o.* 'Soehrenwald'
Olive-green leaves. 20 cm.

*F.o.* 'Solling'
Non-flowering form. Blue-green leaves. 20 cm.

*F.o.* 'Spring Blue' ('Fruehlingsblau')
Rich blue in spring, less bright later. 15 cm.

### *F.o.* 'Tom Thumb' ('Daeumlung')
Dwarf blue to 10 cm.

### *F.punctoria* Sibth. & Sm.: Hedgehog fescue
Probably the prickliest (hence *punctoria*) of the ornamental grasses. Grown for its blue colouring. A loosely tufted perennial to 13 cm. Culms erect, stout, very rigid, smooth; metallic blue. Sheaths longer than the blades; bluish. Blades to 15 cm, rigid, recurved, strongly U-shaped in section, terminating in a very sharp point. Inflorescence produced June and July. Panicles narrowly oblong, up to 5 cm long; spikelets 4- to 7-flowered, the lemmas tipped with a short awn. Looks best if clipped regularly; needs dividing and replanting regularly since clumps tend to become barren in the centre. Perfect drainage, full sun. H5.

### *F.rubra* L. ssp. *rubra*: Red or creeping fescue
A low perennial forming mats, with slender, creeping rhizomes. A common constituent of lawns. Leaves pointed or blunt, tightly inrolled, bristle-like, green or greyish-green. Panicles erect or nodding, lanceolate to oblong, up to 18 cm long, reddish, greyish or green; May–June. Spikelets lanceolate to oblong, the lemmas tipped with a fine awn.

### *F.r.* 'Silver Needles'
Leaves edged white. Quietly charming.

### *F.vivipara* (L.) Sm.
Curious, perhaps amusing, not beautiful. Differing from *F.ovina* or *F.tenuifolia* only in its viviparous habit. A densely tufted perennial to 30 cm. Culms erect, stiff, smooth; becoming rough near the inflorescence. Sheaths rounded at the back, open to the base, smooth to slightly rough. Blades to 20 cm, hair-like, tightly infolded, straight or slightly deflexed. Inflorescence, produced June and July, a contracted panicle, the spikelets abnormal in lacking sexual organs, these being replaced by vegetative growths which may form vestigial roots before falling, the flowering culms gradually bending towards the ground under the weight of the growths. H3.

Not easy to cultivate: a peat-bed plant. The viviparous plantlets seldom root and grow on. Divide and replant regularly.

### *F.v.* 'In'
Dwarf form from Norway. No more than 5 cm tall.

## GAUDINIA P.Beauv.
A genus of 3 or 4 species of annuals or biennials from disturbed ground in southern Europe and the Mediterranean. It bears some superficial resemblance to *Avena*. One or two species are grown as ornamentals and

provide fine heads for drying. Seed should be sown thinly in April where the plants are to grow, in a sunny position in ordinary garden soil. The heads should be picked while still immature.

Plants tufted. Leaves flat. Inflorescence a bilateral raceme on a fragile axis breaking at the base of each internode; spikelets 3–11-flowered, stalkless, in 2 rows, falling entire; glumes unequal, shorter than lemma, the lower 3–5-nerved, the upper 7–11-nerved; lemmas leathery, slightly keeled with a bent awn arising from the back.

### *G.fragilis* (L.) Beauv.
Annual to about 40 cm, stems erect or spreading. Leaves softly hairy, finely pointed, up to 15 cm long, the ligules very short. Panicle, produced May to August, a narrow, jointed spike, up to 20 cm long, green. Spikelets 1–2 cm, the lower glume up to 5 mm, the upper up to 8 mm, the lemmas lanceolate, terminating in an awn up to 2 cm long. Sometimes cultivated for its unusual inflorescence which is attractive in indoor arrangements but must be cut when young since the spike breaks up at maturity.

## GLYCERA R.Brown
A genus of some 40 species of generally tall, aquatic or marshland grasses from the temperate regions. The variegated form of *G.maxima* is much grown for ornament. It grows best with abundant moisture at the roots, as on the bank of a pond or stream, but can be successfully grown in any fertile soil that is not dug. It is easily increased by division in spring, while the species are easily raised from seed sown outside in spring.

Glabrous perennials. Leaves flat, sheaths closed or partly closed. Panicles with a 3-sided main axis; spikelets few- to many-flowered: glumes unequal, transparent, very small to nearly as long as the lemma; lemmas broad, round on the back, without awns, 5–9-nerved, the nerves parallel and conspicuous.

### *G.maxima* (Hartm.) Holmb.: Great water grass, Reed manna grass, Reed meadow grass, Reed sweet grass, Sweet hay
The green-leaved plant is of little garden merit, though quite common in ponds, ditches, canals and other wet places throughout its range, and is a decided delicacy to the palates of horses and cattle because of its sweet taste—hence *Glyceria* meaning 'sweet', and the common name sweet hay—so much so that foolish beasts will often bog themselves down knee-deep in mud in their efforts to get to it.

The variegated forms are among the finest of all variegated garden grasses and should be grown wherever they can be accommodated. They have what is probably the most brilliantly variegated foliage of any grass grown in the garden. Flowers uninteresting. Another virtue is that this is one of the few ornamental grasses (as opposed to sedges, rushes and so on) that can actually be grown in the water rather than merely beside it. It does not, however, need water to grow well, and will thrive in the border, though here the brilliance of its variegation can make it a difficult plant for which to find companions and foils.

A stout, deciduous perennial with vigorously spreading stolons, growing up to 2.1 m under optimum conditions, usually about half that height. Culms erect, smooth. Leaf sheaths entire at first, later splitting, keeled upwards, smooth close to the node, becoming hairy towards the ligule. Ligule not particularly noticeable; blunt but with a small central point. Leaf blades up to 60 cm long, 2 cm wide, with margins parallel coming to an abrupt point; hairless, rough on the margins and more or less rough beneath. Inflorescence, produced June to August, a rather open, much-branched panicle up to 45 cm long, branches closely clustered, slender; green, tinged with yellow or purple. H1.

### G.m. 'Pallida'
Leaves boldly variegated pale creamy-white. H1.

### G.m. 'Variegata'
Leaves boldly variegated with white or creamy-yellow stripes, the amount of white or cream greatly exceeding the amount of green in the leaf. Young leaves in spring are a delightful pinkish colour, which becomes purplish before fading. By comparison with the type, the leaves are rather broad, up to 5 cm across, and the plant is generally rather smaller-growing, reaching no more than 75 cm in height. H1.

## GYNERIUM Beauv.
A monotypic genus from streamsides and wet places in tropical Mexico, the West Indies, Peru and Brazil. The sole species is a gigantic rhizomatous perennial reed up to 10 m tall. It is nearly related to *Cortaderia* but differs in having the leaves distributed along the culm instead of crowded at the base. It is highly ornamental and in cultivation needs a warm greenhouse where it can be grown in a large pot or tub standing in water. The leaves can be as much as 1.6 m long clustered towards the tops of the culms, and the panicle, which resembles that of pampas grass, as much as 1 m long.

Panicle large, dense, dioecious. Main axis erect, branches drooping; female spikelets with long-attenuated glumes and long, silky lemmas; the male spikelets with shorter glumes and lemmas, without awns.

### G.sagittatum (Aubl.) Willd.: Wild cane, Uva grass
A coarse, tufted, reed-like grass to 9 m; stems up to 2.5 cm thick covered with old sheath bases, terminating in a fan-like cluster of leaves. Leaves to 1.8 m long, 10 cm wide, evenly spaced up the stem, the lower ones soon falling.

96

Panicles, produced in later summer, to nearly 1 m long, plumose and generally similar to those of *Cortaderia selloana*, the branches drooping. G2.

## HAKONECHLOA Honda

A monotypic genus of perennial woodland grass from cliffs and mountains in Japan. Although of diminutive stature it is closely related to the tall reeds (e.g. *Phragmites* and *Arundo*) by its rhizomatous habit and by its free-standing culms. The species and its variegated forms are very decorative and are easily grown in a semi-shaded position in ordinary garden soil. They are usually increased by division in spring.

Low, rhizomatous perennial. Leaves linear–lanceolate, finely pointed; ligules membranous with hairy margins. Panicle loose; spikelets stalked; 3–5-flowered; glumes unequal, shorter than lemma, persistent, pointed, the lower glume the smaller; lemma overlapping, longer than the glumes, with a straight awn as long as the lemma.

### *H.macra* (Munro) Makino

A Japanese grass of relatively recent introduction, low-growing but with a rhizome system remarkably similar to that of *Phragmites* though more refined. The typical plant is a fine, lushly pale yellow-green grass with fine, delicate inflorescences, of great garden merit, slowly forming dense clumps. In spite of its very slowly creeping habit, it is non-invasive. The variegated forms are smaller-growing and less vigorous, among the most brightly coloured of all variegated plants, looking good as single specimens at the front of a border, breathtakingly effective when grown in large drifts. In all forms the leaves become stained with vinous reddishness towards autumn, somewhat in the manner of *Imperata*.

Slowly spreading, rhizomatous perennial growing up to 30 cm. Culms erect, very slender; wiry, smooth; bright green. Leaf sheaths rounded at the back, smooth with a fringe of short hairs near the top, sometimes rather purplish in colour. Leaf blades up to 20 cm long, 9 mm wide, flat in section or with loosely involute margins; smooth, tapering at both ends; bright green. Inflorescence, produced August to October, a rather open panicle up to 15 cm long, about one-third as much across, the spikelets yellowish-green. H4.

### *H.m.* 'Albo-aurea'

Of less vigorous growth, the leaves variegated white and yellow, with very little green. H4.

### *H.m.* 'Albo-variegata'

The leaves variegated white, again with very little green. A plant of singularly little vigour, more inclined to fade away than thrive. Ten years ago I and several others had live plants in our gardens but I am now unable to trace a living plant in cultivation in the UK from that original introduction. Material has recently been re-introduced to the UK from Japan via America. H4.

### H.m. 'Aureola'
Leaves brilliant bright yellow with a few slender green lines running through them. The form usually seen. H4.

In practice, nurserymen do not seem to take much care in distinguishing one variegated form from another. Several other varieties are cultivated in Japan and may be worth introducing.

## HELICTOTRICHON Schulk
A genus of about 100 species of perennial grasses from meadows, woodland margins and dry hillsides mainly concentrated in Eurasia but extending to other temperate regions and to mountains in the tropics. Two species are cultivated as ornamentals. Both are showy, with large, open panicles held well above compact clumps of foliage. They are easy to grow in ordinary fertile soil and may be increased from seed sown out of doors in spring, or by division also in spring.

Tufted perennials with distinctly ribbed leaves. Panicles lax, compound; spikelets numerous, erect or spreading, with 2–several fertile florets and 1–2 sterile, much-reduced florets; the fertile florets with sharply bent, dorsal awns; glumes unequal, lanceolate, membranous, the lower 1-nerved, the upper 3-nerved.

### H.planiculme (Schrad.) Bess.
An attractive ornamental grown for its broad leaves and showy, erect panicles. Compactly tufted with erect, fairly stout stems to nearly 1 m tall. Leaves flat or folded, smooth, up to 48 cm long, abruptly pointed. Panicles produced June to July, dense, up to 30 cm long, 6.2 cm wide, the spikelets linear to oblong, 4–7-flowered, about 2.5 cm long, tinged purplish, the lemmas bearded at the base and bearing awns up to 2.5 cm long. H4.

### H.sempervirens (Vill.) Pilger: Blue oat grass
One of the most marvellous of the middle-sized blue grasses, making a rounded hummock of spiky blue leaves overtopped by showy, arching flower-heads. Grown mainly for the blueness of its foliage, it also has a fine architectural quality and looks good in flower, the heads being borne high above the foliage. Specimens need space so that their form can be appreciated; also looks good massed in pebble gardens.

Densely tufted perennial without stolons, growing up to 1.2 m when in flower, usually rather less. Culms erect, becoming arching; blue. Leaf sheaths basal, slightly hairy; blue. Leaf blades up to 30 cm long, 2 cm wide, evenly tapering to a fine point; straight, stiff, slightly hairy; blue. Inflorescence, produced June and July, a drooping, 1-sided panicle up to 15 cm long, arching at the tips of the stems, the spikelets sparsely borne; very pale bluish, becoming light brown. It needs regular grooming—i.e. the removal of old leaves and flower stems. H4.

### *H.s.* 'Glauca'
A name of doubtful authenticity applied to plants questionably bluer than usual.

## HIEROCHLOË R.Brown
A genus of doubtfully as many as 30 species of coumarin-scented perennials from the grasslands and boggy meadows of the temperate and Arctic regions other than Africa. Two or three species are sometimes cultivated for the supposed enchantment afforded by their scented leaves and stems, though they are scarcely ornamental in appearance and suffer moreover the major disadvantage that when once well-suited they run so aggressively as to become quickly more of a pest than a pleasure. They are very readily increased by quite small pieces of root, or by seed sown out of doors in spring. They will grow in most soils and thrive in rich, moist soils.

Erect but sometimes aggressively stoloniferous, sweet-smelling perennials with flat to almost rolled leaves and small panicles with 1 terminal bisexual floret and 2 female florets, the male florets falling together with the bisexual floret; glumes nearly equal, ovate, about as long as the florets, smooth, thin and papery; sterile lemmas as long as the glumes, sometimes with awns arising from between 2 lobes; fertile lemmas similar but awnless; palea rounded on the back.

### *H.odorata* (L.) Beauv.: Holy grass, Vanilla grass
One of the few grasses grown primarily for its scent, perhaps the most fragrant of all hardy grasses. The aroma is best revealed when the leaves are broken or crushed. Its name 'holy grass' comes from the custom, at one time widespread, of scattering aromatic plants on floors, especially in churches. In folklore, this grass was believed to have the power of inducing sleep, and bunches of it were often hung in bedrooms. In cultivation in the southern counties of the UK it is always the first grass to flower. It will tolerate quite dry conditions.

Vigorously spreading, deciduous, perennial grass with far-reaching, white rhizomes which form compact tufts, growing up to 50 cm. Culms erect, slightly nodding at the tip, with very few nodes; slightly hairy, especially close to the flower-head. Leaf sheaths rounded on the back, somewhat rough. Leaf blades up to 30 cm long, 1 cm wide, flat in section, tapering to a fine point; slightly hairy above, smooth underneath, rough on the margins, the lower blades much longer than the upper ones, which are often extremely short; aromatic when bruised. Inflorescence, produced March to May, a loosely branched panicle up to 13 cm long, about half that across, the spikelets rather plump; green or purplish at the base, becoming brown, 3-flowered, the lower 2 flowers staminate, the upper 1 bisexual. H1.

### *H.redolens* (Vahl) Roem. & Schult.

Broadly similar to *H.odorata* but larger and coarser, forming tufts rather than carpets, the slender stems growing to 1.4 m. An attractive grass in woodland openings. H4.

## HOLCUS L.

A genus of 6 or 8 species of annual or perennial grasses from woodlands, grassland and wastelands throughout Europe, the Middle East and North Africa. They are generally aggressive weeds, difficult to eradicate, but two sorts are grown for ornament and neither is likely to become a problem.

Annuals or perennials with flat leaves and contracted panicles. Spikelets 2-flowered, with short rachilla extension, the lower floret bisexual, the upper male, falling entire; glumes about equal, papery, enclosing florets; lemmas polished, the lower awnless, the upper with a hooked or bent awn arising in the upper third.

### *H.lanatus* L.

A species much confused with *H.mollis*, but this is a grass of open habitats, whereas *H.mollis* is a grass of open woodlands. H1.

### *H.mollis* L.

The typical plant is one of the most obnoxious grasses it can be one's misfortune to have in the garden, being popularly known as 'the other couch grass', the true couch grass being *Agropyron repens*. The variegated form, by way of total contrast, is one of the most desirable of all variegated grasses. It can be used in the rock garden, as an edging, in multi-coloured lawns, in grass knot gardens or as ground-cover. It will stand mowing well, once established. Like most white-variegated grasses, it looks best if planted where the late afternoon or evening sun can shine through the leaves.

Tufted perennial with far-creeping rhizomes growing up to 1 m when in flower. Culms erect, but almost as often spreading as erect; slender, smooth; loosely to densely bearded at the nodes. Leaf sheaths rounded on the back; hairless or occasionally softly hairy. Leaf blades up to 20 cm long, 13 mm across; flat in section; hairless or softly hairy. Inflorescence, produced June to August, a narrowly oblong panicle, the branches hairy, the spikelet 2-flowered, bisexual, the upper one staminate. H1.

100

*H.m.* 'Albo-variegatus' (usually sold simply as *H.m.* 'Variegatus')
This variety is less vigorous, both in its top-growth and in the extent to which
the rhizomes creep. The leaves have very broad margins of pure white with a
narrow green strip up the centre. Grows to only 10 cm. Does not flower freely;
flowers best removed by clipping the plant over with garden shears. The plant
needs tidying occasionally during the growing season. H1.

## HORDEUM L.

A genus of 20 to 40 species of annual or perennial grasses from dry soils and
open places throughout the temperate regions. *H.vulgare* (barley) is a major
cereal crop in temperate regions. There are several cultivated variants some
with awns 6 cm long, some without awns (beardless barley) and one with the
grain free from the lemma and palea (naked barley). Some species are
ornamental, with showy, open panicles and rather large spikelets. They are
easily grown in light soil from seed sown in spring. The inflorescence shatters
readily at maturity and heads for dried arrangement should be picked while
immature and hung upside down to dry to minimise this. Dry heads readily
take up aniline dyes.

Low to tall annuals or perennials with flat leaves. Panicle racemose, oblong
to linear. Spikelets 2 or usually 3 together, the central spikelet bisexual, the
others male or barren, the central spikelet stalkless, the lateral spikelets clearly
stalked (all 3 stalkless in the cultivated barleys), the central spikelet 1-flowered
with a bristle-like rachilla extension, the lateral spikelets usually smaller and
reduced to a bunch of 3 awns. Glumes linear to lanceolate, or awn-like, free to
the base: lemmas ovate coming to a long, conspicuous awn.

### *H.jubatum* L.: Fox-tail barley, Squirrel-tail barley

By far the finest of the wild barleys, and one of the most decorative of all annual
grasses. Grown for its beautiful, soft, feathery heads, which arch gracefully,
bearing long, hair-like spikes, particularly on the upper side of the arch. With
age, these twist and curl in a fascinating manner. Pick very early for drying;
shatters very quickly. Takes aniline dyes well, as does *H.vulgare.*

A short-lived perennial, or more usually an annual, growing up to 60 cm.
Culms several, rarely solitary, erect, smooth. Leaf sheaths rounded on the
back, smooth. Leaf blades up to 20 cm long, 6 mm wide; scabrous; upright or
arching. Inflorescence, produced June to July, a dense, nodding spike up to
10 cm long, usually almost as much across; overall of a very hairy or spiky
appearance, the glumes awn-like, up to 5.6 cm long; pale green or purplish,
becoming beige. H2.

### *H.vulgare* L.

Cultivated barley. Is broadly similar but taller, to 1.2 m, and the lemmas may
be awned or awnless, the awn, when present, as much as 15 cm long. Annual.

## HYPARRHENIA Fourn.

A genus of more than 50 species of tall, clump-forming annuals or perennials mainly from the savannah regions of Africa but also from similar habitats in other tropical regions. The genus is remarkable for its elaborate compound panicles. The plants require a warm greenhouse in Britain, and may be raised from seed sown in spring and transplanted into good, rich soil. They will scarcely endure outside in an English summer.

Inflorescence a large, compound panicle composed of pairs of racemes themselves bearing paired, dissimilar spikelets, the racemes enclosed in often colourful spathe-like structures; stalked spikelets usually male 2-flowered, longer than stalkless spikelet, unawned; the lower glume rounded on the back, the lower floret reduced to a transparent lemma; the upper floret bisexual; with a bidentate lemma extending into a stout, hairy, sharply bent awn.

### *H.cymbaria* (L.) Stapf.

A tall grass for the warm greenhouse with ornamental panicles. Perennial with stout stems to 6 m tall. Leaves 45 cm long. Panicles produced late summer or autumn up to 60 cm long, much-branched, dense; the spathes boat-shaped, horizontally spreading, red or purple. G2.

### *H.hirta* (L.) Stapf.

The only species that has any chance outside in the UK, and then only in southern counties in well-drained soils and with protection from severe frosts. Perennial with slender, wiry stems to 2 m tall. Leaves up to 30 cm, glaucous. Panicle produced late summer, loose, sparsely branched, about 30 cm long, the spathes about 5 cm long, narrow, becoming tightly inrolled and reddish. Racemes silky–hairy, white or greyish. H5–G1.

## HYSTRIX Moench

A genus of 6 or 8 species of erect perennials from woods and meadows in North America and temperate Asia, and New Zealand. It is closely related to *Elymus* with which it is sometimes merged, and is easily confused with *Leymus*, though not related to it. One species is grown for its pretty, pinkish, bottle-brush-like panicles. It can be grown from spring division or from seed sown in spring, and needs a sunny position in an open border. The flowers are effective when cut, both fresh or dried.

Leaf blades flat, flexible. Panicle a linear raceme, the spikelets 2–4-flowered, in groups of 1–4 at each node of a tough, flattened rachis; glumes reduced to stump-like awns or absent; lemmas rounded on the back, obscurely nerved, tapering to long, thin awns.

### *H.patula* Moench: Bottle-brush grass

The common name comes from its curious flowers, which are quite stiff and closely resemble a porcupine (Latin = *hystrix*) or that type of bottle-brush used for cleaning babies' bottles. These are quite unlike the flowers of any other cultivated grass, except perhaps *Sitanion hystrix*, from which it differs in having more showy, pink flower-heads, those of *Sitanion hystrix* being greenish-white. It is known purely for its unusual flowers, the plant itself being rather untidy.

Loosely tufted, deciduous perennial, without stolons, growing when in flower up to 1.2 m in the wild, rather less in cultivation. Culms erect, rigid, slender. Leaf sheaths sometimes hairy, sometimes not. Leaf blades up to 15 cm long, 1 cm wide, tapering to an attenuated point. Inflorescence, produced September to October, a sparse spike up to 15 cm long, the spikelets borne in pairs, held horizontally at maturity; light green or pinkish-green. H5.

## IMPERATA Cirillo

A genus of 8 species of rhizomatous perennials from open places in the tropics and warm temperate regions. One species is grown for the ornamental value of its leaves which are stained the colour of blackberry juice, the amount of colouring increasing as the season advances. It is easily grown in ordinary garden soil, and may be increased by seed or by runners. In warm climates it is an aggressive weed, but in the average climate of the UK it runs rather less.

Slender perennials. Panicle spike-like with branches bearing pairs of similar spikelets, each on its own stalk. Spikelets small, 2-flowered, enclosed in long, silky hairs; glumes as long as the spikelet; upper lemma awnless; lower floret reduced to a transparent lemma.

### *I.cylindrica* (L.) Beauv.: Blood grass

Perennial with slowly spreading rhizomes. Stems erect, up to 1.20 cm but usually less than 30 cm. Leaves tightly rolled, rarely flat, narrowly linear, sharp-pointed, up to 60 cm long, often erect or nearly so, light green stained rich vinous red, the amount of colouring increasing as the season advances. Panicles produced August to September, cylindrical, spike-like up to 20 cm long by 2.5 cm wide, surrounded by white hairs. H5–G1. The epithet 'Rubra' sometimes used is superfluous.

## KOELERIA Pers.

A genus of about 35 species of tufted perennials from dry grasslands in the temperate regions. One or two species are ornamental and they are easily grown in ordinary garden soil, doing especially well on chalk soils. They are readily increased by division preferably in spring, but can just as easily be raised from seed sown out of doors in spring.

Low or tall, tufted plants with narrow leaves flat or rolled. Panicle spike-like. Spikelets 2–4-flowered, laterally compressed, the rachilla extending beyond the florets as a slender bristle or bearing at the tip a reduced floret; glumes unequal, the upper as long as the first floret, the lower two-thirds as long;

lemmas lanceolate, strongly keeled, longer than the glumes, awnless or with a vestigial awn.

### *K.cristata* (L.) Pers.: Crested hair grass

Grown for its shining, spike-like panicles. Densely tufted perennials with stiff stems to 50 cm long. Leaves flat or rolled up to 20 cm long, with blunt tips, minutely hairy or hairless. Panicle produced June/July, erect, narrowly oblong, tapering, up to 10 cm long, silvery, green or purplish; the spikelets 2–3-flowered. H1. Var. *glauca* has silvery leaves like *Festuca glauca*.

### *K.vallesiana* (Honck.) Bertol.

Sometimes listed as a British native but only found on limestone hills in Somerset. Densely tufted perennial to 40 cm tall. Culms stiff, slender to stout.

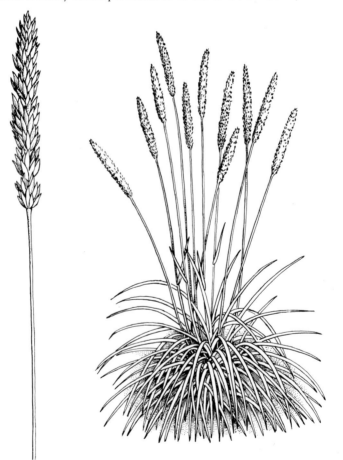

16 *Koeleria vallesiana*

1. *Elymus hispidus*

2. *Carex phyllocephala*
'Sparkler' in the reserve
collection at Longwood
Gardens

3. *Miscanthus sinensis*
'Cabaret' in an American
garden

4.   *Miscanthus gracillimus* 'Morning Light'

5.   *Carex muskingumensis* in Oehme, van Sweden Associates Inc. planting at the Federal Reserve Bank, Washington, D.C.

Ligules remarkably short. Leaves up to 10 cm long, very narrow, blunt-tipped, rolled or flat, hairless. Panicles, produced June–July spike-like, oblong or ovate-oblong, purplish to silvery-green, the spikelets 2–3-flowered. H4.

## LAGURUS L.

A genus of a single species of annual grass from the maritime sands of the Mediterranean. It is often grown as an ornamental and is easily raised from seed sown in spring where it is to grow, or in autumn under glass. It grows best in a light, sandy soil in full sun.

Softly hairy, tufted annual to 60 cm tall. Leaf blades flat, linear to narrowly lanceolate. Panicle spike-like, ovoid. Spikelets 1-flowered; glumes unequal, linear, the upper as long or longer than the floret, both with densely hairy, bristle-like tips; lemmas membranous, hairy at the base, and with a long, bent awn arising just below the tip.

### *L.ovatus* L.: Hare's tail

A popular annual whose heads are decorative both in the garden and for indoor decoration. The heads should be picked young, in dry weather, tied in bunches and hung upside down in a dark, airy room until the stems are stiff. Excellent for dyeing.

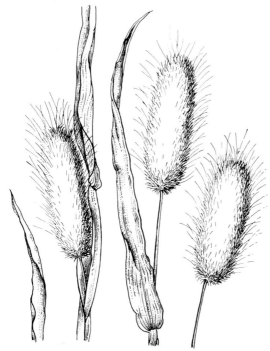

17  *Lagurus ovatus*

Tufted, softly hairy annual, growing up to 60 cm when in flower. Culms usually several; erect, or decumbent becoming erect, sometimes arching at the tip; very slender with few nodes; light green. Leaf sheaths rounded on the back, loose, somewhat inflated, slightly hairy. Leaf blades up to 20 cm long, 1.5 cm across, flat in section; velvety, light green. Inflorescence, produced June to August, a dense, globose, spike-like panicle up to 6 cm long, about 2 cm across, erect or nodding; pale green, rarely tinged pink, becoming beige, the head softly hairy and silky.

### *L.o.* var. 'Nanus'
A delightful miniature form growing to no more than 15 cm.

## LAMARCKIA Moench
A genus of a single species of annual grass from open places in the Mediterranean region and the Middle East. It is much grown as an ornamental and is one of the best small grasses for drying. The flower is more like a toothbrush than a bottle-brush. It comes readily from seed sown in spring where the plants are to grow, preferably on light, sandy soil.

Tufted annual with flat leaves. Panicle oblong condensed, 1-sided, bearing crowded, drooping bunches of spikelets, the fertile ones hidden except for their awns by the more numerous sterile spikelets. Clusters usually of 3 sterile and 2 smaller spikelets, one fertile the other rudimentary. Fertile spikelets 1-flowered, with an awned rudiment; glumes narrow, longer than the lemma; lemma membranous, rounded, 5-nerved, with a long awn; sterile spikelets many-flowered, lemmas empty.

### *L.aurea* (L.) Moench: Golden top
One of the best small grasses for drying, the erect, silky plumes on their tall, wiry stems being most effective. Loosely tufted annual growing to 30 cm. Culms several, very rarely solitary; erect, or decumbent at the base becoming erect; smooth. Leaf sheaths rounded at the back, smooth, slightly inflated. Leaf blades up to 20 cm long, 9 mm wide, flat in section; soft, hairless or very slightly hairy on the upper surface, gradually tapering to a fine point; undulate or twisting. Flowering season March to June. Inflorescence a very dense panicle up to 6 cm long, about half as much across, the branches short and erect, the spikelets of two kinds: the fertile ones about 2 mm long, the awn about twice as long as the spikelet; the sterile ones about 8 mm long, shining whitish, sometimes becoming golden-yellow to purplish.

Easily grown in any fertile soil in sun. Sow seed in spring where the plants are to flower.

## LEYMUS Hochst.
A genus used by some authors for plants here retained in *Elymus* q.v.

# LOLIUM L.

A genus of about 8 species of annual or perennial grasses from the meadows and pastures of temperate Eurasia, introduced to and naturalised in other temperate regions. One species, *L.perenne*, is a common and excellent pasture grass and is sometimes grown for ornament. It is easily cultivated and is best grown from divisions.

Blades flat. Panicle a simple, terminal, flat spike. Spikelets alternate, stalkless in 2 opposite rows, several- to many-flowered; upper glume absent except on the terminal spikelet; the lower as long or longer than the second floret, strongly 3–5-nerved; lemmas rounded on the back, 5–7-nerved, awned or awnless.

## *L.perenne* L.: Perennial rye grass

A common constituent of sports turfs, but also grown for its ornamental panicles which are attractive in the garden and for indoor decoration, fresh or dried. Loosely or densely tufted perennial, stems erect or spreading, smooth, up to 1 m. Leaves up to 30 cm long, smooth, glossy beneath. Panicle produced May to September, 30 cm long, flattened; the spikelets up to 14-flowered, oblong. H1.

# MELICA L.

A genus of about 80 species of mainly woodland perennials from the temperate regions except Australia. Four species are quite often grown as ornamentals for their generally light, delicate appearance. When picked for drying the stems should be taken before the heads are fully open. They are easy to grow in medium loam or light, sandy soils especially if calcareous, in sun or semi-shade, and can be increased by division or by seed sown in spring out of doors.

Generally tall plants with the base of the culm often swollen into a corm-like body; sheaths closed; blades flat, narrow, occasionally with cross-nerves. Panicles usually simple, often scanty, with rather large spikelets. Spikelets 1–several-flowered, the rachilla extending beyond the fertile florets and bearing at the apex a club-shaped tuft of 2–3 smaller, empty lemmas; glumes unequal, thin, papery, almost as long as the lower floret, strongly 3–5-nerved; lemmas convex, membranaceous, awnless or sometimes awned.

## *M.altissima* L.

Highly prized for its decorative qualities in spite of a rather loose, floppy growth. Loosely tufted, deciduous perennial growing to 1 m. Culms erect; sometimes decumbent at the base, becoming erect; stout, but not particularly strong. Leaf sheath rough. Leaf blade up to 46 cm long, 2 cm wide; hairy beneath, the mid-vein very prominent beneath. Inflorescence, produced June to July, a loose, spike-like panicle to 15 cm long, 5 cm across, the spikelets at first furled, later becoming spreading; creamy-white, very conspicuous. H2.

*M.a.* 'Atropurpurea' hort.
Chaffy purple flowers followed by jet black seeds. H2.

*M.a.* 'Alba'
Has white spikelets. H2.

### *M.ciliata* L.: Hairy mellic
Basically, a compact version of *M.altissima*, differing from that species further
in that it prefers dry to damp soils, has blue-green not green leaf blades and
densely hairy spikelets. A loosely tufted perennial to 1 m. Culms erect, slender,
weak. Sheaths rolled, rough to touch. Blades to 45 cm long, rolled or acutely
U-shaped in section, blue-green. Inflorescence, produced June to August, a
dense, white, spike-like panicle to 20 cm long; branches at first narrowly erect,
later spreading; bright brownish. The flowers show off well against the foliage.
H1.

*M.c.* 'Alba'
Has white flowers. H1.

Several very similar species—e.g. *M.glauca* F.Schultz, *M.magnolii* Gren. &
Godr., *M.nebrodensis* Pail. and *M.transsilvanica* Schur. may also be grown for
ornament. They are sometimes treated as subspecies of *M.ciliata*.

### *M.papilionacea* Auct.
Differs from the other cultivated mellics in its generally pink inflorescences, its
inflated spikelets and the white or almost transparent membrane in which
these are contained. A loosely tufted perennial to 45 cm. Culms erect or
decumbent, wiry, smooth. Sheaths rounded on the back, slightly rough in the
upper part. Blades to 20 cm long, flat or slightly V-shaped in section, smooth
above, hairy beneath. Inflorescence, produced June to August, a very loose
spike, the branches widely spaced on the axis; spikelets rich pink, slightly
inflated, contained in a white to transparent membrane. Highly effective when
massed, creating a pink haze of flowers. H2.

### *M.uniflora* Retz.: Wood melick
Common in woods and at the foot of hedgerows, usually on limestone or chalk.
The garden forms are useful as well as decorative.
   Loosely tufted perennial with slowly creeping rhizomes. Culms variable
from erect, to erect becoming arching; very slender, smooth; light green. Leaf
sheaths tubular, tightly fitting, loosely hairy or hairless, the basal sheaths
sometimes tinged with purple. Leaf blades up to 20 cm long, 5 mm wide,
gradually tapering to a fine point, very thin, flat in section with a pronounced
mid-vein on the underside; slightly hairy above, minutely hairy beneath and

on the margins; bright green. Inflorescence, produced May to July, a loose panicle, very sparingly branched, erect, or erect becoming nodding, sometimes the branches falling to one side; the spikelets with delicate chocolate-brown florets. H1.

## *M.u.* var. *albida*
Florets white, not brown. A striking plant that comes true from seed. H1.

18 *Melica uniflora* var. *albida*

## *M.u.* var. *aurea*
Has yellowish leaves. H1.

## *M.u.* 'Variegata'
Has leaves longitudinally striped green and white. A lovely variety needing good soil in shade. H1.

109

## MIBORA Adans.

A genus of a single species of dwarf annual grass from damp, sandy soils in Western Europe and North Africa. It is sometimes grown as a curiosity and comes readily from seed sown in spring in damp, sandy soil.

Leaves flat. Panicle a 1-sided, spike-like raceme. Spikelets 1-flowered, without rachilla extension. Glumes about equal, longer than floret, 1-nerved; lemma rounded, obtuse, hairy.

### *M.minima* (L.) Desv.: Early sand grass, Sand bent

A charming little grass, its bright green foliage being among the first to appear in spring as it flowers very early. Ideal for growing in association with terrestrial orchids and other such plants that like some shade at their roots. Tends to form tufts rather than a turf, although, with time and self-seeding, quite an adequate turf can be produced. In wet situations, it stays green and bright until late summer; in dry soils, dies away early, often coming again in late summer. Probably the smallest of the cultivated grasses, useful as well as beautiful.

Diminutive, tufted annual growing to 10 cm, often about half that height. Culms numerous, erect or spreading; extremely slender, unbranched, smooth; bright green. Leaf sheaths tightly fitting, splitting at the top; green or purplish; round, overlapping. Leaf blades up to 19 mm long, extremely thin, almost hair-like; flat in section or with the margins inrolled; blunt-tipped; bright green. Inflorescence, produced March to May, a 1-sided spike up to 13 mm long, the spikelets almost stalkless, 1-flowered, in 2 rows on each side of the axis; green, purplish or reddish.

## MILIUM L.

A genus of 4 species of annuals and perennials from the woodlands of the north temperate zone of the Old World, and also from eastern North America. It is closely related to *Oiyzopsis* from which it differs by its lack of awns. One species is grown as an ornamental. It is a woodland plant and needs a position in at least some shade. It is easily raised from seed sown in spring where the plants are to grow.

Low to quite tall plants with flat leaves and open panicles. Spikelets 1-flowered; glumes equal, rounded on the back, membranaceous; lemmas shorter than glumes, rounded on the back, obtuse, awnless, obscurely nerved.

### *M.effusum* L.: Wood millet

A widespread native of both Britain and North America: with its silken leaves, one of the most graceful of native grasses. The typical plant is useful in semi-shaded situations where the light, bright green of its foliage and greenish, open inflorescence is effective against a darker background. The variety with yellow leaves is one of the most desirable of all garden grasses, the leaves being of an even colour and holding that colour well through the year. It is one of the earliest grasses into growth in the spring, and looks superlative used *en masse* as ground-cover in slightly shaded areas. Also unexpectedly effective when used to underplant white-variegated shrubs.

Loosely tufted, deciduous perennial with slowly creeping rhizomes, growing up to 60 cm when in flower. Culms erect, or decumbent becoming erect; usually slender, rarely stout; smooth. Leaf sheaths rounded on the back, smooth. Leaf blades up to 30 cm long, 15 mm wide; flat in section, gradually narrowing to a point, somewhat undulate on the margins; slightly rough on the nerves and on the margins. Inflorescence, produced May to July, a very loose, nodding panicle up to 45 cm long, the branches borne in clusters; flexuous, spreading; pale green, very rarely purple. H1.

### *M.e.* 'Aureum'
Although accorded the status of a garden variety, this is probably a true botanical variety since it comes true from seed. The leaves are evenly suffused golden-yellow, lasting well into late summer. H1.

### *M.e.* 'Variegatum'
Leaves variegated white. A striking plant, but a weak grower. H1.

## **MISCANTHUS** Anderss.
The hardy species of *Miscanthus*, and their many garden varieties, are among the best of ornamental grasses, being attractive in leaf and flower, the flowers appearing late in the year when most other grasses are over, and lasting on the plants till well into winter. They are grown as much for their bold, architectural qualities as for their late flowers. The flowers, lasting at least as long, possibly longer, than those of the pampas grass, are of a quite different shape, so that where both are present in the same garden, the one shows off the virtues of the other. If grown as specimens, they need plenty of space to develop. Their character is completely lost if they are crowded by other strong-growing plants.

A genus of about 20 species of robust perennials from marshes and open places in South-East Asia and thence westward into Africa. Several species have large, showy panicles and these are popular as ornamentals. They will grow in most soils but do best in good loam. To flourish they need adequate moisture and a regular regimen of organic manure. Though usually increased by division which is essential for named sorts, they come readily from seed sown under glass.

Generally large plants, tufted or rhizomatous, with flat blades and generally large, terminal, plumose panicles of slender, spike-like racemes. Spikelets small, borne in pairs with unequal stalks along a slender, continuous rachis; each spikelet surrounded by a spreading beard of long hairs arising from the

111

callus; glumes firm, hairy; lemmas transparent, enclosed by the glumes, the upper lemma awned.

### *M.floridulus* (Labill.) Warb.

Generally similar to *M.sinensis* with which it has been much confused in the past. Differs in its extended panicle-axis, in its oblong to broadly pyramidal panicle, in its smaller spikelets and in its less strongly recurved spikelet stalks. The margins of the leaves becoming purple, the blades stained purplish late in the season. A tall, robust grass useful for creating a subtropical effect. H5.

### *M.nepalensis* (Trin.) Hack.

A desirable and highly ornamental dwarf species. Forms a tufted perennial to about 1 m high, the stems slender. Leaves flat or folded, stiff, hairless, linear, finely pointed, about 30 cm long, the margins smooth. Panicles produced August/September, loose to dense, spreading, up to 15 cm long and 8 cm across, composed of many slender, nodding racemes individually up to 13 cm long, golden or yellow; the spikelets, surrounded by fine, silky, golden or yellow hairs. H5–G1.

Like a miniature *M.sinensis* and useful in smaller gardens. Recently re-introduced from the Himalayas by Tom Schilling, the curator of Wakehurst Place. Somewhat frost-tender.

### *M.sacchariflorus* (Maxim.) Hack.

A tall and impressive grass of subtropical appearance. Vigorous, erect, densely tufted perennial with stout, steadily but not far-reaching stolons, growing up to 2.4 m in flower. Culms erect, with nodes not particularly swollen. Leaf sheaths rigid, light brown, splitting early in the season and tending to look untidy. Leaf blades up to 1 m long, 2.5 cm wide, evenly tapering to an attentuated point; olive-green with a markedly white midrib; rough on both surfaces and with sharply appressed teeth along the margins. Inflorescence, produced August to October, a much-branched panicle up to 30 cm long, of silky texture, the spikelets lacking awns; white, reddish or purplish. H5–G1.

### *M.s.* 'Aureus'

Leaves striped golden-yellow. The variegation is not a particularly effective one, and the plant is smaller-growing than the type plant, reaching a mere 1.5 m in height. H5–G1.

### *M.s.* 'Variegatus'

Leaves clearly marked with rather narrow, pure white stripes. It is not the most effective of white-variegated grasses, but there are few other grasses of similar vigour that are variegated at all and for this reason this variety is worth cultivating. Only slightly less vigorous than the type plant. H5–G1.

### *M.sinensis* Anderss.: Eulalia grass, Japanese silver grass

The most widely grown of the cultivated species of *Miscanthus*; also the one with the greatest number of garden varieties. There are two ways of distinguishing this species from *M.sacchariflorus*: the first and least reliable is that this species is definitely clump-forming, whereas *M.sacchariflorus* is of rhizomatous habit; the more certain way is that in this species the spikelets are distinctly awned—that is, there is a long, coarse, hair-like projection on the back of each individual flower part. Another difference is that, in *M.sacchariflorus*, the leaves are glabrous, whereas in *M.sinensis* the underside of the leaf is distinctly hairy: this is probably the best diagnostic characteristic when the plants are not in flower. Like *M.sacchariflorus*, this is an excellent grass for specimen planting, much as one might use a shrub, as well as for screening. Some varieties lend themselves better to one use, others to the other. Many of the varieties are valued for their flowers which, in some cases, do not appear until as late as November, when all other grasses have finished flowering and when relatively few plants at all are in flower in the garden. The flowers will remain intact through winter until cut to the ground in spring. This species contains some of the finest of the larger-growing, variegated grasses. All require plenty of space when grown as specimens, so that they can develop properly and so that their stately beauty can be appreciated in relation to the space surrounding them.

A vigorous, clump-forming perennial to 4 m in the warmer parts of the USA, seldom above 2 m in the UK. Roots both coarse and fibrous, not stoloniferous. Culms erect, smooth, exceptionally strong. Leaf sheaths rigid, rolled, shattering early in the season. Ligule short, long-haired. Leaf blades up to 1 m long, 2.5 cm wide; margins almost parallel for most of the length of the leaf, closing in fairly abruptly to a point; hairy on the undersurface, margins scabrid; blue-green with a distinct white mid-vein. Inflorescence, produced October to November, a somewhat fan-shaped panicle up to 30 cm long, wider at the top than at the bottom; at most about three-quarters as much across as tall; whitish, often tinged red, the spikelets distinctly awned. H5.

### *M.s.* 'Autumn Fire' ('Herbstfeuer')
*Gracillimus* has good whitish flower-heads and brilliant autumn foliage.

### *M.s.* 'Cabaret'
A stunning, white-variegated form in the style of *M.s.* 'Variegatus' but much more showy. H5.

### *M.s.* 'Cascade' ('Kascade')
*Gracillimus* type with rose-pink, pendent flowers.

### *M.s.* var. *condensatus*
Not a particularly well known or widely cultivated variety. It differs from the

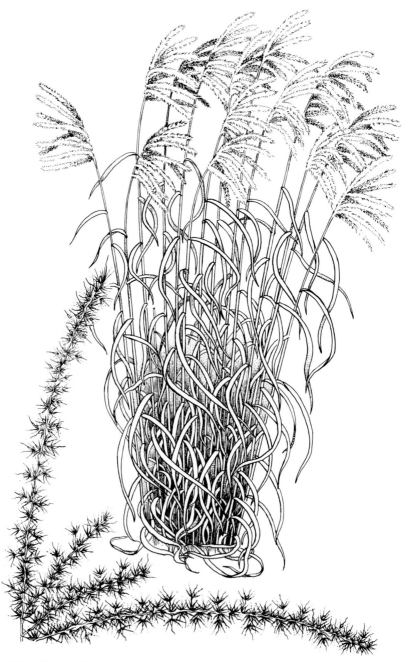

19 *Miscanthus sinensis*

type only in that the culms are much stouter, being almost twice the diameter of those of the type, and the leaves are much broader, up to 7.5 cm across. These differences greatly enhance the architectural value of the plant, without in any way detracting from its beauty in flower. H5.

### M.s. 'Flamingo'
Generally similar to 'Cascade' but smaller-growing and with red stems and lovely autumn colour.

### M.s. 'Goldfeder'
A gold-margined form. Slow-growing to little more than 1.5 m. H5.

### M.s. 'Goliath'
A strong-growing selection with extra-large panicles produced in September.

### M.s. 'Gracillimus'
One of the most delightful varieties, in many ways untypical of the species. Of very slender habit, the leaves of well-established plants being little more than 1 cm across, delightfully curled, the inflorescence also being somewhat curly. The plant is smaller-growing than the type, up to about 1.2 m, but just as hardy. It is not really suitable for hedging or screening, looking far better when grown as an isolated specimen where its curious habit of growth can be fully appreciated.

### M.s. 'Graziella'
An improved *gracillimus* type, flowers at first rose-pink fading to silvery-white. Autumn colour reddish-brown. Reliably free-flowering.

### M.s. 'Grosse Fontane'
A strong growing selection with unusually long leaves creating a fountain-like effect. Flowers reddish at first.

### M.s. 'Herbst Feuer'
A selection remarkable for its good autumn colour. H5.

### M.s. 'Klein Fontane'
A low-growing *gracillimus* type remarkable for its early flowering season, July–August.

### M.s. 'Malapartensis'
A form with somewhat bronze foliage, the panicles rich vinous purple at first. H5.

### *M.s.* 'Morning Light'

One of the finest of the newer cultivars, generally similar in size and form to *M.s.* 'Gracillimus', but has a band of white running the length of each margin, making the blade look narrower. The overall effect of the plant when seen from a distance, is silvery. Flowers September–October. Obtained from the private garden of Dr Masato Yokoi in Japan and introduced to the US National Arboretum at Washington by Dr John Creech and Sylvester March in 1976. According to Dr Yokoi this plant has been cultivated in Japan for over 100 years, often in small containers as a companion to bonsai plants. The Japanese have no varietal name and refer to this form merely as 'narrow-variegated'. The name 'Morning Light' was given it by Kurt Bluemel, America's leading grasses nurseryman. H5.

### *M.s.* 'Natsubo'

A variegated variety in which the leaves are striped white. The variegation is not dramatic, and the plant seems to have given way to *M.s.* 'Variegatus' (see below), in which the variegation is rather better. Grows to 1.5 m. H5.

### *M.s.* 'November Sunset'

A late-flowering *gracillimus* type. 2–2.5 m tall. A Kurt Bluemel introduction.

### *M.s.* 'Purpureus'

Leaves tinted brown, becoming red in autumn. Flowers pinkish. 1.2 m.

### *M.s.* 'Red Feather' ('Rotefeda')

Plumes flamingo pink.

### *M.s.* 'Sarabande'

Flowers in September.

### *M.s.* 'Silver Feather' ('Silberfeder', 'Silber Faine')

A relatively recent introduction, reputedly more free-flowering than the type plant, but otherwise very similar. Ideal for hedging and screening, but also good as a single specimen plant, the flowers appearing in September and October and lasting through winter into spring. 2 m. H5.

### *M.s.* 'Silver Arrow' ('Silberfeil')

A Heinz Klose introduction, with very tall, ascending flower stems.

### *M.s.* 'Silver-red' ('Rotsilber')

Another *gracillimus* type with silver-striped leaves and lovely red flowers produced on strong stems high above the leaves. Mid-September.

### *M.s.* 'Silver Spider' ('Silberspinne')

An elegant plant with very narrow leaves and wide-open flower-heads.

*M.s.* 'Silver Tower' ('Silberton')
Tall, stiff spikes with silvery plumes. 2.5 m.

*M.s.* 'Sioux'
Silvery-pink flower-heads.

*M.s.* 'Siren' ('Sirene')
Very tall, strong-growing form, the flowers produced high above the leaves. 2.6–3 m.

*M.s.* 'Strictus'
This cultivar is very similar to the highly popular *M.s.* 'Zebrinus' but differs in its narrower, more upright habit of growth. It has the same distinctive bars of yellow across the leaves. Its habit makes it useful as a specimen in smaller gardens where *M.s.* 'Zebrinus' would prove too spreading in habit; it is also preferable for hedging and screening purposes. H5.

*M.s.* 'Tiger Tail' ('Punktchen')
Leaves transversely banded creamy-white.

*M.s.* 'Undine'
Silvery-white flowers and good autumn colour. Similar to 'Graziella'.

*M.s.* 'Univittatus'
This variety is virtually a variegated form of *M.s.* 'Gracillimus'. The whole habit of growth and flowering is identical, the only difference being that, on this plant, the leaves have a broad yellow median stripe. Its garden uses are the same as for *M.s.* 'Gracillimus'. H5.

*M.s.* 'Variegatus'
This is the extremely popular and widely cultivated variegated form of the plant. It differs from the type in that it has an extremely broad median stripe of a rich creamy colour, and the leaf blades are striped silvery-white. It is one of the finest of all the larger, variegated garden grasses, and is equally effective as a specimen, or planted *en masse* as a hedge or screen. It is only slightly less vigorous than the type. H5.

*M.s.* 'Yaku Jima'
A dwarf, clump-forming selection, always the last to flower. H5.

*M.s.* 'Zebrinus'
Resembles the type plant, but the leaves have horizontal zones of yellowish-white. H5.

117

### M.transmorissonensis
A useful newly introduced species from high mountains in Taiwan. Flowers early, June/July, and stays small, under 1.2 m. Most attractive. H5.

### M.yakushimensis
A dwarf species to less than 1 m in flower. Introduced to the UK by John Bond, the Keeper of the Gardens at Windsor, who had it from those great plantsmen Robert and Jelena de Belder, who themselves got it from Yakushima Island, Japan. Densely tufted perennial to less than 1 m in flower. Stems erect, stiff, slender. Leaves linear, U-shaped in section tapering to a fine point, with a broad white central stripe, up to 50 cm long, 4 mm wide. Ligule short, membranous. Panicles loose, open composed of up to 7 very slender, linear racemes; September and October. H4?

### M. Sp. nov.
Another dwarf species growing at the Savill Garden in Windsor Great Park which Mr Bond tells me also came from Robert and Jelena de Belder, and also from Yakushima Island. It is, however, quite distinct from *M.yakushimensis*, being, in effect, a dwarf *M.floridulus*. H4?

### M. × oligonensis (M. sinensis × M. oligostachys)
'Dumbo' ('Zwergelefant')
In effect a dwarf *M.floridulus*. Grows 100–140 cm, plumes silvery-pink, very freely produced.

'July' ('Juli')
A July-flowering hybrid. Plumes silvery-red.

'Weather-cock' ('Wetterfane')
Leaves turning reddish in early winter.


## MOLINIA Shrank.
A genus of 2 species of tufted Eurasian perennials, natives of wet moorlands. The genus is related to *Hakonechloa* through *M.japonica* and is easily confused with *Eragrostis* from which it differs by the long rachilla internodes. In the field little confusion occurs as the two genera never grow in the same place. One species is grown for ornament. It enjoys damp, acid soil and is readily increased by dividing the rootstock.

Tufted perennials, the culm internodes unequal, the lowest section swollen into a food storage organ, those next ascending reduced to leaf-bearing segments, the topmost internode being most of what is visible. Panicle open or contracted, spikelets 2–5-flowered, glumes shorter than lemma, 1–3 nerved; lemmas membranous.

118

### *M.caerulea* (L.) Moench: Purple moor grass

Deservedly one of the most popular garden grasses, especially in its finest variegated forms. A native of acid heathlands and, though valuable as fodder, disliked by farmers because it is a host plant to the fungus which causes ergot of rye, itself the cause of the alarming and deadly disease of ergotism, popularly called 'St Anthony's fire'.

Densely tufted perennial forming large tussocks and growing up to 45 cm when in flower. Culms erect, usually slender, rarely stout; stiff and somewhat wiry; smooth, the basal internode becoming swollen. Leaf sheaths round on the back, smooth except in the upper part, which is slightly hairy. Leaf blades up to 45 cm long, 13 mm wide, tapering evenly to a narrow point; slightly hairy above, rarely hairless, the margins slightly hairy; the blades falling from the sheaths in earliest winter. Inflorescence, produced summer though autumn, a variable panicle, dense or loose, up to 40 cm long, often very much shorter; green, yellowish, brown or dark to light purple; lacking awns. H1.

### *M.c.* 'Aureo-variegata'

This somewhat suspect name has been used to describe a variegated form in which the leaves are striped a creamy to yellowish-white. The variegation on *M.c.* 'Variegata' is so variable that this is probably merely a selected form of that, not worthy of varietal status. H1.

### *M.c.* 'Bog Witch' ('Moorhexe')

Narrow, upright foliage and tall, needle-like flower stems topped with dark flowers.

### *M.c.* 'Fountain' ('Fontane')

An *altissima* type with inclining stems creating a fountain-like effect.

### *M.c.* 'Fountain-spray' ('Strahleonquelle')

Stems curve to create a fountain-like effect.

### *M.c.* 'Heather Bride' ('Heidebraut')

Produces narrow columns of stiffly erect, straw-coloured stems topped with yellowish flowers and dainty seedheads.

### *M.c.* 'Karl Foerster'

A tall, *altissima* type.

### *M.c.* 'Mountain's Friend' ('Bergfreund')

An *altissima* type with burning yellow autumn foliage.

### *M.c.* 'Nana-variegata'

A miniature replica of the next, resembling it in every way but only growing about 7.5 cm tall. H1.

*M.c.* 'Ramsay' ('Dauerstrahl')
Has tall, yellowish flower stalks splayed like the rays of the setting sun.

*M.c.* 'Skyracer'
A Kurt Bluemel introduction with very tall flower spikes. *Altissima* type.

*M.c.* 'Transparent'
Has curiously transparent flower-heads.

*M.c.* 'Variegata'
The form most commonly cultivated. A fine variety, the leaves longitudinally striped white. The degree of variegation is somewhat inconstant, some plants being finer than others. Generally smaller than the typical plant. H1.

*M.c.* 'Windplay' ('Windspiel')
An *altissima* type that moves gracefully in the wind. Compressed, golden-yellow heads.

## MUHLEMBERGIA Schreber

A genus of 150 or more species of annuals or perennials from open grasslands in subtropical and warm temperature regions of the New World, especially Mexico and southern USA with a few (8 or 10) species in Asia. Many species are highly ornamental, grown for their thread-like leaf blades and slender stems which combine to create an enchanting weeping effect. In Britain they are really best treated as conservatory plants and grown in large pots or Versailles tubs to be stood out in summer. They are easily raised from seed sown in a little warmth.

Low to tall, tufted or rhizomatous plants with simple or much-branched culms; leaves thread-like, flat or rolled; panicle open. Spikelets small, stalked, 1-flowered, awned or awnless; glumes obtuse to acuminate plus or minus as long as the lemmas; lemmas firm, narrow, 3-nerved, awned or awnless, the awn straight or bent.

### *M.mexicana* (L.) Trin.
Tufted, greyish-green perennial to 1 m with a tough, knotted, scaly rhizome. Stems slender, erect, branched; leaves flat linear, finely pointed, up to 20 cm long. Panicles, produced July and September, narrowly lanceolate, erect or nodding, up to 15 cm long, much-branched, the branches thickly set with spikelets, the spikelets nearly stalkless, the lemmas as long as the glumes, shortly bearded at the base. Called 'mexicana' by Linnaeus who thought it came from Mexico. It comes from Canada and the USA. H2.

120

6. *Sasa glaber*
'Tsuboi' by kind permission
of Mr. Peter Addington

7. *Miscanthus sinensis* 'Variegatus'

8. *Carex oshimensis* 'Evergold'

9.  *Carex elata* 'Aurea' at Longstock Water Garden

10.  *Arundo donax*
at Longwood Gardens

11.  *Koeleria vallesiana*

12.  *Miscanthus sinensis*

13.  *Bouteloua gracilis*

14.  *Hakonechloa macra* 'Albo-aurea'

15.  *Glycera maxima* 'Variegata'

# NARDUS L.

A genus of a single species of tufted perennial from the moorlands of Europe. It stands alone in the tribe Nardeae, and is morphologically something of a puzzle showing both pooid and bambusoid affinities and yet plainly belonging to neither. Its spikelets are anomalous anywhere. It is occasionally grown for ornament for its distinct 1-sided spikes. It is easily grown in most garden soils and can be raised from seed or increased by division.

Tufted perennial with membranous ligules and filiform blades. Panicle a 1-sided raceme. Spikelets alike, 1-flowered without rachilla extension: lower glume reduced ring on the rachis, upper glume lacking; lemma 3-nerved, awned from the tip; palea shorter than lemma.

## *N.stricta* L.: Mat grass

Low, tufted perennial, with erect, wiry stems to 30 cm tall. Leaves green or greyish-green, the sheaths shiny, persistent, blades sharply pointed up to 30 cm long. Panicles spike-like, up to 8 cm long, green or purplish, the spikelets narrow and finely pointed, the lemma bearing an awn up to 4 mm long, flowering June/August. H2.

# NASELLA Desv.

A genus of some 15 species of perennials from the grasslands of South America, especially the Andes. It is occasionally grown for ornament but requires a warm, sheltered place in the garden.

Slender, tufted perennials with narrow blades and small panicles. Similar to *Stipa* but differing in the gibbously ellipsoid florets; the lemma coriaceous, the margins overlapping, the awn curved or bent.

## *N.trichotoma* (Nees) Hack.

Grown for its attractive panicles. Tufted perennial with exceptionally slender, erect stems to 50 cm tall, the leaves filiform, bristle-like, tightly rolled, up to 40 cm long, pale green, smooth or rough. Panicles, June to September, up to 25 cm long, open, loose, with fine, wide-spreading branches, the spikelets borne on long stalks, shiny, the glumes finely pointed, the lemmas with awns 6 cm long. H4?

# OPLISMENUS Beauv.

A genus of 5 or more species of trailing, annual or perennial grasses from forest shade in the tropics and subtropics. They are unique among grasses in that they produce a sticky secretion on their awns to achieve dispersal of their seeds. One or two species and their varieties ape *Tradescantia* in their mode of growth and these used to be widely grown as edgings in conservatories and as basket plants. They present no particular difficulties in cultivation but need a minimum temperature of 15.5°C (except for *O.ondulatifolius* which is hardy in

Zone 5), and must be kept shaded from strong sun. They are usually increased by detaching rooted pieces of stem.

Creeping/trailing, much-branched, shade-loving grasses with thin, flat, generally ovate blades and erect flowering culms bearing 1-sided racemes along a central axis. Spikelets paired, the lower often much reduced; glumes half as long as the spikelet or a little more, terminating in a viscid awn; lower lemma shortly awned, upper lemma with the margins clasping the palea.

### *O.compositus* (L.) Beauv. Basket-grass

A low, creeping, very leafy perennial, the stems slender, trailing, rooting at the nodes, up to 1.5 m long, freely branched. Leaves narrowly ovate, contracted at the base, up to 15 cm long, 2.5 cm wide, of thin texture, slightly hairy. Summer, autumn and winter, panicles up to 30 cm long, with up to 10 racemes, each up to 5 cm long, the racemes spreading, slender. Spikelets lanceolate. G2.

### *O.hirtellus* (L.) Beauv.

A creeping perennial, with slender stems up to 1 m long, branched, rooting at the nodes. Leaves narrowly ovate, contracted at the base, up to 13 cm long, 2.5 cm wide, somewhat hairy. Summer, autumn and winter, panicle up to 15 cm long with up to 10 dense racemes, each up to 2.5 cm long. G2.

### *O.h.* 'Variegatus'

Has the leaves striped white. G2.

### *O.imbecillicus* (R.Br.) R. & S. Idiot grass

Sprawling perennial growing to about 15 cm, spreading indefinitely. Culms decumbent, becoming erect only to flower; much branched, indefinitely long; nodes clearly marked; roots forming at almost every node and the plant frequently creeping along, as it were using its roots as stilts to support the culms. Leaf sheaths rounded, overlapping, rather loose; purplish at the base. Leaf blades up to 5 cm long, 13 mm wide, usually narrower; slightly auriculated, evenly tapering to an abrupt point. Inflorescence, produced at any time throughout the year, a sparse, spike-like, short-branched panicle. G2.

### *O.i.* 'Variegatus'

Has the leaves variously striped white and usually tinged pink. An attractive grass for greenhouse or conservatory. Called *O.i.* 'Vittatus' in the USA. G2.

### *O.undulatifolius* (Ard.) Beauv.

Very leafy, creeping perennial with slender, rooting stems up to 1 m long, freely branched. Leaves more or less hairy, ovate, rounded at the base, up to 5 cm long, 2 cm wide. Panicle, produced July to September, loosely spicate, up to 10 cm long, composed of up to 10 short, dense clusters of spikelets, the

122

spikelets oblong-ovate. Hardy in the extreme south and west of the UK but generally needing a cool greenhouse. H5–G1.

## ORYZA L.

A genus of about 20 species of annual or rarely perennial grasses from the swamps and humid forests of the tropics and subtropics. One species, *O.sativa* (rice), usually grown in flooded fields, is the staple diet of two-thirds of mankind. It is scarcely an ornamental plant, but a couple of varieties are grown for decoration. They should be treated as tender annuals and the seed sown in heat in January or February, hardened off and then stood out in June at the edge of a pond with the pot submerged.

Often tall, moisture-loving grasses with flat blades and open panicles of simple, raceme-like spikes. Spikelets flat, 1-flowered with 2 sterile lemmas less than half the length of the spikelet; fertile lemma coriaceous, awned or awnless.

### *O.sativa* L.

20  *Oryza sativa*

This tropical grass has been cultivated as a food crop throughout the torrid zones for so long that its true origins seem to be lost.

Vigorous, loosely tufted annual up to 2 m in the tropics, usually well under half that height when cultivated in the cooler parts of the world. Culms stout, erect, arching, smooth. Leaf sheaths rounded on the back, slightly rough. Leaf blades up to 1.5 m long, 25 mm wide, broad along most of their length, gradually tapering towards the tip; arching, the highest point usually occurring at about half their length; slightly rough on both surfaces. Inflorescence, produced July to October, up to 45 cm long, a loosely branched panicle, the branches at first ascending, becoming spreading and 1-sided at maturity. The heads look very effective if dried when the rice is well swollen.

### O.s. 'Nigrescens'
A garden variety, believed to have originated in Japan. Leaves a rich, dark purple. Once grown at the Royal Botanical Gardens, Kew but no longer grown there since it failed to set viable seed.

### O.s. var. *rufipogon*
Grown for its decorative, long, red-awned inflorescence. Needs to be kept in the greenhouse if it is to make sufficient growth for flower-heads to form.

## ORYZOPSIS Michaux
A genus of some 35 species of perennials from the woodlands and hillsides of temperate and subtropical areas in the northern hemisphere, mainly the Middle East. The genus intergrades with *Stipa* but is distinguished by its dorsally compressed floret. The grains are sweet and considered by some a delicacy. One species is sometimes grown for ornament. It will grow in ordinary garden soil, thrives in damp soils and can be increased by division or raised from seed sown out of doors in late spring.

Tufted, usually rather large but low perennials with stiff, flat spreading leaves, and loose, open, spreading panicles of awned spikelets. Spikelets 1-flowered, the florets lanceolate to ovate, strongly dorsally compressed; glumes about equal; lemma about as long as the glumes, oval or oblong, dark in colour, the awn soon falling, short, straight.

### O.miliacea (L.) Aschers. & Schwein f.: Smilo grass, Rice grass
A light, airy, very graceful grass from the warmer parts of the Mediterranean. Its general appearance is similar to that of *Deschampsia caespitosa* (q.v.) from which it can be distinguished by having a 1- not 2-flowered spikelet. Whereas *D.caespitosa* is a woodland grass, and will grow in shade, this plant enjoys a position in full sun.

Densely tufted perennial with short rhizomes, growing up to 1.2 m when in flower. Leaf sheaths smooth, dark green. Leaf blades flat, up to 45 cm long, 1 cm wide, rough on the upper surface, smooth on the underside; leaf margins parallel for three-quarters of the length of the blade, then tapering to a point. Inflorescence, produced May to October, an exceptionally loose, open panicle, the spikelets green with a distinct green stripe on the glumes. The culms are erect, but tend to arch outwards gracefully under the weight of the inflorescence. H4.

## PANICUM L.

A very mixed genus of some 450 species of annuals or perennials with a pantropical distribution and some outlying species in temperate North America. The genus is very varied in form ranging from low cushions (*P.koolauense*) to almost shrubby (*P.turgidum*), and varying in leaf form from scale-like (*P.cupressifolium*) to very broad (*P.latissimum*) but is constant in the uniformity of the spikelets. A few species are quite ornamental and can be grown in ordinary garden soil. The annuals should be raised from seed sown in heat and set out when all danger of frost is past, and the perennials may be raised from seed or increased by division.

Annuals or perennials of various habits, with usually flat leaves and a generally open panicle. Spikelets 2-flowered, dorsally compressed, symmetrical; lower glume shorter than spikelet, upper glume longer than spikelet; lower floret sterile, the lemma similar to the upper glume; upper floret fertile, the lemma firm, clasping the margin of the palea.

### *P.capillare* L.: Witch grass

Another of the North American tumble grasses, grown for its huge but brittle flower-heads, which break off from the main axis as soon as the seed is ripe. A loosely tufted annual to 80 cm, culms several, erect, or decumbent becoming erect; sheaths hispid, blade up to 25 cm long, undulate at the margins, sometimes twisting, rough on both surfaces and both margins. Inflorescence, produced August to October, a diffuse but densely flowered panicle, about half the size of the entire plant; greenish to light brown. Very distinct in its flower-heads, the branches very fine and the spikelets so tiny that the whole head seems to be made of a mass of thread-like branches: when grouped the heads create the effect of a cloud hovering above the foliage.

### *P.clandestinum* L.

Interesting not only for its fine foliage but also for its axillary panicles which remain closed and are self-fertile (self-fertilisation being the clandestine act of the specific epithet). Clump-forming perennial, the stems erect or spreading, branched, up to 1.2 m; leaves broad, ovate, rounded at the base, finely pointed, up to 20 cm long, 3 cm wide, hairy at the base. Terminal panicles, produced August to September, loose, open, up to 15 cm long, 10 cm wide, the spikelets

125

elliptic, minutely hairy, the lower glume a third of the length of the spikelet, the upper glume ± the length of the lower lemma. Reasonably hardy in southern Britain. H4.

### *P.mileaceum* L.: Millet, Hog millet, Indian millet, Common millet, Broom-corn millet

Grown as a food crop for both man and beast in China, Japan, India, parts of southern Europe and some parts of North America, where it is also grown in a small way as a fodder crop. It makes an attractive garden grass and is ideal for indoor decoration, green or dried.

Loosely tufted annual growing to 60 cm when in flower. Culms usually several, very rarely solitary, smooth. Leaf sheaths coarsely hairy, splitting very early in the season. Leaf blades up to 45 cm long, 2 cm wide, the margins slightly undulate, slightly hairy above, smooth below, rather oval in outline. Flowering season July to October. Inflorescence a much-branched panicle, the branches tending to run parallel so that the spikelets occur in a rather flat plane at the tip of the inflorescence, which tends to bow under the weight of the head; usually green, occasionally purple. H4.

A form with purple inflorescences is occasionally sold either as *Panicum violaceum* or as *P.m.* 'Violaceum' though the standing of the name is dubious.

### *P.obtusum* H.B.K.: Vine mesquite

Tufted perennial with creeping stolons, and densely hairy nodes which root readily. Stems erect or spreading, thin and wiry, up to 75 cm tall. Leaves flat, hairless or slightly hairy, linear, finely pointed, up to 23 cm long, 6 mm wide. Panicles produced August/September narrow, up to 12.5 cm long, composed of several dense, erect, 1-sided racemes, the spikelets on one side of the axis, short-stalked, elliptic, the lower glume shorter than the spikelet, the upper and lower lemma about equal. H3.

### *P.virgatum* L.: Switch grass

A grass of tremendous character and many virtues. Its narrow, upright habit of growth makes it an ideal accent plant. It has an almost unique delicacy among the large grasses. The feathery inflorescences are at first narrow, with the branches tightly ascending, gradually becoming more diffuse as the branches spread away from the main axis and become drooping, producing the effect of an extremely diffuse inflorescence. It is singularly free-flowering, producing an enormous number of flowering culms. The leaves turn a brilliant glowing yellow in autumn and persist on the plant through winter, having turned an attractive light brown. It is best sited in the middle of a mixed border, or else grown as a specimen.

Vigorous, upright perennial to 2 m tall when in flower, with short, stout, scaly rhizomes. Leaf sheaths green, glabrous, persistent. Leaf blades up to

60 cm long, 2 cm wide; flat, glabrous but sometimes softly hairy towards the base. Inflorescence, produced September to November, a very loosely structured panicle up to 50 cm long and the same across at maturity. H3.

### P.v. 'Haense Herms'
Reddish-brown leaves and a fountain-like habit of growth. Good autumn colour.

### P.v. 'Red Bronze' ('Rotbraun')
A form with light brown leaves. Interesting and useful. 60–80 cm.

### P.v. 'Rotestrahlbush'
Seems to be the same as 'Haense Herms'.

### P.v. 'Rubrum'
Produces clouds of dainty chestnut-brown seedheads above leaves which are tinted red in summer and which become a blaze of crimson in autumn. It is not as exciting a plant as catalogues sometimes make it sound. Less vigorous than the type plant, it grows to a height of only 1 m. H3.

### P.v. Strictum
This variety is even narrower in its habit of growth than the type plant, and of slightly smaller stature, growing no more than 1.2 m tall. It differs so little from the type that the type plant is probably to be preferred. In small gardens, however, where space is a problem, the slightly smaller size of this plant might be an advantage. H3.

## PASPALUM L.
A genus of about 330 species of annual or perennial grasses from savannah and forest margins in chiefly the New World tropics. The genus is closely related to *Panicum* and *Seteria*, and is distinguished by its lack of a lower glume. Only one or two species are grown for ornament, and need a warm, sheltered position in full sun and light soil. They can be increased by division or raised from seed sown in heat under glass.

Generally tufted, hairless plant with flat or rolled leaves and panicles of 1-sided racemes arranged like the fingers of a hand at the top of the culms, the racemes bearing 2–4 rows of adpressed spikelets. Spikelets single or paired, oval or circular, 2-flowered; lower glume usually absent, upper glume and sterile lemma about equal; fertile lemmas obtuse, coriaceous.

### P.ceresia (Kuntze) Chase
A beautiful grass grown for its unusual, colourful panicles. A tufted perennial of loose habit, hairy at the base, with slender, ascending stems up to 75 cm tall.

Leaves glaucous, lanceolate or linear-lanceolate and finely pointed, up to 45 cm long, 3 mm wide, sometimes hairy above. Panicles, produced in summer, composed of up to 4 racemes, ascending or arching, each individually up to 7.5 cm long, the raceme axis flat, ribbon-like, purplish, with yellowish-bronze translucent margins, up to 8 mm wide, the spikelets solitary, concealed by long, silky, silvery hairs; anthers bright yellow; stigmas purple. H5–G1.

### *P.dilatatum* Poir.: Paspalum, Dallis grass, Water grass

Grown for its most unusual panicles. Has been grown out of doors at the Royal Botanical Gardens, Kew for many years, surviving severe frosts. Tufted perennial to 2 m with moderately stout, ascending stems. Leaves flat, hairy at the base, linear, finely pointed, up to 45 cm long, 1 cm wide, the sheaths compressed. Panicle, produced in summer, up to 26 cm long composed of up to 20 racemes, the racemes each up to 10 cm long, dense, green or purplish, collected together near the top of the stem. Spikelets paired, with a fringe of white hairs. H4.

## PENNISETUM Richard

A genus of about 120 species of annuals or perennials from savanna and woodlands in the tropics and the warm temperate regions. One species, *P.glaucum* (Pearl millet), is the most drought-resistent of all cereal crops and another, *P.clandestinum* (Kikuyu grass), is grown for pasture. Several species have highly ornamental panicles and are well worth growing. They need a sunny position and light, well-drained soil, and can be increased by seed or division for the perennials. The tender species need a warm greenhouse.

Low to tall, loosely tufted plants with erect, often branched stems and usually flat leaf blades and dense, spike-like panicles. Spikelets 2-flowered, single or in 2s or 3s, enclosed by an involucre of often plumose bristles united at the base if at all, falling together with the spikelets. Lower glume shorter than the spikelet, often minute or absent; upper glume about as long as or shorter than the sterile lemma; lower floret male or sterile, upper floret fertile, its lemma smooth, enclosing the palea.

### *P.alopecuroides* (L.) Spreng.: Fountain grass

A grass of great charm, its flower-heads arching outwards like water spraying out from a fountain. A loosely tufted perennial to 1 m, culms erect, becoming arching towards the tip. Sheaths rounded, slightly hairy, slightly inflated; dark green; blades to 15 cm, scabrous. Inflorescence, produced August and September, to 15 cm long, 10 cm across, a spike-like panicle with ascending branches, erect, arching at the top, seemingly hairy, brown becoming bright red at the tip. H5–G1.

128

### *P.a.* 'Hamelin' ('Hameln')

A low-growing (30–60 cm) early-flowering variant. Flowers August–September.

### *P.a.* 'Moudry'

A later-flowering form with showy, long blackish-brown heads.

### *P.* 'Burgundy Giant'

This is one of the most remarkable grasses to make its debut in the last decade. It is a strong-growing grass to 1.5 m, the whole plant—leaves, stems, flowers—deep burgundy: the colour of the best form of *Phomum tenax* 'Purpureum'. The leaves are broad, up to 3.5 cm wide, and are borne on stiff, stout stems. The panicle, produced from July till October, can be as much as 35 cm long, and nods gracefully. G2.

The plant is probably only truly perennial in Zone 10 in the USA or as a conservatory or greenhouse plant in the UK, its main use being as a horticultural annual. At Longwood Gardens it has been found to come readily from stem cuttings rooted under light mist in summer. It is not to be confused with the much smaller and daintier *P.setaceum* form known as 'Rubrum' or 'Cupreum'. The original plant is of garden origin at the Mane Selby Botanic Gardens in Sarasota, Florida. I am indebted to Rick Darke, Curator of Plants at Longwood Gardens for information on this cultivar.

### *P.latifolium* Spreng.

Grown for its broad leaves which create a subtropical effect. Needs a warm greenhouse. Perennial with short, thick rhizomes and stout, erect stems to 2.7 m, branched in the upper part, heavily bearded at the nodes. Leaves flat, the sheaths smooth, the blades lanceolate, narrowing towards the base, finely pointed, up to 75 cm long, 6 cm wide. Panicles produced, August to October, at the tips of the branches, dense, drooping, up to 5 cm long, carried at the tips of thread-like, flexible stalks, the axis studded with minute stumps; spikelets solitary. G2.

### *P.orientale* Rich.

The most widely cultivated of the ornamental species of *Pennisetum*: certainly among the top ten for beauty of flower. Shows to best effect when grown as an isolated specimen.

Densely tufted, deciduous perennial grass with slowly creeping rhizomes growing up to 1 m when in flower, but usually rather less, about half that height being more typical. Culms erect, or decumbent becoming erect, slightly hairy. Leaf sheaths rounded on the back; slightly hairy. Leaf blades up to 1 m long, 6 mm wide; dark green; arching, flat in section, slightly hairy above and on the margins. Inflorescence, produced July to September, a spike-like panicle up to 40 cm long, about 7.5 cm across at most; somewhat lax, the bristles much longer than the spikelets; very fine, feathery, pink or purplish. H5.

### *P.villosum* R.Br. ex Fresen: Feathertop
A perennial generally treated as an annual in Britain and the colder parts of the USA, or a short-lived perennial in the warmer parts. The flower-heads splay out from the leaf tuft like feathers in a feather duster. Grows to 60 cm, culms several, erect becoming arching, smooth. Sheaths round, smooth; blades up to 45 cm long, flat in section, arching. Inflorescence, produced August to September, a spike-like panicle to 23 cm long, borne at the tips of arching stems; very bristly; the bristles far longer than the spikelets, giving the feathery appearance; rich pink to purple. Colour fades on drying. H5–G1.

## PHAENOSPERMA Benth.
A genus of a single species standing alone in the tribe Phaenospermateae, widespread in Eastern Asia from Assam to Japan. It is ornamental, grown for its leaves which are broad and deeply veined giving a pleated appearance. It needs a sheltered position in light shade, and is easily raised from seed or increased by division. It is not particularly frost-hardy.

Tufted perennial with membranous ligules and broad, flat, lanceolate blades with well-defined nerves running obliquely from the midrib, with less well-defined cross-nerves and a falsely petiolate base which is twisted so as to bring the underside of the leaf to the top. Inflorescence a panicle with all the spikelets alike. Spikelets 1-flowered, without rachilla extension and lacking awns; glumes unequal, the lower half as long as the upper, the upper as long as the spikelet: lemmas also as long as the spikelet, rounded on the back. Grain spherical with longitudinal grooves and a small knob on the top.

### *P.globosa* Munro ex Benth.
Stems erect, up to 1.5 m, usually about half that. Leaves up to 60 cm long, 4 cm wide, green above, glaucous beneath. Panicles produced June/August, lanceolate, with spreading branches, up to 50 cm long; spikelets 4 mm long. Grown for its unusual broad pleated leaves, curious panicles and strange grains. H5–G1.

## PHALARIS L.
A genus of 15 or so annuals or perennials from the north temperate zone, mainly the Mediterranean region. Several species are grown for ornament. They grow well in ordinary garden soil. The annuals can readily be raised from seed sown where it is to grow, and the perennials can be increased by division.

Usually erect, tufted or running plants with flat blades. Panicle spike-like to ovoid. Spikelets laterally compressed, 2–3-flowered, the lower 2 florets reduced

130

to lemmas, the upper floret fertile; glumes equal, longer than and enclosing the lemma; sterile lemmas half as long or less than the fertile lemma, fertile lemma leathery, awnless.

## *P.arundinacea* L.: Reed canary grass

The white-variegated form of this grass, popularly known as gardeners' garters, is by far the commonest of the variegated grasses. Though spectacular, it tends to be invasive. Mentioned in early herbals as being cultivated for its brightly variegated leaves, it was probably the first of the variegated grasses to be brought into gardens. The plant's invasive character can be used to advantage as ground-cover, particularly where large areas of a single and relatively weed-free ground-cover are wanted: this quality could well be more widely exploited in amenity plantings. It is also useful in wet situations, such as ponds or streamsides, where it will be sufficiently vigorous to compete with other invasive plants. Grown in the border, it not only needs careful placing in relation to surrounding plants, since its variegation is so bright, but also some care in confining it. All the variegated forms show themselves to best advantage when grown among other plants, rather than when isolated as specimens, and they look brightest when grown among green plants rather than when contrasted with plants of darker foliage.

Extensively spreading, stoloniferous perennial grass growing up to 2 m when in flower. Culms erect or bent at the base, becoming erect, smooth, with 4 to 6 nodes, each noticeably swollen, the culm changing direction from the horizontal to the vertical gradually at each node. Leaf sheaths smooth, rounded on the back; green or greenish-white. Leaf blades up to 32 cm long, 2 cm wide, flat in section, firm; growing away from the culm in a gracefully arching fashion, tapering to a narrow point; light green or greenish-white. Inflorescence, produced June to August, a lanceolate panicle, dense in the upper portion, looser at the base, up to 25 cm long.

## *P.a.* 'Dwarf's Garters'

Another variation on *P.a.* 'Picta' which has not till now been differentiated by a varietal name. It is essentially similar to *P.a.* 'Picta', differing only in that it is dwarf-growing, seldom exceeding 30 cm in height, and proportionately less invasive. H1.

## *P.a.* 'Feesey's Form'

This variety has not till now been distinguished by a varietal name, and would appear to have arisen as a sport of *P.a.* 'Picta'. It differs in that while the leaves are similarly longitudinally striped green and white, the green is much paler than in *P.a.* 'Picta' and there is a far higher proportion of white, some leaves having only 1 or 2 very thin green stripes on them. It is vastly superior to *P.a.* 'Picta' as a garden plant, and is not invasive, spreading only slowly and gradually forming quite dense clumps which are easily controlled. Originally distributed by Mervyn Feesey. H1.

### P.a. luteo-picta: Voss

A variety in which the leaves are longitudinally striped golden-yellow. Much less often seen than *P.a.* 'Picta', equally beautiful but probably rather less dramatic in its variegation. Slightly smaller-growing than the type plant, but equally invasive. H1.

### P.a. 'Picta' Gardeners' garters

The ubiquitous gardeners' garters, described by Gerard in his *Herbal* together with the yellow-variegated form. The leaves are longitudinally striped white, one side of the blade usually being predominantly white, the other predominantly green, the proportion of green to white being roughly equal on most leaves. An exceedingly invasive plant. H1.

### P.canariensis L.: Canary grass

Widely cultivated in the cool temperate regions of the world for birdseed, the seeds being particularly liked by canaries, hence the Latin name. Probably of more value for drying than in the garden. Grow in an out-of-the-way corner, and leave a few flower-heads each season to seed themselves.

Tufted annual growing up to 1.2 m under optimum conditions, usually rather less. Culms usually several, erect or decumbent becoming erect; slender to stout, stiff, smooth. Leaf sheaths rounded on the back, the upper ones somewhat inflated; smooth or sometimes hairy. Leaf blades up to 23 cm long, 12 mm across; flat, rough, narrowing to a fine point. Inflorescence, produced June to September, a dense, ovoid, spike-like panicle; green and white.

## PHLEUM L.

A genus of some 15 species of annual and perennial grasses from dry grasslands in the north temperate region and in South America. None is particularly ornamental though the spike-like flower-heads dry well and take dyes exceptionally well. Easily grown in an open position in the garden. The annual species should be raised from seed sown thinly in spring where the plants are to grow, while the perennials can be increased by division.

Tufted plants with erect culms, flat blades and dense, cylindrical panicles. Spikelets 1-flowered, strongly laterally compressed; glumes equal and longer than the floret which they enclose; membranous, strongly keeled, shortly awned; lemmas membranous 3–7-nerved, truncate or obtuse, awnless.

### P.pratense L.: Timothy grass, Cat's-tail

A useful ornamental grown for its decorative spikes which are useful for picking and drying. Tufted perennial with quite stout stems, often swollen and bulbous at the base, erect or ascending to 1.5 m. Leaves flat, hairless, up to 45 cm long, 1 cm wide, slightly rough. Panicles, produced June to August, cylindrical, dense, bristly, up to 30 cm long, greyish or purplish, the spikelets oblong; glumes oblong bearing a short rigid awn and fringed with stiff hairs. H3.

## *P.subulatum* (Savi) Aschers & Graebu.

Slender annual grown for its attractive heads. Culms erect or ascending, tufted or solitary, up to 50 cm tall. Leaves hairless, narrowly linear and finely pointed, up to 10 cm long, minutely scabrid above. Panicle, produced June–July. Narrowly cylindrical, quite dense, up to 10 cm long, green or purplish, the spikelets elliptic, overlapping, usually hairless. H2.

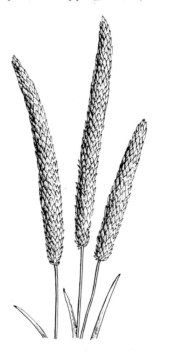

21  *Phleum subulatum*

## PHRAGMITES Adans.

A genus of 3 or 4 species of perennial reed from marshes and riversides in temperate and tropical regions around the world. One of the diagnostic characters of the genus is that the spikelets emerge in the juvenile form and mature on the panicle. The species are highly ornamental, with large, showy panicles, but are too aggressively invasive to be admitted to any but the largest

133

gardens unless carefully confined and strictly regulated. In cultivation they grow best in containers submerged in ponds or as marginals, but they will generally grow adequately in good, deep garden soil.

Tall perennial reeds with creeping rhizomes and extensively colonising, creeping, leafy stolons. Blades linear, flat. Panicles large, showy. Spikelets several-flowered, the lowest floret male or empty, middle floret bisexual, upper ones more or less reduced, the rachilla covered with long silky hairs: glumes soon falling, 3–5-nerved, shorter than lowest lemma; lemmas narrow, hairless.

## *P.australis* (Cav.) Steud.

One of the great colonising grasses of the world, forming extensive mono-specific stands over vast tracts of wetlands. It has an extraordinarily wide distribution, being found in the temperate regions of both the northern and southern hemispheres (hence the specific epithet *australis*), and extending marginally into the tropics. In the wild and even in cultivation it steadily and persistently invades lakes, ponds and waterways turning them back into dry land. The culms have traditionally been used as 'straw' for thatching.

The type, though graceful in flower, is far too invasive for the garden. Some of the varieties, however, are well worth a place, provided they are contained. The variegated forms are effective foliage plants, while the flowers have a special charm: apart from their delicate pinkish or purplish colour, there is a fascination in the way in which all in the inflorescences in a clump become 1-sided on the same side, owing, presumably, to the direction of the prevailing wind. The plant is most vigorous when grown in wet conditions, and the charm of the plant and its reflection in water is surpassed by few other grasses. The varieties, grown in mixed borders, particularly together with shrubs, seem more in place in the garden. One of their bonus points is the way their leaves turn a good autumnal russet.

Robust, erect perennial, spreading rapidly by both rhizomes and leafy stolons, growing up to 3 m when in flower. Culms erect, stout, rigid, closely clasped by the leaf sheaths, the nodes scarcely swollen, usually unbranched, smooth. Leaf sheaths rounded on the back, overlapping. Ligule reduced to a dense fringe of short hairs. Leaf blades up to 60 cm long, 2.5 cm wide, flat in section, contracted at the base, expanding and then gradually contracting towards a flexuous tip; tough and fibrous in texture, falling from the culms in winter, the culms standing until well into the following season. Inflorescence, produced August to October, a loose, much-branched panicle, up to 60 cm long; at first erect, symmetrical, becoming nodding, 1-sided; pinkish-purplish becoming brown; persistent. H1.

## *P.a.flavescens* Cust.

Differs from the type only in that the overall colour of the inflorescences is yellowish. Generally rather less effective than the type plant. H1.

22  *Phragmites australis*

### *P.a.giganteus* (Gay) Husnot

A giant variety with flowering culms growing up to 6 m, and larger in all its parts than the type. A native of the Mediterranean, this is more tender than the type. An imposing plant, comparable to *Arundo donax*. Sometimes known as *Arundo phragmites* var. *pseudodonax*. H1.

### *P.a.humilis*

Differs in its dwarf stature, seldom growing to as much as half the height of the type. H1.

### *P.a.* var. *striatopictus* Reichb.

Leaves longitudinally striped yellowish-white and green. Less vigorous than the type, but not, perhaps, of sufficiently dramatic variegation to justify its inclusion in the garden. H1.

### *P.a.* 'Variegatus'

A dramatically variegated form, the leaves longitudinally striped rich, bright yellow in spring and early summer, the colour fading to pure white by the time the flowers emerge. It is less vigorous than the type, growing to little more than 1.2 m. H1.

## POA L.

A genus of between 300 and 500 species of annual or mainly perennial grasses from meadowlands throughout the cool temperate and cold regions, and from mountains in the tropics. The genus is remarkably uniform, making it sometimes difficult to distinguish between species. Several are highly ornamental either for the blue of their leaves or for their panicles. They are easily grown in ordinary garden soil and can be raised from seed or increased by division.

Low or fairly tall grasses with narrow blades either flat or folded ending in a navicular point. Panicle open. Spikelets laterally compressed, 2–several-flowered, the uppermost floret reduced or rudimentary; glumes unequal, membranous, 1–3-nerved; lemmas membranous, keeled, acute, awnless.

### *P.bulbosa* L.: Bulbous meadow-grass

Occasionally cultivated for its curious bulbs. Tufted perennial to 60 cm, stems erect or spreading, slender; leaves folded or flat, up to 5 cm long, 2 cm wide, abruptly pointed, the sheaths green or purplish, the inner basal sheaths thickened and fleshy, forming a bulbous swelling at the base of the shoot. Panicles, produced March and April, oblong, dense, up to 6 cm long, 2.5 cm wide, the spikelets ovate, 3–6-flowered, coloured green, gold, purple and white, the lemmas lanceolate with a fringe of short hairs on the keel and margin. H1.

16.  *Phalaris arundinacea* 'Picta'   17.  *Carex siderostica* 'Variegata'

18.  *Milium effusum* 'Aureum'

19.   Grasses in a woodland setting. The New American garden, Washington, D.C. Photo James Van Sweden: reproduced by courtesy of Oehme, Van Sweden Associates Inc.

20.   Pennisetums in the Federal Reserve garden, Washington, D.C. Photo John Neubauer. Reproduced by courtesy of Oehme, Van Sweden Associates Inc.

*P.b.* var. *vivipara* Koel.

Has the upper part of the spikelet replaced with a plantlet. A curiosity: of no beauty. H1.

### *P.colensoi* Hook.f.

A blue-leaved New Zealand species sometimes mistaken for *Festuca glauca*. It is a good blue, retaining the purity of its colour throughout the year, even in winter looking better than most grasses. Inflorescence quite pretty, borne well above the foliage, so delicate it does not detract from the beauty of the plant.

Densely tufted perennial growing to 25 cm. Culms erect or arching, very slender; smooth, grooved; blue. Leaf sheaths purplish; rounded at the back, grooved, with a conspicuous sheathing membranous ligule. Leaf blades up to 15 cm long, 2 mm wide, filiform, the margins inrolled, usually curving; clear blue. Inflorescence, produced June to August, a broadly ovate panicle up to 5 cm long, the branches rather spreading, the spikelets blue becoming brownish. H4?

### *P.labillardieri* Steud.

A fascinating but still uncommon species from Australia and New Zealand. The New Zealand plants seem hardier than the Australian ones, since it grows in sub-alpine meadows there. Has similar qualities to *Helictotrichon sempervirens*, forming mounds of bright bluish foliage, but differs from the plant most noticeably in its much narrower, filiform leaves. It will probably become as popular as that plant once it is better known and is more widely available. Needs a specimen position for its architectural form to be appreciated.

Densely tufted perennial, growing up to 1 m when in flower. Culms erect, slender, smooth. Leaf sheaths filiform, smooth, lacking ligules. Leaf blades up to 60 cm long, 4 mm wide, involute, filiform, rather ragged; blue-green. Inflorescence, produced in summer, a rather loose panicle up to 20 cm long, less than one-third of that across; the branches very sparse, whorled about the main axis; the spikelets very few. H5?

### *P.pratensis* L.: Smooth meadow-grass, Kentucky blue-grass

Perennial with slender creeping rhizomes forming tufts or patches. Stems slender or stout, erect up to 2.8 m tall: leaves green, hairless or minutely hairy; ligules very short: blades blunt or abruptly pointed, up to 30 cm long, rough or nearly smooth. Panicle produced May to July, pyramidal or oblong, erect or nodding, open or dense, up to 20 cm long, 10 cm across, green or purplish; branches in groups of 3 to 5; spikelets ovate to oblong, shortly hairy on the keel, with long kinked hairs at the base. Very variable, with numerous strains. H3.

137

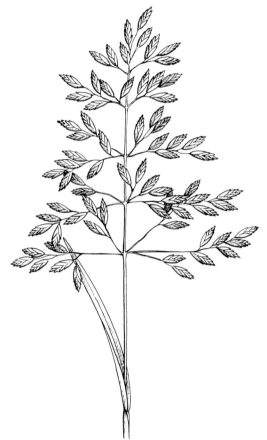

23  *Poa pratensis*

## *P.tasmanica* Hort.

Relatively newly introduced, this is the smallest of all the blue grasses, ideal for a sink, trough or rock garden. A dwarf, mat-forming perennial to 10 cm. Culms erect, smooth, blue, rapidly drying to russet. Sheaths rounded, overlapping, blue to purplish. Blades to 10 cm, usually less; filiform; palest blue. Inflorescence a narrow blue spike, florets white; February to March in Britain. Frost-hardy; dislikes winter wet. H5.

## POLYPOGON Desf.

A genus of 15 to 20 annual or perennial grasses from damp places throughout the warm temperate regions and from tropical mountains. It is very similar to *Agrostis* with which it interbreeds but differs in its deciduous spikelets. One species is grown for its highly ornamental, silky panicles. It is easily grown in fertile soil in sun. Seed should be sown in spring where the plants are to grow.

Decumbent or low grasses with flat blades and dense, bristly, spike-like panicles. Spikelets 1-flowered, without rachilla extension, falling entire: glumes about equal, longer than floret, 1-nerved, chartaceous, with a straight, slender, apical awn; lemmas much shorter than glumes with a straight, slender, apical awn shorter than the awn on the glume.

### *P.monspeliensis* (L.) Desf.: Annual beard grass

A highly decorative annual, producing a wealth of blooms, prized for their lovely silky appearance.

Loosely tufted annual, growing up to 76 cm when in flower. Culms several, rarely solitary; erect, or decumbent becoming erect, varying from slender to stout, usually tending towards stout; often branched near the base; smooth but sometimes becoming rough near the panicle. Leaf sheaths smooth, the upper ones somewhat inflated. Leaf blades up to 15 cm long, 8 mm wide; flat in section, tapering to a fine point; rough on the nerves. Inflorescence, produced June to August, a very dense, spike-like panicle up to 15 cm long, narrow, cylindrical, densely covered in very fine bristles; green or yellowish, becoming light brown.

## RHYNCHELYTRUM Nees

A genus of about 15 species of annual and perennial grasses from the savannahs of Africa. One species is sometimes cultivated for its highly coloured, very ornamental panicles. Several other species would be equally ornamental. Easily grown in ordinary garden soil.

Small to quite large plants with leaf blades flat or thread-like, and showy panicles with slender branches. Spikelets laterally compressed, silky-hairy: glumes unequal, upper glume gibbous as long as the spikelet, papery to leathery, thinner towards the tip, more or less swollen on one side below and tapering to a beak above; lower glume small; lower floret male, its lemma similar to the upper glume but narrow and less swollen, cartilaginous.

### *R.repens* (Willd.) C.E. Hubbard

Exceptionally beautiful, grown for its unique bright rose-pink flower-heads. Loosely tufted, short-lived perennial or annual growing to 30 cm in cultivation. Culms decumbent, becoming erect or spreading, the nodes clearly marked rooting where they touch the ground; slender. Leaf sheaths rounded at the back, smooth. Leaf blades up to 30 cm long, 7 mm across; flat in section, evenly tapering to a long point. Inflorescence, produced July to October, a loose panicle up to 15 cm long, about half as much across, packed with long, dense hairs greatly exceeding in length the spikelets; cream, mauve, pink or purplish. H5–G1.

## SACCHARUM L.

A genus as generally understood of some 40 species of usually tall, tufted or rhizomatous perennials from riversides and valley bottoms throughout the tropics and subtropics. One species, *S.officinarum*, and two segregates, *S.barberi* and *S.sinense*, produce sugar cane.

The genus has traditionally been split among several other genera whose distinctions seem to have little value: the awned species were referred to *Erianthus*, the species with coiraceous glumes to *Narenga* and the species with pedicelled spikelets to *Lasiorhachis*. These divisions are not maintained here.

### S.hostii Griseb.

This imposing, elegant grass could almost be described as a fastigiate pampas grass. Seldom seen or offered, it is well worth growing if you have the opportunity. In spite of its height, it is a narrow grass, not taking up much ground-space. Its general habit of growth is rather similar to some of the species of *Miscanthus*, and its flowers very much resemble a rather tightly formed, reddish-purple pampas plume.

Narrowly erect, tufted perennial with both coarse and fibrous roots, occasionally producing not very vigorous stolons. Culms erect, up to 2 m tall, slender, joints scarcely swollen. Leaf sheaths smooth, rigid. Leaf blades up to 45 cm long, 2 cm wide at the base, tapering narrowly and evenly towards the tip; a rough, coarsely hairy texture beneath, smooth above; dark, sometimes almost bronzy-green, with a striking white line down the centre. Inflorescence, produced August to September, a rather dense, stiff panicle, up to 30 cm long and 15 cm wide; a rich reddish-purple colour. G2.

### S.officinarum L.: Sugar cane

Sometimes grown for ornament in warm greenhouses, the highly decorative panicles being much-used in house decoration, especially when dyed. Perennial to 7 m; stems solid, erect or ascending, up to 5 cm in diameter. Leaves up to 2 m long, 5 cm wide, without hairs, erect or drooping. Panicles up to 1 m long pyramidal, dense or loose, fragile, the spikelets oblong, enclosed in white hairs.

A variable species, differing in the size and colouring of the leaves and panicles and the shape of the internodes. Usually propagated by cuttings. G2.

### S.ravennae (L.) Beauv.

One of the most neglected of the larger-growing grasses, every bit as lovely as pampas grass and the cultivated forms of *Miscanthus*, but unfortunately more winter-tender. It is of value not only for its architectural form, but also for its foliage and flowers. In many ways of similar garden value to pampas grass, but the flowers are narrower and it has the added bonus of good autumn colour.

Vigorous, stoutly tufted perennial with both fibrous and coarse roots, not stoloniferous. Culms erect, up to 1.75 cm wide; green. Leaf sheaths rigid;

24  *Saccharum officinarum*

green. Leaf blades up to 75 cm long, 2.5 cm wide; deeply U-shaped in section, wide for most of their length, narrowing abruptly to an attentuated point; coarsely hairy on both surfaces; mid green with a clear white median stripe. Inflorescence, produced August to September, a rather erect panicle up to 60 cm long, 23 cm across; densely hairy, especially in the lower part of the panicle; silvery-white or beige. H5–G1.

*S.r.* var. *purpurascens* hort.
A form with panicles of a rich purplish colour. H5–G1.

## SESLERIA Scop.
A genus of about 25 species of perennial grasses from mountainous terrain in Europe, mainly centred on the Balkans. One or two species are ornamental and are occasionally grown. Easy in good soil in an open position.

Panicles capitate or spike-like, subtended by usually 2 scarious bracts. Spikelets 2–5-flowered: glumes about as long as lowest lemma; lemmas rounded 2–5-toothed, the teeth often drawn out into short awns.

### *S.caerulea* (L.) Ard.
A pleasing grass for the rock garden or front of the border.

Its appeal is the uniquely coloured inflorescence early in the year, its bi-coloured leaves, the upper surface being green the under surface a whitish-blue.

Densely tufted perennial with stout rhizomes, growing up to 15 cm when in flower. Culms erect or oblique, slender, wiry, smooth, the nodes occurring only near the base. Leaf sheaths persistent, smooth, keeled. Leaf blades up to 20 cm long, 5 mm wide, of equal width along most of their length, then narrowing abruptly to a blunt, somewhat thickened and hooded tip; flat in section or V-shaped, strongly keeled beneath; the upper surface and margins rough, shining green, the underside blue, smooth. Inflorescence, produced March to June, a dense, ovoid, spike-like panicle up to 32 mm long, usually very much less, of a brilliant, unexpected purple when in full flower. H1.

## SETARIA Beauv.
A genus of around 100 species of annual or perennial grasses from woodlands and grasslands throughout the tropics and subtropics. One species, *S.italica* (Foxtail millet), is a major cereal crop in China and is much grown in Europe for birdseed. Several species are grown as ornamentals either out of doors or in greenhouses. The greenhouse species generally have dramatic pleated leaves: they need to be grown in rich loams and given abundant water, and require a minimum winter temperature of 10°C. The hardy species are mainly annuals with showy, spike-like heads. They are ideal for cutting and drying but must be culled while still green otherwise they soon shatter. They can be grown in ordinary garden soil from seed sown in spring where the plants are to grow.

Plants of various size and habit, large or small, slender or stout, blades linear to ovate. Inflorescence a panicle varying from narrow and densely spike-like to rather open. Spikelets 2-flowered, short-stalked, and subtended by 1–several bristles which persist after the spikelets have fallen; the lower floret male or sterile, the upper female; glumes unequal, the lower broad and half the length of the spikelet, 3–5-nerved, the upper as long as the sterile lemma, the fertile lemma hard and brittle.

### *S.italica* (L.) Beauv.: Foxtail millet, Italian millet

Annual. A spectacular species that has been regarded as sacred in China since at least 2700 BC. Apparently known to lake-dwellers in Europe, who presumably cultivated it as a grain crop. Unknown wild anywhere. A loosely tufted

25 *Setaria italica*

plant to 60 cm. Culms erect, often nodding under the weight of the inflorescence. Sheaths round, hairy, blades to 30 cm long, hairless but minutely rough; slightly blue-green. Inflorescences, produced August to October, a very dense, flat, spike-like panicle to 10 cm long, heavy, densely packed with long bristles; green or purplish. Heads ripen in autumn: pick and dry well.

### *S.lutescens* (Weigel) F.T. Hubb.: Yellow bristle grass, Common bristle grass

Probably the finest ornamental *Seteria*, with its brilliantly foxy-red bristles, which contrast well with the glaucous foliage. Densely tufted annual growing up to 76 cm when in flower. Culms erect, slender, smooth becoming rough near the panicle. Leaf sheaths smooth, compressed, keeled in the lower portion. Leaf blades up to 30 cm long, 8 mm wide; broad for much of their length, coming to a fine point; mainly hairless, but hairy towards the base, rough on the margins; arching; glaucous green. Inflorescence, produced July to October, a very dense, cylindrical, spike-like panicle, the branches very short, bristles numerous; several times longer than the branches, giving a softly bristly appearance to the inflorescence, the overall colour yellowish to reddish.

26 *Setaria verticillata*

### *S.plicatilis* (Hochst.) Hack.

The flower-heads are typical of the genus, but this plant has the added interest of broad, pleated leaves. A loosely tufted perennial to about 1 m in cultivation. Culms erect, moderately stout; smooth becoming rough towards the panicle. Sheaths compressed and keeled. Blades to 45 cm long, 2.5 cm wide; closely pleated, rough. Inflorescence, produced in summer, a dense, cylindrical, spike-like panicle, erect becoming nodding, to 30 cm long, 6.5 cm wide, the bristle much longer than the branches; green or pinkish; silky. Most unusual in leaf and flower. Needs a well-drained site with plenty of moisture at the roots. H5–G1.

### *S.verticillata* (L.) Beauv.

A curiosity, sometimes grown for its retrorsely barbed panicles. A loosely tufted annual. Culms slender, erect, up to 60 cm tall. Leaves up to 10 cm long, flat, hairless, the ligule with a dense fringe of hairs. Panicle, produced August to October, spike-like or cylindrical, very dense, very bristly, the bristles 1–3 together, retrorsely barbed, the spikelets oblong, blunt, the upper glume as long as the spikelet.

## SITANION Raf.

A genus of 3 or 4 species of perennial grasses from western North America from Mexico and Canada, from habitats ranging from semi-desert to alpine meadow. Only 1 species is commonly grown for ornament and is valuable in borders for its bristly spikes. It is easily grown in ordinary garden soil and may be raised from seed sown in spring, or increased by division. The spikes dry and dye well and should be culled while immature otherwise they soon shatter.

Low to tall, tufted perennials with slender stems, membranous ligules and blades flat or rolled. Panicle a very bristly spike, the spikelets 2–several-flowered, borne usually in pairs alternating on opposite sides at each joint on the fragile main axis; the axis breaking at each joint at maturity; lowermost floret in one or both spikelets of a pair reduced to an awn: glumes side by side, bristle-like, 1–2-nerved, the nerves drawn out into awns; lemmas rounded on the back, 5-nerved, 2-toothed, the central nerve drawn out into a long, slender awn with sometimes 1 or more further awns.

### *S.hystrix* (Nutt.) J.G. Smith.: Squirrel tail

One of only three species of *Sitanion*, all natives of the USA, and all formerly included under *Elymus*. The one described here is grown for its bottle-brush-type flower-heads, somewhat similar to those of *Hystrix patula*, but green or whitish-green in colour, not pink. The whole plant turns a good autumnal brown once touched by frost. Flowers not suitable for picking since they shatter early.

A loosely tufted perennial to 60 cm when in flower. Culms erect, or decumbent becoming erect; rather slender; smooth but becoming rough close to the panicle. Leaf sheaths rounded, keeled, somewhat inflated. Leaf blades up to 30 cm long, 6 mm wide, slightly U-shaped; the nerves prominent, the margins rough. Inflorescence, produced July to August, a spike-like panicle conspicuous for its extremely long awns, giving the flower-head much the appearance of a bottle-brush or porcupine. H2.

## SORGHASTRUM Nash

A genus of about 16 or 20 species of annuals and perennials from savannah and forest margins in Africa and tropical America. The species are generally similar to those in *Sorghum* but differ in that the panicles have no stalked spikelets, the stalk alone being present, these barren stalks being diagnostic of the genus. Several species are ornamental, and their cultivation is as for *Sorghum* (q.v.).

### S.nutans (L.) Nash

A beautiful grass needing greenhouse treatment in the UK. Stems stout, to 1.2 m. Leaves finely pointed, to 60 cm long, up to 1 cm wide, rough. In summer, panicle rather dense, narrow, contracted, yellowish or ochrous, to 35 cm long, the raceme axis and spikelet stalks hairy. Spikelets lanceolate, the awn bent. G2.

## SORGHUM Moench

A genus of about 20 species of annuals and perennials from savannah and forest margins in the tropics and subtropics of the Old World, with one species occurring in Mexico. *S.bicolor* is a major cereal crop in the tropics. Several species are ornamental, with broad leaves and showy panicles. The hardy species are best grown in warm positions in rich but light soil. The annuals, several of which are excellent in subtropical bedding schemes, should be sown in January under glass, then hardened off and finally set out in June. Several perennial species can be grown in warm greenhouses in large pots, in rich soil and need plenty of watering.

Tufted, rarely rhizomatous, grasses with stout to robust stems, membranous ligules and mostly long, flat blades. Panicle large, its primary branches single or compound, bearing short, dense, spike-like racemes with hairy internodes. Spikelets in pairs, the spikelets dissimilar in each pair, 1-stalked and fertile, the other stalkless and male or sterile, 2-flowered, the lower floret always sterile. Stalkless spikelet with glumes equal, leathery, the upper boat-shaped: lemmas enclosed by the glumes, the upper one usually awned: stalked spikelets narrower and awnless.

### S.bicolor (L.) Moench.: Sorghum, Great millet

Like many tropical plants, this has a multitude of uses. The grain is made into

146

flour, or simply boiled for human consumption; it is also used for stock and poultry feeding, as well as for making a rather potent alcoholic beverage. The juice of the stems is used for making a singularly strong alcoholic drink, as well as for the making of molasses and syrups. The dried panicles are used for making brooms. Its main horticultural use is for foliage effect as a subtropical bedding plant.

Extremely vigorous, erect annual. Culms up to 6 m tall under optimum conditions, seldom over 2.5 m in the UK and similar cool climates; very stout, up to 2 cm thick, solid, smooth. Ligules very large, prominent. Leaf sheaths tightly clasping the culm; green at first, rapidly becoming light brown; splitting and becoming ragged early in the season. Leaf blades exceptionally broad, up to 10 cm across, 1 m long, rarely more; flat in section, undulate at the margins, arching, gradually tapering; mid green with a broad white median stripe. Inflorescence, produced in summer, a much-branched loose panicle, very variable in size and shape, up to 25 cm long, usually about half as wide, sometimes more, sometimes less; erect, nodding or pendulous; green, whitish-beige or pinkish. Grains large, variable in colour, from green through browns to almost black.

## SPARTINA Schreber

A genus of perhaps 15 species of perennials mainly from intertidal mud flats, but occasionally from dunes and freshwater swamps, along the temperate and subtropical Atlantic and Pacific coasts of America, and the Atlantic coast of Europe and Africa. They are generally very easily grown but have little ornamental value, except for *S.pectinata*, which grows best in damp ground near water. Increase by division in spring.

Tufted or rhizomatous, often tall perennials with stiff, slender stems, the leaves flat or rolled, the panicle erect, with few to many straight spikes. Spikelets strongly flattened, 1-flowered, stalkless, overlapping on one side of the axis only without rachilla extension; glumes 3, unequal, narrow, acute to shortly awned; lemmas firm, keeled; lodicules often lacking.

### *S.pectinata* Link: Prairie cord grass, Freshwater cord grass

An American native of marshes and sloughs from New England to the Great Plains. The culms are much used for thatching and covering hay stacks. Useful because it is one of the few grasses that will grow happily in either fresh or salt water marsh lands as well as in normal garden soils. Cultivated for its gracefully arching blades, over which the narrow inflorescences, borne on their wiry stems, look most attractive and for its autumn colour, the blades turning a showy bright yellow.

Vigorously rhizomatous perennial, forming large clumps or, rarely, extensive stands, and growing up to 2 m under optimum conditions, seldom above 1.2 m in garden cultivation. Culms erect, thin, wiry and rather whippy. Leaf sheaths rounded on the back, splitting early; green. Leaf blades up to 60 cm long, 2 cm wide, flat in section, very scabrid on the margins, gradually tapering along their lengths, gracefully arched; light green to yellowish-green. Inflorescence, produced May to July, up to 25 cm long, composed of between 2 and many closely appressed spikes racemose on the main axis; light green becoming beige.

### *S.p.* 'Aureomarginata'
The margins of the blades marked with broad, yellow bands. This plant was long cultivated under the incorrect name of *Spartina cynosuroides* 'Aureomarginata'. The gold variegation is not particularly dramatic since the plant has rather yellowish-green leaves anyway. H2.

## SPODIOPOGON Trin.
A genus of 9 species of perennial, rarely annual, grasses from open hillsides in tropical and temperate Asia including Japan and Thailand. Related to *Saccharum* with which it has some evident affinities. One species is sometimes grown as an ornamental for its hairy panicles. It is easily grown in ordinary garden soil, and may be raised from seed sown under glass, or increased by division in spring.

Plants with long, creeping, scaly rhizomes and slender to stout stems; membranous ligules and flat leaf blades. Panicles composed of spike-like racemes, the primary branches flexible. Spikelets in pairs, 1 stalked, 1 stalkless, 2-flowered, the lower floret male, the upper bisexual: glumes firm, hairy; lemmas transparent, enclosed by the glumes.

### *S.sibiricus* Trin.
Perennial with scaly, creeping rhizomes and erect stems to 1.5 m. Leaves up to 38 cm long, 2 cm wide, linear-lanceolate, green or stained purplish. Panicles, produced August and September, narrowly lanceolate, up to 20 cm long, the racemes 2 cm long; spikelets narrowly ovate, the glumes densely covered with fine white hairs, the awns up to 1.5 cm long. Grown for its attractive hairy panicles. H2–3?

## STENOTAPHRUM Trin.
A genus of about 7 species of annual or perennial grasses from coastal regions throughout the tropics. One species, *S.secundatum* with a far-reaching, creeping habit, is widely used for lawns in warm, humid regions. It may be grown as a basket grass indoors, or as ground-cover under staging in greenhouses, or set out in summer in subtropical bedding schemes, where it will quickly cover a large area. Can be easily increased from cuttings taken any time except winter and rooted in sand in a warm greenhouse. They need rich soil and plenty of water.

Plants usually creeping with leafy stems, leaves flat or folded, ligules ciliate. Panicle sparse, spike-like, made up of very short racemes of few single spikelets, these alternating in 2 rows on one side of the axis. Spikelets stalkless, awnless, falling entire, 2-flowered, the lower floret male or barren, the upper fertile; glumes membranous; lemmas coriaceous.

### S.secundatum (Walt.) Kuntze.: St Augustine grass

Native mainly of the Caribbean, extensively used in some of the drier parts of the tropics as a lawn substitute. The South American landscape designer Roberto Burle Marx used both the type plant and its variegated form to produce bi-coloured lawns. In cooler climates, often grown as a house or greenhouse plant, occasionally as a summer bedding plant. The creeping stems form a curious zig-zag pattern, and on vigorous plants cascade over the side of the pot. It is highly effective when used as a foreground plant in summer bedding schemes, where, if the soil is rich, it will form extensive clumps.

Vigorously stoloniferous perennial growing up to 15 cm. Culms compressed, creeping, ascending only at flowering. Leaf sheaths compressed, hairless. Leaf blades flat in section or slightly V-shaped, up to 15 cm long, 15 mm wide, the margins parallel, terminating abruptly in a rounded tip; hairless. Inflorescence, produced August to September, an erect or slightly curved raceme up to 10 cm long; whitish or pale green.

### S.s.variegatum Hitchc.

Has the leaves longitudinally striped creamy-white. Needs rich soil to thrive. G2.

## STIPA L.

A genus of some 300 species, nearly all perennials, from steppes in the temperate and warm temperate regions. One species, *S.tenacissima*, is used in paper making, including cigarette papers. Several species are grown as ornamentals for their attractive, feathery awns, in some species as much as 50 cm long. They are excellent in arrangements when green or dry, and take dyes exceptionally well. The species listed here are all hardy in the UK and are easily grown in ordinary, well-drained garden soil. They can be raised from seed or increased by division.

Plants tufted, leaves pleated or rolled, with prominent ribs. Panicle terminal, often slender. Spikelets 1-flowered, glumes narrow, 3, about equal, much longer than the lemma; lemma narrow, strongly convolute, terminating in a prominent, persistent awn, the awn usually thick and twisted in the lower part, and thinner and straight in the upper part.

### S.arundinacea Bentham

This charming grass from Australia and New Zealand is quite hardy in

149

southern Britain. Seemingly unknown in the USA. It is grown for its delightful colouring, the leaves gradually becoming streaked with orange and light, bright brown as the summer advances, this being especially pronounced in long, hot summers, the whole plant turning orangey-brown through winter. The open, airy inflorescence is a bonus. Makes interesting and unusual ground-cover, but can be easily controlled when desired.

Loosely tufted perennial growing from slowly creeping, scaly, branching rhizomes, reaching up to 1.5 m in its native countries, seldom exceeding 45 cm in cultivation in the UK. Culms erect to arching, very slender, smooth. Leaf sheaths rounded, slightly rough. Leaf blades up to 30 cm long, 6 mm wide; very leathery, somewhat involute; the nerves well marked, somewhat rough; dark green. Flowering season July to September. Inflorescence a very open, drooping panicle, the slender branches produced in whorls about the main axis; the branches unbranched or very rarely branched, the spikelets sparse, purplish. H4.

### S.calamagrostis Auct.
One of the most free-flowering of all the perennial grasses. Its inflorescences open in June and remain looking beautiful right through the winter. The flower-heads are the epitome of grace, and pick well, looking delightful when fluffed out by the warmth of a room. Forms a dense mound covered with graceful flowers. A plant no garden should be without.

Densely tufted, deciduous perennial growing up to 1 m. Culms erect becoming arching, smooth. Leaf sheaths round, splitting early and turning brown very early in the season; slightly rough. Leaf blades up to 30 cm long, 6 mm wide; flat in section or very slightly V-shaped, evenly tapering to a fine, long point; arching; hairy above, smooth below. Inflorescence, produced June to October, a loose, spreading panicle tending to become somewhat 1-sided; up to 30 cm long, about half as much or more across; somewhat bristly, giving a light feathery appearance; white or tinged purplish. H3.

### S.gigantea
One of the most magnificent of all garden grasses, frequently offered by nurserymen but all too seldom grown. The flower-heads are the great glory of this grass over a long season, being borne high above the rounded hummock of dark foliage. The golden, long-awned, 2-pronged spikelets glisten in the sun and almost dance in the slightest breeze. Best planted as a specimen: looks good grown in an island bed in a lawn.

Densely tufted perennial growing to 2 m or more when in flower, the foliage usually rather less than half that height. Culms erect, stout, rigid, smooth. Leaf sheaths rounded, slightly rough. Leaf blades up to 45 cm long, 6 mm wide, rolled or somewhat U-shaped in section, arching, evenly tapering to a long fine point. Inflorescence, produced June to July, an extremely loose, open panicle

27  *Stipa calamagrostis*

28  *Stipa gigantea*

up to 45 cm long, three-quarters as much across, with many branches, the branches freely branching and bearing large spikelets, each up to 25 mm long; purplish, with long awns up to 15 cm. H5.

### *S.pennata* L.: Feather grass

Among the most desirable of garden grasses, being attractive in both leaf and flower. The leaves grow in a narrow, upright bunch, splaying open at the top. The inflorescence owes much of its grace to its sparseness and its quite exceptionally long awns, these looking like streamers trailing out from the flower-head. If the seeds are watched closely, it will be seen that they work themselves into the ground to the right depth for germination by the twisting and turning motion of the awns, which twist one way in wet weather and contract in dry.

Densely tufted perennial growing up to 76 cm when in flower. Culms erect, or erect becoming arching, slender to moderately stout; slightly rough towards the panicle, otherwise smooth. Leaf sheaths rounded on the back, smooth becoming hairy on the upper part. Leaf blades up to 60 cm long, 6 mm wide; U-shaped in section, rarely flat; mid green, evenly tapering to an exceedingly attenuated point which tends to be light, whitish-green or even slightly brown in colour. Inflorescence, produced July and August, a very loose panicle bearing relatively few flowers: its great charm being due to the awns, the inner one being about 30 cm long; the lower part smooth, the upper part feathery.

### *S.p.* var. *longissima*
Has rough awns. H4.

### *S.splendens* Trin.: Chee grass

One of the largest of the ornamental species of *Stipa*, yet so different from the others that there is some doubt about its taxonomic status, its overall garden effect being rather that of a gigantic *Deschampsia caespitosa*. Important in its native Russian steppe lands because, although of poor quality as a fodder grass, it is extremely drought-resistant and in years of severe drought is the only green feed available to many cattle. The flowering culms are much used for matting, fencing and the walls of the summer tents of nomadic peoples, as well as for fuel. The top growth is of increasing importance in the manufacture of paper.

Grown in gardens for its enormous panicles which, in spite of their great size, appear airy and delicate. The foliage is attractive, and the flowers make a perfect foil each for the other. An ideal specimen plant, but probably looks at its best when planted in closely related clumps of three or five.

Very robust, mound-forming perennial without stolons, flowering culms growing up to 2 m tall, the mound itself usually about half that height. Culms erect, very slender, rather wiry. Leaf sheaths basal, polished. Ligules elongated, pointed. Leaf blades up to 50 cm long, no more than 1 cm wide, very slender, partially rigid; rich dark green. Inflorescence, produced May to July, a well-filled panicle up to 50 cm long, about the same across, borne well above the foliage; purplish, rarely whitish. H3.

## TAENIATHERUM Nevski

A genus of 1 or 2 species of annual grass from hot, dry places in the Mediterranean and Middle East. Ornamental because of its long, silky awns, it is excellent in arrangements whether green or dried. Easily grown in a sunny position in well-drained soil. Seed should be sown in spring where the plants are to flower.

Tufted plants with leaves flat or rolled, narrowly linear, membranous ligules, the panicle a dense bristly spike with a continuous axis and the spikelets in two rows. Spikelets stalkless, 2-flowered, the lower bisexual and fertile, the upper rudimentary and sterile; glumes side by side, awn-like; lemma lanceolate, rounded on the back, with a long, flexuous flattened awn.

### T.caput-medusae (L.) Nevski

Stems erect or ascending to 60 cm. Leaves flat or rolled, hairy, finely pointed up to 13 cm long. Panicles, produced June to July, spike-like, erect or nodding to 15 cm long, the spikelets with very long awns; the lemmas drawn out into a fine, usually spreading awn up to 10 cm long.

### T.crinitum (Schreb.) Nevski

Stems erect or ascending to 45 cm. Leaves flat or rolled, hairy or hairless, finely pointed, up to 13 cm long. Panicles, produced July to August, spike-like, erect, up to 15 cm long, the spikelets long-awned; glumes rough, erect or spreading, lemmas smooth or rough, attenuated into a long rough awn, 11.5 cm long.

## THYSANOLAENA Nees

A genus of a single species of very large, perennial grass from scrublands in tropical Asia, closely related to *Phragmites*. In its native lands it is planted as screens and fences, and in cooler climates it is sometimes grown as an ornamental in large greenhouses, more for its fine foliage than for its flowers. It needs a warm, humid greenhouse, and may be grown in tubs or in the greenhouse borders. It needs plenty of water.

Tall, tufted, bamboo-like grass with stout, solid stems, scarious ligules; leaf blades broad, flat and many-nerved, and the panicle large and much-branched. Spikelets very small, very many, all alike, immature at emergence, 2–3-flowered, the second flower fertile; glumes much shorter than spikelet, often less than half as long, thin, 1-nerved; fertile lemma rounded on the back, 3-nerved, fringed with hairs.

### *T.maxima* (Roxb.) Kuntze

Robust, leafy perennial to 3.6 m. Leaves flat, up to 60 cm long, 6.5 cm wide, lanceolate, finely pointed. Panicles up to 60 cm long, 30 cm wide, pale green, yellowish or brown. Flowers late summer. G2.

## TRICHOLAENA Schult.

A genus of 4 species of annual or perennial grasses from sandy, stony places from the Mediterranean to India. It is related to and sometimes confused with *Rhynchelytrum*, from which it differs in that the lower glume is somewhat remote from the upper, and in the firmer beaked and gibbous upper glume and lower lemma. Some species are grown as ornamentals and require a warm, sunny position in light, sandy and very well-drained soil. They are best raised from seed under glass and set out in early summer.

Tufted plants with rigid, branched stems, ciliate ligules, the blades flat or rolled, and open panicles of silky spikelets. Spikelets small, 2-flowered, the lower usually male, the upper fertile; glumes unequal, lower glume tiny; upper glume and lower lemma similar, blunt, awnless; upper lemma smaller.

### *T.teneriffae* (L.f.) Parl.

Perennial to 60 cm with hard, slender stems. Leaves glaucous, with a firm hardened point, up to 15 cm long, 2 cm wide. Panicles produced July to September linear, contracted or loose, to 11.5 cm long, the spikelets pale green or purplish, with silky hairs longer than the spikelet. G1.

## TRIPSACUM L.

A genus of about 14 species of robust perennials from woodlands and damp places in Central America, southern USA through to Paraguay. It is closely related to Maize (*Zea*) and *Tripsacum* × *Zea* hybrids occur. One species is grown as an ornamental both for its broad, flat leaves which can create a subtropical effect, and for its curious panicle. Can be raised from seed or increased by division, and will thrive in ordinary garden soil. In spite of its tropical or nearly tropical origins it will endure severe frost in the southern UK.

Tall, usually rhizomatous perennials with stout stems, ciliate ligules and broad, flat blades. Inflorescences terminal and axillary, composed of usually digitate racemes, the short lower part of the raceme female, the upper, longer part male. Spikelets unisexual, awnless; female spikelets single, stalkless, sunk in a cavity in the internode; lower glume leathery, closing the cavity in the internode, upper glume thinner; lemmas enclosed by glumes: male spikelets 2-flowered, stalkless or nearly so, in pairs at each joint; glumes firm, enclosing the lemmas.

### *T.dactyloides* L.: Gamma grass, Buffalo grass

This native of the USA is little known or grown in gardens, yet it is well worth including where there is room, because it is so different in character from all others. It is a most effective garden grass, the broad, luxuriant foliage affording a striking contrast to the remarkably sparse inflorescences. An interesting plant in and out of flower. The leaves emerge a rich, emerald green in spring, but rapidly become tinged with red and light brown, although the midrib remains a clearly defined white line. The leaf sheaths assume a similar colouring, but are slightly slower to assume these tints than the blades. The flowers, in spite of their sparseness, are very attractive, the exserted anthers being a rich blood-red, while the pistils are foxy-brown.

Robust perennial with thick, knotty rhizomes, growing to 3 m in the USA, usually no more than 2 m in the UK. Culms erect, stout at the base, narrower higher up, sparsely jointed. Leaf sheaths glabrous, tightly rolled around the culms. Leaf blades up to 60 cm long, 2.5 cm wide, broad along most of their length, sometimes terminating in a rather blunt point, sometimes splitting towards the tip; flat in section, scabrid on the margins, arching; with a clearly defined white midrib against a luxuriant rich green. Inflorescence, produced August to October, a unilateral, terminal raceme composed of 3, rarely fewer, spikes, up to 25 cm long, the spikelets unisexual, the pistillate part forming the lower quarter of the length of the spike, the staminate part the upper three-quarters. H3.

## UNIOLA L.

A genus of 4 to 8 perennial grasses from arid, often sandy places, in Central America from the southern USA to Equador. Several species may be grown as ornamentals. Some bear a superficial resemblance to *Bromus unioloides* (so-named from its similarity to *Uniola*), but differ in having awnless lemmas, and other species resemble *Briza maxima* but differ in having flattened not fattened spikelets. They grow best in sun. They can be raised from seed or increased by division.

Usually tufted, often tall, erect perennials with flat or rolled leaves, ciliate ligules, and large, showy panicles composed of many crowded, overlapping racemes on a central axis. Spikelets 3–many-flowered, very flat, sharply keeled; glumes lanceolate; lemmas 3–9-nerved, coriaceous, leathery.

### *U.latifolia* Michaux: American wild oats

A native of rich woodland in the USA. The inflorescence has some resemblance to *Briza maxima*, except that the very large spikelets are distinctly flattened as though they had been ironed. The broad, rich green leaves are an added attraction. Will tolerate more shade than most garden grasses.

Loosely tufted perennial with stout, slowly spreading rhizomes, growing up to 1.2 m in its native woodlands, rather less in cultivation in the UK. Culms erect becoming arching, smooth. Leaf sheaths rounded on the back, rather loose, slightly inflated, especially the lower ones. Leaf blades up to 20 cm long,

19 mm wide; flat in section, smooth, the margins slightly rough; somewhat stiff but very slightly arching. Inflorescence, produced in August, an open, drooping, 1-sided panicle up to 20 cm long, sparsely branched, the branches bearing few, very large, flattened spikelets, each up to 13 mm long; at first green becoming tawny.

## ZEA L.

A genus variously put at 1–4 species of tall, robust annual, rarely perennial, grasses of unknown wild provenance in Central America. *Z.mays* is the staple cereal crop of the tropical world. It is not known in the wild and is thought to have been domesticated about 7000 years ago from a species resembling *Z.mexicana*. It is the only important grain crop contributed to the world by the Americas. Though the wild species of *Zea* (formerly put in the genus *Euchlaena* Schrad.) and maize seem to the naked eye to have little in common, under the microscope their coincidence of identity is indisputable. It is peculiar in that it only makes growth during the hours of darkness (most grow in daylight) and in that it will not flower until it has put on a certain number of leaves. Several cultivars of *Z.mays* are grown as ornamentals and some are common elements in subtropical bedding. They are best treated as half-hardy annuals, raised individually in pots from seed sown under glass in January, hardened off and set out in June, or from seed sown in May where the plants are to grow, though the latter will result in very much smaller plants.

Robust, tall grasses with stout stems, broad, conspicuously distichous leaves and monoecious panicles; the male flowers (tassels) in large, spreading terminal panicles composed of numerous spike-like racemes, the female panicle (cob) occurring in leaf axils, the spikelets in longitudinal rows around a thickened axis, the whole cob enclosed in a large, leaf-like bract, the very long styles protruding from the top in a mass of silky threads.

### *Z.mays* L.: Corn, Maize, Indian corn, Sweet corn

Erect annual, up to 2.4 m tall. Culms erect, very stout, up to 3 cm across at the base, usually solitary, sometimes branching, occasionally producing small shoots around the base. Leaf sheaths tightly clasp the culms. Leaf blades up to 60 cm long, 11.5 cm wide, flat in section, hairy above, smooth on the underside, margins ciliate, arching, somewhat undulate, broadly oval in outline; rich green with white median stripe. Flowers, produced June to August, unisexual. The male staminate inflorescence (tassel) is terminal on the culm, a symmetrical branched raceme. The female, pistillate inflorescence (silk) axilliary, largely hidden by the leaf sheaths, the styles being extremely long and protruding from the top of the pistillate flower as a mass of silky threads.

The type is seldom cultivated as an ornamental, although the broad leaves have considerable merit as foliage plants in subtropical bedding schemes. The majority of garden varieties are grown either for their coloured leaves or for

157

their variously coloured ears. Both look well grown among other grasses or as a vertical accent in a low-level bedding scheme.

### *Z.m.* 'Curagua'
Robust with exceptionally broad, green leaves.

### *Z.m.* 'Golden Bantam'
Dwarf, with rich, golden-yellow grains. Well suited to the shorter growing season of the UK. Good to eat.

### *Z.m.gracillima*
A dwarf, green-leaved variety of no particular garden merit.

### *Z.m.gracillima variegata*
The smallest of the variegated varieties, growing to only 60 cm, leaves striped clear white. A particularly useful variety for small gardens.

### *Z.m.* 'Harlequin'
Leaves striped green and red, with deep red ears. Of medium vigour, growing to about 1.2 m.

### *Z.m.* 'Indian Corn'
The ears contain kernels of many colours, these being excellent for drying and arranging together with ornamental gourds.

### *Z.m.japonica*
One of the earliest variegated forms to be grown as an ornamental. Leaves striped white. Rather less vigorous than the type plant, growing to about 1.2 m.

### *Z.m.japonica* 'Quadricolor'
Of relatively recent introduction, vastly superior to variety. Leaves variegated green, white, yellow and pink. Slightly more robust.

### *Z.m.* 'Multicoloured Pierrot'
Another variety in which the ears bear kernels of many colours: again, excellent for drying for floral work.

### *Z.m.* 'Strawberry Corn'
Bears delightful little ears only 5 cm long and 4 cm across, of a rich reddish-mahogany colour, enclosed in straw-coloured husks. Both decorative and edible.

# ZIZANIA L.

A genus of 3 species of tall annuals or perennials from marshes and shallow water in Eastern Asia and North America. Two species are cultivated for ornament, the annual *Z.aquatica* in particular making a tall, handsome grass especially decorative at the edge of lakes and ponds. It is easily grown in shallow water and should be raised from seeds sown in spring under glass in pots standing in water and then hardened and planted out. Alternatively, seeds can be sown in spring directly into soft mud in shallow water.

Tall annuals or perennials with stout, robust stems, membranous ligules, long, flat leaf blades and large, showy panicles, the lower branches with all male, the upper with all female spikelets. Female spikelets awned, linear, the lemmas clasping the keels of the palea; male spikelets narrowly oblong, pendulous, 5-nerved, awnless or shortly awned.

## *Z.aquatica* L.: Wild rice, Annual wild rice, Canadian wild rice, Water rice, Water oats

Wild rice is native to most of the Eastern and Mid Western States of the USA, where people still gather the grains which they use to make a type of flour. As an ornamental, it is useful in that it is one of the few large-growing waterside grasses which you need never fear will cut the hand: being an annual, its spread is quite easily controlled. Grown for its shear luxuriance; the contrast of the enormous, open panicles and the rich, lush foliage.

Vigorous, clump-forming annual up to 4 m tall in flower. Culms erect; sometimes decumbent at the base, becoming erect, stout. Leaf sheaths rolled, glabrous. Leaf blades up to 1.2 m long, 6.5 cm wide, flat in section; margins parallel for about three-quarters of the length of the blade, which then tapers towards the tip; a luxuriant light green. Inflorescence, produced June to October, a huge, much-branched panicle up to 50 cm long, the branches up to 20 cm long, widely and loosely branched, more or less symmetrical; light brown.

## *Z.a.angustifolia* Hitchc.

Differs from the type plant only in that it is smaller in all its parts.

# 6 Bamboos

The bamboos cultivated out of doors in Europe and North America form an essentially distinct and cohesive group within the grasses, the distinguishing feature being their copiously branched woody culms. In a world-wide context bamboos may be herbs, shrubs, trees or climbers and include a few distinctly odd genera: *Myriocladus* for example looks like a bromeliad on top of a cane, *Glaziophyton* is reed-like, though will sprout typical bamboo shoots from the base after burning, *Nemolepis* is grass-like, while *Guadella* is a look-alike of *Aframomum*, a genus in Zingiberaceae, and *Puelia* has one species with root tubers and another which though basically bamboo-like produces only a single large leaf at the tip of a long, slender cane.

The woodiness of bamboo stems is different in kind from the woodiness of the trunk of a typical tree. The stems are like those of other grasses but stiffened with fusoid cells which give them great flexible strength and hardness. These cells are highly specialised and are found in no other group of plants. The hardiness of bamboo culms is such that they will quickly blunt any sharp instrument taken to them, and their flexible strength is proverbial and is in part derived from their tubular construction. Many can bend over under the weight of wind and rain so that their tips touch the ground, yet spring up again once wind and rain have passed: a more rigid tree — a pine perhaps — would simply snap.

It seems probable that the bamboos were in evolutionary terms the fore-runners of the modern grasses (just as tree Ranunculaceae were the fore-runners of the lowly buttercup). The pattern seems to be that the bamboos evolved as forest plants and that they have gradually adapted themselves to aquatic and forest margin habits as well, though there is some dissenting opinion on this. They have conspicuously failed to adapt to those habitats which we call grassland. They seem to need the moister, shadier conditions associated with forest.

Typically, bamboo culms are hollow (solid in *Chusquea*) and divided into cylindrical segments by the nodes (joints), the lowest internodal section usually being disproportionately long. Generally the lower half of the culm is clad in leaf sheaths which usually terminate in a rudimentary blade, while the upper half is copiously branched, the branches arising at the nodes. It usually appears as though many branches come from each node but in fact only a single branch arises at each node (except in *Chusquea*) though that branch itself branches so near the base as to appear many-branched. The number of branches is diagnostic, the number of branches typically arising at the mid-culm region is known as the branch complement. The branches themselves branch, sometimes many times. This extraordinary branching system is unique to bamboos. The leaves are linear to oblong, usually with cross-nerves and a false petiole but are too uniform throughout the tribe to be of any really diagnostic value. In general, hardy bamboos have tessellated leaves, the tessellation being clearly visible if the leaf is held up to the sun.

The root system of bamboos is now well understood, and this understanding makes it possible to be certain about which bamboos run and which do not. The type of root system is diagnostic. The same terminology is used for bamboo roots as of sedges. The roots may be either sympodial (pachymorph) or monopodial (leptomorph), the latter being the running type. Sympodial rhizomes turn upwards at the tip which then produces a culm, the extension of the rhizome then arising from a lateral bud. Such a root system produces a tight clump of culms, and bamboos with this type of root system are known as caespitose. Monopodial rhizomes travel indefinitely, the culms arising from the lateral buds. Bamboos with this type of root system are classed as running and are capable of colonising very large areas. A very few species are amphipodial and possess both types of rhizome. *Chusquea* is unique among bamboos in general in having both sympodial and monopodial species.

The flowers of bamboos seem at a casual glance to be just like those of grasses but they are invariably small and are never showy. The inflorescence usually consists of a small panicle or raceme—the raceme often reduced to a single spikelet—borne at the tips of the lateral branches; the spikelet often laterally compressed. The fruit is usually a caryopsis (a grain) though in a few eccentric bamboo genera (*Olmeca, Melocalamus, Dinochloa, Melocarma* and *Ochlandria*) it is a berry. It is often a problem with bamboos that flowers and fruits have been seen so infrequently that little reliance can be placed on some of the information available.

The flowering of bamboos is still a considerable mystery, not only to laymen but also to botanists. Many flower either annually or else seem to be more or less continuously in flower, while others flower only periodically, at intervals of anything from 20 to 120 years. It is sometimes stated that each species of bamboo has its own period for flowering, but the timing does not seem to be that precise. Similarly it has sometimes been claimed that all bamboos of the same species all over the world will flower at the same time, but there is little real evidence to support this. Again, there is a widely held belief that bamboos die after flowering but generally this is not true. The flowering culms tend to lose their leaves or to be leafless, and in those bamboos in which flowering occurs at intervals, flowering culms may be produced to the exclusion of the leafy culms so that the plant may look dead. In fact the rootstock, if well

161

established, normally survives. After flowering the plant will usually revert to producing leafy culms. The cutting down and removal of old flowering culms seems to speed this process, but, conversely, you cannot stop a bamboo from flowering by cutting off its flowering culms.

In general bamboos are easy to grow well provided that their basic requirements are met. They evolved to fill a forest or forest margin econiche so their main needs are dappled shade to shield them from direct sun, shelter to protect them from desiccating winds and always adequate moisture at the roots: they also enjoy atmospheric humidity and seem to grow extra well beside a pond or stream. They grow best in good, deep, loamy soils, and respond well to being generously fed, either with farmyard manure or with a good general, balanced fertiliser — or both; but if you use fertiliser it helps if you also apply good garden compost since this leaves a residue of humus.

When planting bamboos it is really worth the trouble of taking out a hole 1 m across and 50 cm deep, filling the bottom of the hole with old farmyard manure and back-filling with a mixture of manure and earth. The bamboo will then grow away so much better than if you simply try to jam it into the smallest hole you can. It also pays to mulch bamboos generously — at least 10 cm thick — of well-rotted manure or compost. Not only does this feed the plant but, more importantly, it shades the roots and ensures that there is an even level of moisture available at all times.

Beyond that the most important single consideration throughout the first year after planting, whether the plant is pot-grown or a bare-root transplant, is to keep it watered. All the old gardening books advise one to cut a bamboo down to the ground immediately after planting, the thinking being, perhaps, that if there are no leaves they will not be able to dry out. Modern thinking is that the plant needs its leaves to supply it with energy derived from sunlight and that therefore the fewer leaves or stems you remove the better. There is also the debatable question as to whether bamboos are best planted in spring or autumn. Provided that you are putting out strong, well-grown plants from pots it really seems to make little difference: the important thing is to plant early enough in autumn or late enough in spring for the ground to be warm enough for the roots to get established. Avoid planting in winter. In the longer term the appearance of bamboo clumps can be greatly enhanced if the dead canes are regularly removed.

The propagation of bamboos is generally straight forward: you divide them as you would any other perennial plant except that you have to take special steps to deal with the extraordinary toughness of the roots. With running bamboos — those with monopodial rhizomes — all you need do is find a suitably small culm or tuft of culms growing at a little distance from the main clump, sever the connecting rhizome which can usually be done with a sharp chop with a spade, and then dig up the small plant, roots and all, and re-plant it where you want it. It is with the caespitose bamboos — those with sympodial rhizomes — that you are likeliest to have real problems. In theory all you do is remove a wedge-shaped piece from the clump — like the first slice from a cake — and plant that, back-filling the hole left behind so that the bamboo will grow back into it. In practice the culms may grow so close together you can't find room to get a spade between them and the rhizomes may be so tough you need to take an axe to them. With ingenuity and patience you can usually sever a sufficient slice to grow on. Having acquired your propagating material is only half the battle: the other half is looking after the young propagule until it is properly established and that means not only ensuring that it never lacks water but also that it is sheltered from winds.

As for the decorative garden uses of bamboos, that is plainly a highly subjective matter. The most usual reason for growing a particular bamboo is simply that you like it. But beyond that they do have some quite specific merits. They were first widely cultivated in Britain by the Victorians who valued them because they could so easily create a jungle-like effect. In the smaller gardens of today that is not perhaps an effect most of us would deliberately seek. On the other hand no other plants can so quickly give a garden a subtropical appearance, especially when grown together with *Trachycarpus fortunei*, phormiums, *Fatsia japonica* and cordylines.

Some species can be very effective as screens or hedges — *Pleioblastus (Arundinaria) simonii* being one of the species most often used in this way. One of the loveliest dense screens I have ever seen is made of *Arundinaria spathacea (murieliae)*: it surrounds a nursery area at Longstock Water Gardens, Stockbridge, Hampshire. Just as good a screen, but lacking the grace of *Arundinaria spatheacea*, is *Sinarundinaria nitida* with slender, erect canes and small, narrow leaves. For a light screen — one which interrupts one's view rather than obscuring it — *Semiarundinaria fastuosa* is unbeatable. I have seen it used in this way in a courtyard garden in London. One would have expected it to keep out all the light but in fact it carried most of its foliage well above window height and created an exotic air of mystery.

A few species make lovely specimens for a lawn or the centre of a circular bed. For such a purpose one would choose a narrowly caespitose bamboo, and one with a fountain habit such as *Arundinaria spathacea (murieliae)*. Perhaps no other bamboo can lend such grace to a garden: the culms are covered in a greyish-white, mealy bloom and the foliage is a froth of light green bending outwards. When the weight of rain rests on the leaves the canes may bend so far that the foliage touches the ground. *Phyllostachys nigra* 'Boryana' is similar but less elegant and far more vigorous. These bamboos can lend enchantment to a town garden when grown in tubs. Used in this way they can do duty for a small tree. *Phyllostachys flexuosa* may sound even more exciting but it actually lacks the desired fountain habit. Instead the culms flop outwards from ground level, making it the most inconvenient of bamboos. It is one of the virtues of these bamboos that they quickly create a mature effect.

It remains only to remark that the naming and identification of bamboos is fraught with difficulties. Part of the problem is that since their flowers are so seldom seen, diagnosis, at least in Britain and over much of the USA, has to rely on vegetative characters that are by no means obvious. One needs a good hand lens (×10 or better) to identify bamboos accurately, and you need to make the identification at the right season, that is when the new culms have grown to their full height but before they shed their sheaths. Often there are bristles on the sheaths and on the culms and it is important to notice whether these are present or absent, dark or light and so on.

## A–Z of Bamboos

### ARUNDINARIA Michaux

A genus as now defined of about 50 species from northern India through the Himalayas to Japan, and North America and South Africa, inhabiting forest and forest margins and damp grasslands. Rhizomes monopodial, forming thickets rather than clumps but not generally unduly invasive. Culms erect, hollow, round and lacking the grooves or flattening found in some genera and *Phyllostachys* in particular; sheaths persistent, with dark, rough bristles and clearly developed blades. Branch complement 3–7, foliage developing from the top down. Leaves more or less tessellated. Inflorescence racemose or paniculate, but occasionally reduced to a single spikelet: spikelets many-flowered with 1–3 glumes. Stamens 3. Stigmas 3.

### *A.amabilis* McClure

This is the legendary 'lovely' bamboo of China, a plant of such commercial virtue that for nearly a century its canes were more in demand than those of any other bamboo. They have a catalogue of merits; they are naturally straighter than those of any other bamboo; they taper only slightly; long sections of the culms are free from branches; the nodes lack prominence; and the canes have remarkable stiffness. They were the preferred material in England and America for split-and-glued fishing rods, and in Germany for hop poles, and the majority of the garden canes from the Orient were of this species. In America the culms are still used for rug poles. Its commercial superiority gave its introduction into the USA a high priority and it took F. A. McClure 20 years to track it down. Its culms are commonly known in trade as tsingli or tonkin canes suggesting that canes of it may first have reached the West from the Tonkin Province of Indo China (now North Vietnam).

In cultivation in the UK it is an attractive bamboo and seems reasonably hardy south of London but is badly hit in hard winters. It is distinct because of its seeming to produce leaves of two different sizes.

Rhizomes monopodial but forming a fairly dense clump which only runs a little at the edges. Culms erect to the tip, not bending, 3–12 m, 10–20 cm in circumference; sheaths hairy; nodes not prominent, the nodes on the lower one half to two-thirds of the culm without branches; branch complement 1–3, typically 3 with the central one dominant, branches thin: leaves 180 × 20 mm or 360 × 40 mm, dark green above, paler beneath with bristles on both margins. H2.

### *A.aristata* Gamble

This is the awned or bearded bamboo from Sikkim and Bhutan in the north-western Himalayas. Interesting in that in the wild it behaves just like a perennial grass and might almost be called a deciduous bamboo. It springs up with the spring, flowers, sets seed and dies down with the coming of the winter frosts. In the milder climate of the UK it remains above ground all the time.

Rhizomes monopodial forming a compact clump. Culms erect, 5–8 m tall and 40–60 mm in circumference, brownish-green or yellowish, becoming speckled, smooth to the touch; sheaths soon falling, tapering, bristly at the base with auricles and bristles at the top, blade small; nodes with white, waxy bloom below; branch complement 3–7, branches and branchlets dull reddish: leaves 100 × 10 mm mid green, visibly tessellated, with a distinct twist towards the tip. H2.

### *A.falconeri* (Munro) Rivière

This is considered by many who have grown it to be the most beautiful and ornamental of the bamboos that can be grown out of doors in the British climate. It is distinct because of the absence of visible tessellation on the leaves and also in its habit: it forms an exceptionally close clump with the slender canes densely packed, the outer canes flexuose and arching outwards, the inner ones straight and erect. The whole plant is luxuriantly furnished with leaves and these are decidedly glaucous. Like most thin-leaved species it needs to be grown in semi-shade and preferably in a humid atmosphere. It is a native of the north-eastern Himalayas. It is somewhat anomalous among *Arundinaria* and may better belong with some of the species now in *Chimonobambusa*.

Rhizome monopodial, forming a densely caespitose clump. Culms 7–10 m or more, 60–100 mm in circumference, greenish-yellow maturing dull yellow; nodes not prominent, purplish below, lacking white bloom. Sheaths not persistent, purplish, longer than the internodes; branch complement 3–7, branches smooth and slender, leaves 160 × 16 mm, often smaller, thin and papery, pale green, lacking hairs and with no visible tessellation. H2–3.

### *A.jaunsarensis* Gamble

A tall, graceful, vigorous bamboo of particular utility where a dense screen is required quickly, since it has a strongly running rootstock. It is usually in flower, though in the late 1970s it seemed to have a major flowering, which no doubt depleted its vigour. It is not a particularly hardy bamboo, and the severe

165

winters that have occurred in the UK since 1979, coming on top of its flowering, have seemingly killed many once fine stands.

Rhizomes monopodial forming an extensively running but dense thicket. Culms erect, up to 6 m, 20–50 mm in circumference, eventually somewhat arching at the apex, bearing longitudinal ridges: nodes with white, waxy bloom below: sheaths deciduous, purplish-brown, with auricles and bristles: branch complement 5, the branches only on the upper two-thirds of the culm, those at the top opening first: leaves small, abundant, bright green, visibly tessellated, about 100 × 10 mm: sheaths smooth, with auricles and bristles. H2.

### *A.j.* 'Pitt White'

This belongs here. It is a plant of far greater vigour and more drooping habit, producing canes as much as 10 m tall and 120 mm in diameter, bearing abundant foliage causing the upper part of the plant to weep under the weight of the leafage, and producing great billowing, green cascades. A lovely clone, less inclined to travel at the root than the typical plant. H2.

### *A.maling* Gamble

A very striking Indian bamboo making a dense clump of slender canes, each straight as a ramrod and conspicuously marked with white, waxy bloom and bedecked with an airy pattern of small, delicate-looking leaves. It is a thin-leaved species requiring shade and shelter.

Rhizomes monopodial forming a dense clump. Culms erect, straight, to 5 m, 100 mm in circumference; glaucous, rough to the touch; nodes not prominent, with extensive white, waxy bloom below; sheaths persistent, tapered, blades long and narrow, ligule fringed: branch complement 5; leaves 180 × 20 mm, glaucous beneath, slightly downy towards the base; sheaths with auricles and bristles; ligule minutely downy. H2.

### *A.spathacea* (Franchet) McClintock

This Chinese plant is one of the loveliest and most decorative of all bamboos. It is of medium size, and forms a tight clump of slender canes which rise erect at first but then arch over and bow down under the sheer weight of an abundance of small, light green leaves, so that in every gentle breeze it looks like a living fountain of greenery. If there were one bamboo of which it might be said it should be in every garden then this would be the one. It needs shelter from wind and abundant moisture at the root. The specific name refers to a passing spathe-like quality in the culm sheaths when they stand out from the culm. Often confused with *Sinarundinaria nitida*, but has larger, greener leaves than that species, more prominent sheaths and has greater overall bright greenness.

Rhizome monopodial forming a dense clump. Culms erect and unbranched

166

at first, branching in the first year and weeping when mature, to 4 m tall, 40 mm in circumference, fresh pale green; nodes not particularly prominent, with white, waxy bloom below; sheaths soon falling, greenish-purple and downy when young, soon becoming smooth and parchment-coloured, standing out from the culm before falling and conspicuous at this time; branch complement 5, middle one dominant; leaves visibly tessellated, light green, 15 × 2 cm or less; sheaths often purplish, smooth, without bristles; ligule downy. H2.

Several enchanting and extremely useful dwarf forms were at one time in cultivation, but many of these flowered between 1978 and 1980 and sub-sequently died. They may no longer be in cultivation.

### *A.spathiflora* Trin.

A seldom-grown species of no particular ornamental merit. Closely related to, and generally similar to, *A.aristata* from which it differs in that the culms are somewhat zig-zag, and are grey, covered in white bloom at first but become, at maturity, pinkish in sun, with dark bands below the nodes. H2.

### *A.tessellata* (Nees) Munro

Interesting in being the only African bamboo in general cultivation in Europe; it is the only bamboo indigenous to South Africa. The name *tessellata* might lead one to expect very clearly marked leaves, but the tessellation is no more distinct than in the leaves of other hardy bamboos. It is very distinct among bamboos in its general appearance; and can always be told apart from other bamboos by its pure white culm sheaths—unique among hardy bamboos.

Rhizome monopodial producing a tight clump of closely packed culms. Culms erect, up to 7 m tall, 6–8 cm in circumference, smooth, with a deep purple ring below each node; lower nodes closely crowded, upper nodes more distant; unbranched and leafless in the first year; culm sheaths persistent, longer than the internodes, thick, nearly white, with auricles and bristles; blades long and narrow; branch complement 5–7, nearly circling the node; branches short, rather erect, purplish: leaves 14 × 2 cm, visibly tessellated, dark green; sheaths with auricles and bristles; ligule ringed, 1.5 mm. H2.

### BAMBUSA Schrader

A genus of about 120 species of tropical or subtropical shrubs or scramblers, natives of forest habitats in Africa, Asia and America. Rhizome sympodial, much-branched, forming clumps. Culms hollow, round: sheaths thick, decidu-ous with or without bristles: branch complement several to many but usually one branch dominant, sometimes with recurved, hook-like thorns at the node. Leaves lacking visible tessellation: leaf sheaths with auricles and rough bristles. Inflorescence many-spiked; spikelets 2–many-flowered with 1–3 glumes. Stamens 6: stigmas usually 3. *B.vulgaris* is the archetypal bamboo commonly grown around villages to provide a ready source of construction materials and most of the everyday needs of the villagers.

### *B.glaucescens* (Willdenow) Holttum

One of the most variable of Chinese bamboos, often cultivated for the decorative qualities of its many cultivars. Not particularly frost-tolerant but some cultivars are fine enough to deserve greenhouse or conservatory cultivation.

Rhizome sympodial, running to form generally diffuse thickets. Culms ascending, to 5 m, 6–9 cm in circumference, thin-walled and rough to the touch when young, becoming somewhat arching at the top when mature; sheaths green at first becoming yellowish, without markings; stiff; the hairs soon falling, the auricles conspicuous and the bristles smooth (rough in other species); blades triangular; nodes prominent, with white, waxy bloom beneath; branch complement many at each node, branches arising from the base of the culm and all nodes; slender; leaves variable in size from 11 × 1.2 cm to 16 × 2 cm, silvery beneath: sheaths smooth, without auricles but with smooth bristles. H5–G1.

### *B.g.* 'Alphonse Carr'

Differs in having culms bright yellow, striped vivid green.

### *B.g.* 'Fernleaf'

Remarkable for its many tiny leaves, the leaves plainly arranged in two ranks. Known in the USA as the fernleaf hedge bamboo.

### *B.g.* 'Golden Goddess'

A form with golden canes.

### *B.g.rivierorum*

The dwarfest of the many forms of *B.glaucescens*, growing to 1.5 m, the internodes apparently solid, the foliage similar to that of *B.g.* 'Fernleaf'.

### *B.g.* 'Silverstripe'

Distinguished by its canes being bright yellow with thin but conspicuous vertical stripes; culm sheaths dark brownish-green. It is the tallest of the various forms of this bamboo in cultivation.

### *B.g.* 'Silverstripe Fernleaf'

In effect a variegated form of *B.g.* 'Fernleaf', the leaves being striped white.

### *B.g.* 'Stripestem Fernleaf'

Similar to *B.g.* 'Fernleaf' but the culms pale reddish to yellow, irregularly striped green at first.

## *B.g.* 'Willowy'

A cultivar that grows to about 6 m and has the habit of a fountain. Canes erect but arching over at the top and forming a veritable cascade under the sheer profusion of small, green leaves.

## CHIMONOBAMBUSA Makino

A genus of 6 species from the forests of China and Japan. Rhizomes monopodial, slowly but persistently invasive. Culms hollow, round in section except in *C.quadrangularis* where it is square: conspicuously late in emerging, the new culms arising in autumn often not surviving the winter. Sheaths lacking bristles, persistent or fugacious: nodes 2-ridged, swollen, with root thorns between ridges: branch complement 3–7, developing from the top down. Leaves visibly tessellate except in *C.falcata*. Inflorescence paniculate, made up of clusters of single spikelet racemes; spikelets many-flowered.

## *C.falcata* (Nees) Nakai

An interesting species from the mountains of Bhutan and Sikkim, with deep crimson, new shoots and almost grey, mature culms. It is too tender to grow outside in most of the UK and not perhaps quite ornamental enough to warrant conservatory space. The leaves lack visible tessellation.

Rhizomes monopodial forming a tightly caespitose clump. Culms erect but arching over at the fringe of the clump, to 6 m tall, 5–9 cm in circumference, hollow, round in section; nodes at first hairy, later smooth, with white, waxy bloom below; sheaths fugacious, equal to or longer than internodes, dark red at first, later straw-yellow; ligule 12 mm long; branches numerous, developing from the top down; leaves up to 16 × 1.2 cm, not visibly tessellated, with a curious twist at the tip; ligule up to 6.5 mm. H3.

## *C.hookeriana* (Munro) Nakai

A charming and highly ornamental Indian species, valued for its abundance of delicate foliage and its canes which are bright golden-yellow splashed with stripes of pink and green. In the UK it generally requires conservatory culture.

Rhizomes monopodial, and forming rather loose clumps tillering (producing runners) at the edges. Culms up to 10 m tall, generally less, 9 cm or more in circumference, glaucous, slight golden-yellow at maturity, striped pink and green; nodes not prominent, with white, waxy bloom below; sheaths persistent, longer than the internodes, smooth; branches many. Leaves up to 30 × 4 cm, occasionally with thin, white stripes as though variegated, not visibly tessellated; ligule 2–3 mm. H5–G1.

## *C.marmorea* (Mitford) Makino

An enchanting and decorative, semi-dwarf Japanese bamboo, usually growing to no more than 1.25 or 1.5 m in the UK but capable of colonising quite large areas. It is however amenable to tub culture, and can be most ornamental when used in this way in town gardens or on terraces. Called the marbled bamboo by Marliac, the marbling being on the culm sheaths. The leaves appear to be gathered in bunches, and each has a distinctive twist at the tip. It is usually the first bamboo to produce new shoots, often as early as January or February in the UK.

Rhizome monodial forming a low, shrubby thicket that spreads persistently. Culms to 3 m but usually less, 2 cm in circumference, very thick-walled, pale green mottled or marbled brown and white at first, maturing dull to deep purple when grown in sun; nodes prominent, very close together, about 15 cm apart; sheaths persistent, marbled pinkish or purplish at first, the colouring soon fading, hairy at the base at first. Branch complement 3, the middle one dominant, short and rather erect; leaves up to 16 × 1.2 cm, usually much less, visibly tessellated; ligule tiny. H2.

### C.m. 'Variegata'
Differs in that the leaves are variably striped white: not an effective or showy variegation.

### C.quadrangularis (Fenzi) Makino
This elegant Chinese bamboo is usually grown for its square canes, though in Britain at any rate this is a feature which is scarcely remarkable. It needs a hotter climate for the stems to acquire their squareness, but this bamboo is interesting for other reasons. It has quite conspicuous nodes which bear curious, hook-like protruberances—actually the buds of incipient aerial roots. It is also remarkable among cultivated hardy bamboos in being the only one whose branches you can snap off in your hand: for all other bamboos you need pruning shears at the very least.

Rhizome monopodial but vigorous and far-running, forming a diffuse clump. Culms erect or ascending, up to 10 m tall and 12 cm in circumference, obtusely square in section especially in the lower part of the culm, somewhat rough below the nodes; nodes prominent with a sharp band of blackish-purple immediately below and bearing hook-like, incipient root buds; sheaths fugacious, thin, hairless; branch complement 3–7, branches often articulated at the branch nodes; leaves up to 14 × 2 cm, usually less. H3.

### CHUSQUEA Kunth
A genus of about 100 species from the montane woodlands of Central and South America. Shrubs, erect or lax, or climbers. Rhizomes usually sympodial and forming dense clumps but sometimes monopodial and running; rarely amphipodial. Culms solid, round. Sheaths long-persistent, lacking bristles: branch complement several to very many, sometimes encircling the culm.

Leaves narrow. Inflorescence paniculate: spikelets with 1 fertile floret: glumes 4, lacking awns; stamens 3; stigmas 2.

## *C.breviglumis*

This may or may not warrant specific status and is regarded by McClintock as a variety *C.culeou*, var. *tenuis*. It is distinct horticulturally in its smaller stature, no more than 1.5 m tall with culms at most 2 m, the culms always arching never erect, and in the longer leaves, as much as 15 cm, the minute, hyaline, marginal teeth confluent with the margin. The pattern of the tessellation also differs from *C.culeou*. An enchanting dwarf. H2.

## *C.culeou* Desvaux

This is the most striking and ornamental bamboo, at its most arresting when the new culms have just reached full height, for at that stage they are unbranched and wrapped in parchment-white sheaths. Unfortunately it is difficult to obtain. It comes from Chile and is the only South American bamboo generally grown in Britain. It is remarkable for its hardiness, and for its ability to withstand sustained periods of drought. In the wild it flowers and produces seed annually. It takes 2 to 3 years to settle down if moved. The culms are solid. Freeman-Mitford lists some 16 species of *Chusquea* while Camus describes nearly 70: hopefully some of these may also prove hardy.

Rhizome monopodial forming densely caespitose clumps. Culms erect and tapering, solid up to 10 m but more usually 8 m, to 13 cm in circumference; nodes quite prominent, hairy, with white, waxy bloom below: sheaths large, white, longer than the internodes: branch complement several to many almost encircling the culm, themselves unbranched, developing in the second season and bursting out through the culm sheaths: leaves 10 × 1 cm, visibly tessellated, the midrib conspicuous below. The margins beset with minute, soft, white, hyaline teeth. H2.

## *C.cumingii* Nees

According to McClintock differs from *C.culeou* in that the leaves lack the conspicuous midrib, but he concedes it may be the same as *C.culeou* in which case the correct name for *C.culeou* would be *C.cumingii*. H2.

## INDOCALAMUS Nakai

A genus of about 10 species from Southern China and Malaysia either woodlanders or thicket-forming in open scrub. Differs from *Sasa* (q.v.) in floral characteristics: stamens 3 (not 6) and stigmas 2 not 3.

## *I.tessellatus* (Munro) Keng

An almost indispensable bamboo for anyone seeking to create a subtropical effect in the garden for, although semi-dwarf in stature, this species has the largest leaves of any hardy bamboos. The culms can grow up to 2 m in length, but are bent over and bowed down by the sheer weight of the large leaves so that they rarely reach half that height.

Rhizomes monopodial and invasive. Culms up to 2 m long and 4 cm in circumference, thick-walled, bright green, much covered in a heavy, waxy bloom, bent over sometimes almost to the horizontal; nodes not prominent; sheaths persistent, pale green at first maturing dull straw-yellow; branch complement 3 to 5, the centre one dominant, the others much reduced; leaves to 60 × 10 cm, with clearly marked tessellation visible to the naked eye, bright, shining green above, dull greyish-green beneath; with a line of fine hairs on one side of the midrib; sheaths sometimes purplish towards the tip. H2.

## OTATEA (McClure & E.W.Smith) Calder & Soderstrom

A genus of 2 species from the forests of Mexico to Honduras. Rhizomes monopodial but forming good clumps when young. Culms solid and erect at first becoming hollow and arching at maturity, the upper internodes shallowly grooved on one side; sheaths lacking bristles, soon falling. Branch complement 3 initially, later several to many. Leaves narrow, without visible tessellation. Inflorescence paniculate. Stamens 3; stigmas 2.

### *O.acuminata* (Munro) Calder & Soderstrom

Popularly known as the Mexican weeping bamboo this is one of the most delicate, airy and enchanting of all bamboos and more worthy of tub culture than any other. It produces myriads of small, green leaves, and the flexuous stems are bent under their weight, often weeping right down to ground level. It is thin-leaved and needs shade and shelter from winds.

Rhizomes monopodial and forming reasonably close clumps. Culms up to 6 m × 12 cm in circumference, usually much less, erect, flexuous and arching, solid at first becoming hollow, round but flattened on alternate sides below the nodes; sheaths hairy, without auricles or bristles; nodes not prominent; branch complement 3 at first, many later; leaves 18 cm × 6 mm or less, long-acuminate, pendent; sheaths downy. H5–G1.

## PHYLLOSTACHYS Siebold & Zuccarini

A genus of 45–60 species from Japan and the Himalayas, mainly woodlanders. Rhizomes monopodial and clumps at best diffusely caespitose. Culms close or spaced, internodes flattened on either side, alternately, nodes prominent; branch complement 2, unequal, or sometimes with a third, small, almost vestigial central branch. Sheaths quickly falling, those lowest on the culm remaining longest, bristles rough or absent. Leaves lanceolate, slender-pointed, clearly tessellated, 60–200 mm long, bristles rough but soon falling. Inflorescence racemose, spikelets 1–3-flowered with usually 2 glumes and 5–13 florets.

## *P.aurea* (Carrière) Rivière

Always an interesting bamboo because of its compressed and swollen inter-nodes, it is known in the USA as the fish-pole bamboo because of its popularity for that purpose. It has also been widely cultivated in the Orient for making into walking sticks and parasol handles. The epithet *aurea* given it by Carrière is curious since the typical plant has definitely green culms and the forms with yellow culms all have long-established varietal names. It is always an attrac-tive plant in the garden, and is remarkably tolerant of both frost and drought.

Rhizomes monopodial forming diffuse but not uncontrollable thickets. Culms up to 8 m × 12 cm in circumference, stiffly erect, tapering towards the tip, smooth, bright green at first becoming dull yellowish-green in sun, the internodes deeply grooved and swollen below each node, the lowest progres-sively compressed and swollen; nodes prominent; sheaths persistent at the base of the culms otherwise fugacious; branch complement 2, one dominant, one much reduced; leaves up to 15 × 2 cm, yellowish-green, one margin covered with bristles. H2.

## *P.a.* 'Albo-variegata' (*P.a.* 'Variegata')

Has leaves flecked with white. An interesting and desirable cultivar.

## *P.aureosuleata* McClure

A little-grown but quite decorative Chinese bamboo distinct for its rather erect branches and the green and yellow stripes in the grooves.

Culms up to 6 m × 10 cm in circumference, erect and often somewhat zig-zag, rough to the touch, olive- to greyish-green, with well-defined grooves below the joints, these grooves striped green and yellow; nodes with white, waxy bloom below; sheaths striped yellow and green; branch complement 3, branches almost erect; leaves exceptionally up to 15 × 2 cm, usually half as much; sheaths without auricles or bristles. H2.

## *P.bambusoides* Siebold & Zuccarini

This is the archetypal phyllostachys bamboo with big, flexible culms and delicate leafage. Probably a native of China, it is now naturalised in Japan, India, Burma and elsewhere and is commonly known in the warmer regions of the world as the giant timber bamboo. It is the largest growing and commer-cially most valuable of the bamboos. In British gardens, where it seldom exceeds 6 m, it is sometimes confused with *P.viridi-glaucescens*, from which it is distinct in its larger leaves, and in the purple mottling of its culm sheaths, which are also distinguished by a ring of long, kinked hairs.

Rhizome monopodial forming a loose clump. Culms up to 20 m high and 30 cm in circumference, but more usually under 6 m in cultivation in Britain, erect, pea-green; nodes fairly prominent, nearly without waxy bloom; sheaths mottled purple, soon falling, with small auricles and kinked hairs; branch complement 2; leaves visibly tessellated up to 20 × 4.5 cm; sheaths persistent with kinked bristles. H2.

### *P.b.* 'Albo-variegata'
Has leaves with white markings but is not a conspicuously variegated plant.

### *P.b.* 'Allgold'
Culms yellow with some green stripes. Of smaller stature.

### *P.b.* 'Castillonis'
Has straw-yellow culms with the grooves green.

### *P.b.* 'Castilloni-inversa'
Has green culms, the grooves yellow.

### *P.b.* 'Marliacea'
Has the culm internodes longitudinally wrinkled.

### *P.congesta* Rendle
One of the smaller cultivated *Phyllostachys*, of no particular ornamental merit.

Rhizome monopodial forming a diffuse clump. Culms up to 8 m × 16 cm in circumference, erect, tapering, greyish-green: sheaths dark green with pale purple clouding; nodes not especially prominent with white, waxy bloom below; branch complement 2; leaves up to 12 × 1 cm, often smaller, downy below near the base; sheaths with no bristles or auricles. H2.

### *P.flexuosa* (Carrière) Rivière
Sometimes called the Chinese weeping bamboo, this is a species, which, although of modest stature, needs a lot of space to display itself properly. Only a few of the culms at the centre of the clump grow erect. All the others spread out sideways and arch over, the tips often touching the ground. In a small space this habit can be, frankly, a nuisance. *P.flexuosa* is sometimes mistaken for *P.nigra* since its canes mature almost black-purple, but in *P.nigra* the canes are more erect and the nodes more prominent.

Rhizome sympodial and forming loose clumps. Culms erect or spreading, flexuose, up to 7 m × 10 cm in circumference, somewhat ribbed; nodes not prominent, with white, waxy bloom below; sheaths with some darkish markings, and with a tuft of hairs; branch complement 3; leaves visibly tessellated, 15 × 1.5 cm, downy near the midrib; sheaths without bristles. H2.

### *P.heterocycla* (Carrière) Mitford
Better known under its old name of *P.pubescens* this is another archetypal bamboo. It is known in Japan as the 'noble' bamboo, and in that country, and

174

also in China, is recorded as throwing canes as much as 24 m tall with a basal diameter of 60 cm. In cooler latitudes it is scarcely so noble and tends to produce at least some of its new canes too late in the season to mature before the frosts. It needs abundant moisture at the roots and a very sheltered situation.

Rhizome sympodial forming a diffuse clump. Culms to 20 m × 60 cm in circumference, more usually less than half that, erect but curving from the ground, tapering, greyish at first becoming green or yellowish-orange, nearly orange in sun, round in section; nodes with only one ridge; sheaths very thick, soon falling, dark greenish-brown, hairy and with a tuft of bristles on each side at the tip; branch complement 2; leaves 20 × 1 cm; sheaths with bristles but no auricles. H3.

### *P.h.* 'Bicolor'
Has yellow stripes on the culms.

### *P.h.* 'Nabeshimana'
This is the so-called tortoiseshell bamboo because of the curious, almost bizarre way in which the basal internodes are compressed and grossly swollen on alternate sides, the nodes being diagonal instead of horizontal and running into each. Only a small proportion of the culms actually exhibit this character, and the plant needs gross feeding to produce this effect at all.

### *P.makinoi* Hayata
This is probably the tallest and most dramatic bamboo that can be grown out of doors in Britain. The culms which are distinctly glaucous can reach 10 or 12 m, even in Britain, and are almost as thick as your wrist at ground level. The culms are well-spaced, with most of the foliage produced at the top.

Rhizomes sympodial and forming diffuse clumps of well-spaced canes. Culms erect up to 18 m and 9 cm in diameter, round in section, glaucous and waxy when young; sheaths not persistent, spotted black; nodes with 2 prominent ridges; branch complement 3; leaves ovate-lanceolate, acuminate at the tip, not visibly tessellated. H3.

### *P.nidularia* Munro
Another tall-growing bamboo, similar to *P.viridi-glaucescens*, differing in its more erect culms, in its more prominent nodes which have thick, brown hairs and in the larger blades to the culm sheaths. China. H2.

### *P.nigra* (Loddiges) Munro
This is the black-stemmed bamboo, grown mainly as an ornamental for its striking, jet-black canes. It is generally a delightful bamboo, the canes arching

over gracefully and producing luxuriant masses of foliage. It was the first bamboo introduced to Europe.

Rhizome sympodial forming a dense clump. Culms erect, up to 5 m high and 8 cm in circumference, usually less, with a pair of deep grooves below each node, olive-green at first, becoming mottled with dark blotches in the second year and turning deep, shining black in the third; nodes somewhat prominent, clearly marked with a fine white line with white bloom below; sheaths fugacious, hairy to begin with, becoming smooth, pale pink fading to dull straw; branch complement 2, branches usually much-branched; leaves visibly tessellated, 13 × 1.8 cm, bluntly rounded at the base, tapering evenly to a fine point, of thin texture, one margin markedly bristly. H2.

### P.n. 'Boryana'
Much taller-growing than *P.nigra* itself, to almost twice the height; culms green at first changing to yellow with some purple splashing. A tall and luxuriant bamboo, and the best of all bamboos to grow as a specimen.

### P.n. var. *henonis* (Mitford) Stapf.
Similar to *P.n.* 'Boryana' but canes maturing to rich brownish-yellow. Makes large, dense clumps and is equal value to *P.n.*'Boryana' as a specimen.

### P.n. 'Othello'
A most dramatic form with very black culms, very tightly packed together in caespitose clumps. Distributed by Kurt Bleumel from material introduced into the USA by the National Arboretum, Washington.

### P.nuda McClure
A most ornamental species with tall, ascending, naked culms of a lovely sea-green and an abundance of rich green leaves. A tall but fairly invasive species. H2.

### P.viridi-glaucescens (Carrière) Rivière
A strong-growing bamboo forming large thickets of well-spaced culms, which in cold climates are rigidly erect but in warmer climates tend to lean and arch. A single clump will occupy 1000 sq m or so, making it suitable only for the largest gardens.

Rhizome sympodial forming a large, diffuse, thicket-like clump. Culms ascending or erect, sometimes arching, up to 7 m × 13 cm in girth, deep green at first becoming yellowish-green at maturity; nodes not especially prominent, with white, waxy streaks below; sheaths streaked violet, with auricles and bristles; branch complement 2, occasionally 3 but the third much reduced; leaves visibly tessellated, to 2.8 × 1 cm. H2.

### *P.viridis* (Young) McClure
In effect a smaller-growing version of *P.heterocycla*, from which it differs in having shorter culms, generally thicker than in *P.heterocycla*, the young ones somewhat dimpled, and in the fewer but very much larger leaves — often 12 × 4 cm. H3.

## PLEIOBLASTUS Nakai
A genus of about 20 species of woodland and meadow bamboos from China and Japan, formerly included in *Arundinaria*. Rhizomes monopodial forming thickets, invasive in some species. Culms erect, hollow but thick-walled, sometimes appearing almost solid, round in section; sheaths persistent with smooth, whitish bristles; branch complement 3–7; leaves visibly tessellated; inflorescence a spike or raceme; stamens 3; stigmas 3.

### *P.chino* (Franchet & Savatier) Makino
A variable species often cultivated in one or other of its many forms and variants. None is particularly ornamental, being usually drab in foliage, though the variegated cultivars have a place in some gardens.

Rhizomes monopodial, far-running and invasive. Culms erect, up to 4 m × 4 cm in girth, dark green, with purplish blotches; nodes prominent, with white, waxy bloom below; sheaths persistent, downy when young; branch complement 3–7, but sometimes 1; leaves up to 25 × 2.5 cm, visibly tessellated and dark green on both sides. H2.

### *P.c.* var. *angustifolius* (Mitford) Muroi
A smaller-growing form seldom exceeding 2 m; leaves narrower, often with occasional white stripes especially early in the season.

### *P.c.* 'Argenteo-striatus'
A dwarf form to 1 m with leaves brightly striped cream.

### *P.c.* var. *humilis* (Makino) Suzuki
A form of very dwarf stature to no more than 1.2 m. Often confused with *P.humilis* (q.v.).

### *P.c.* 'Laydekeri'
A dwarf form to 1.2 m, with leaves mottled creamy-white.

### *P.c.* var. *vaginatus* (Hackel) Muroi & Okamura
The most commonly grown form. Culms up to 15 m, purplish, and leaves up to 15 × 1.5 cm, though generally smaller.

### *P.glaber* (Munro) Nakai

A fairly nondescript bamboo that is, however, in its variegated form, the most exciting of all variegated bamboos. Rhizomes slender, creeping but not invasive, culms more or less distant from one another, up to 3 m tall, 12 mm round. Culm- and leaf-sheaths, nodes and internodes glabrous. Ligules with a few long usually kinked hairs. Leaves linear-lanceolate up to 12 cm long, 1.4 cm wide, broadly cuneate at the base, gradually tapering to a point, glabrous on both surfaces, the margins fringed with forward-pointing bristles at the base. H4?

### *P.g.* 'Tsuboi'

Smaller-growing, the leaves dramatically longitudinally striped creamy-white.

### *P.gramineus* (Bean) Nakai

Quite distinct among medium-sized, hardy bamboos in having the narrowest leaves in proportion to their length: the leaves are thin so it is a species which needs to be grown in shade. Quite decorative but too invasive for small gardens.

Rhizomes monopodial forming dense thickets inclined to run vigorously at the edges. Culms erect, up to 5 m × 6 cm in girth, pale green at first becoming deep green and finally yellow; nodes not prominent with white, waxy bloom below; sheaths rough, long-persistent; branch complement often 2 near the base, more higher up, branches almost pendent; leaves visibly tessellated, 25 × 1.25 cm, sharply tapered at the tip, bright green, paler beneath. H2.

### *P.hindsii* (Munro) Nakai

Sometimes confused with *P.gramineus* but really quite distinct in its carriage, the tall canes carrying all the foliage at the top, in its much coarser, broader leaves and in the way in which ragged portions of the sheaths remain clasping the culms. A striking plant, but curious rather than ornamental. Less invasive than *P.gramineus*.

Rhizomes sympodial and forming wide-spreading clumps of closely packed culms. Culms erect 5 m × 6 cm in girth, bright deep green at first with a glaucous-white bloom, maturing dull olive-green; nodes not prominent; sheaths coarse, soon tattering and the basal portions remaining attached to the culms; branch complement 3–5 in the first year, becoming many, erect and carrying all the foliage at the top of the plant; leaves visibly tessellated, up to 28 × 1.6 cm, coarse in texture, wedge-shaped at the base, tapering to a long, fine tip, dark green above, greyish beneath. H2.

### *P.humilis* (Mitford) Nakai

'Humilis' means humble or lowly and this bamboo is therefore lowly or of low stature. It makes up for it by being vigorously invasive. It has a certain charm but its ornamental merits are more than outweighed by its invasiveness.

Rhizomes sympodial and far-running, forming dense, low thickets. Culms up to 1.5 m high and 3 cm in girth, dark green. Sheaths purple at first, soon falling; nodes not prominent, with white, waxy bloom below; branch complement usually 2 or 3, rarely 2, the branches arising low on the culm; leaves visibly tessellated, 20 × 1.8 cm, pale green above, dull pale green below, slightly downy beneath. H2.

### *P.h.* forma *humilis*
A form in which the branches are borne higher up the culm, the branches being short and bushy.

### *P.h.* 'Pumilus'
A form with brighter green leaves and bearded culm bases.

## *P.pygmaeus* (Miguel) Nakai
This is even dwarfer in stature than *P.humilis* and can be every bit as much of a menace in the garden. It is quite pretty, but utterly treacherous and is safest confined to pots.

Rhizome sympodial and invasive, making a carpet-like, low thicket. Culms up to 40 cm high and 0.9 cm in girth, solid, round, slender, flattened at the tip, bright green, purplish at the tip; sheaths persistent, dull green becoming straw-yellow; nodes prominent, purplish, fringed with tiny bristles, with white, waxy bloom below; branch complement 1 or 2, branches arising from the lower nodes only, oddly long in relation to the length of the culms; leaves visibly tessellated, up to 8 cm × 8 mm, rounded at the base, the tip ending in a fine point. H2.

### *P.p.* var. *distichus*
A commonly cultivated variant with hollow culms and growing up to 1 m. The leaves are in 2 rows on the branches, and bunched together towards the tips giving this bamboo a distinctive aspect.

## *P.simonii* (Carrière) Nakai
An attractive bamboo with narrow, willowy leaves and a graceful habit. It runs at the root but is not unduly invasive.

Rhizomes sympodial and spreading to form small thickets. Culms erect, up to 8 m × 6 cm in girth, hollow and thin-walled, olive-green, somewhat arching; sheaths very persistent, dull green tinged purple at first turning parchment-coloured; nodes merely a thin, straw-coloured ring; branch complement 1 at first, later many, lowest branches longest, upper ones shortest; leaves up to 25 × 3 cm, clearly tessellated, vivid green above, green beneath on one side of the midrib, greyish on the other. H2.

### P.s. 'Variegatus'
Of lesser stature, and occasional leaves longitudinally striped white. Not a showily variegated plant.

## P.variegatus (Miguel) Makino
This is one of those botanical oddities, a species which is variegated, merely because the original diagnosis pertains to the form which reached the Western world first. The green-leaved version is var. *viridus*. The species is a highly ornamental semi-dwarf, with a good variegation—probably the best of the white-variegated bamboos. It has a mound-forming habit of growth and makes a dense, weed-proof patch of colour. In moist soils it runs a bit but is easy to control.

Rhizomes sympodial, closely branched and running steadily, forming low, dense thickets. Culms erect, up to 1.3 m × 2 cm in circumference, pale green, though the new culms come through white with green tips; sheaths persistent, thick, parchment-coloured; nodes not prominent, with some white, waxy bloom below; branch complement 1 or 2 produced from the lower nodes, long in relation to the length of the culms; leaves up to 14 × 1.4 cm, the upper surface strongly variegated with dark green and brilliant, creamy-white stripes and bands, the lower surface similarly marked but more subdued, the variegation variable, some leaves almost entirely green, others almost entirely white, bluntly rounded at the base, tapering to a fine, somewhat folded point, covered in fine, white hairs on both surfaces. H2.

### P.v. 'Nana' (P.v. 'Pygmaeus').
With leaves green and grows to no more than 30 cm: probably the dwarfest bamboo in cultivation.

### P.v. var. viridus (Makino) McClintock
The green-leaved version of the species: a little taller and more vigorous.

### P.v. forma glaber
Differs in having hairless leaves.

## P.viride-striatus (André) Makino
This is as much the best yellow-variegated bamboo as *P.variegatus* is the best white-variegated one, and, like *P.variegatus*, it is the species which is variegated, the green-leaved form being known as *P.kongosanensis*, though I am unable to trace that this is in cultivation. The gold colour of the leaves shows best when the plant is grown in full sun, and is always brightest on plants cut to ground level early each spring. When grown in shade the leaves go almost green and look decidedly chlorotic. You can usually find a flowering spike or two on established plants, but I have never found seed.

Rhizome sympodial, running slowly but steadily and forming a dense clump with untidy edges. Culms erect or ascending, up to 1.5 m × 2 cm in girth; sheaths peristent, hairy at the base, less hairy at the tip; nodes hairy, with some white, waxy bloom below; branch complement 1 or 2, branches erect, arising from the lowest nodes only; leaves up to 18 × 3.5 cm, edged with fine bristles on both margins, bright green broadly striped rich golden-yellow, the lower surface being a pale imitation of the upper one, the amount of yellow on each leaf variable but always greater on one side of the midrib than on the other. H2.

### P.v-s. 'Feesey's Form'
A dwarf form growing to no more than 75 cm, originally distributed by Mervyn Feesey.

### P.v-s. 'Allgold'.
A form with leaves entirely gold. Very dramatic, but less easy to grow and scorches in full sun even in Britain.

## PSEUDOSASA Nakai
A genus of perhaps 6 species from southern China, woodland plants but forming thickets in open country. Rhizomes monopodial, running aggressively in some species and forming extensive thickets. Culms erect; sheaths persistent, usually without bristles. Branch complement 1 or exceptionally 3 but then 1 dominant, lower nodes without branches. Leaves tessellated without bristles. Inflorescence paniculate. Stamens 3 (rarely 4). Stigmas 3.

### P.japonica (Steud.) Makino
This is almost certainly the most widely planted bamboo in Europe and to a great many people it quite simply is bamboo, which is a pity, as it is dull, drab, and utterly uncharming. It is known in Japan as the 'female bamboo', though why this bamboo should be female more than another seems to be a secret of the inscrutable Orient. It was introduced to France by von Siebold in 1850 and quickly spread to other European countries. It is sometimes claimed that this was the first bamboo to reach Europe, but that honour belongs to *Phyllostachys nigra*. The Japanese record white- and gold-variegated forms, but these do not seem to have reached the West.

Rhizome sympodial, slowly forming large, dense, ragged clumps. Culms erect but arching at the tips up to 6 m high and 6 cm in girth, thin-walled, olive-green at first later dull, matt green, unbranched in the first year; sheaths long-persistent even into the third season, with rough hairs at first, green becoming pale beige; nodes not prominent, sometimes oblique, with a little white, waxy bloom below; branch complement 1, or 2, or 3; leaves visibly tessellated, very broad for such tall canes, up to 36 × 3.5 cm, edged with fine hairs on one margin only, the midrib yellow and conspicuous, dark, glossy green above, one-third of the lower surface the same colour, the other two-thirds silvery-grey. H2.

### *P.j.* 'Tsutsumiana' Yanagita

An amusing and ornamental variety in which the internodes are swollen on alternate sides at about one-third of the way up from one node to the next, otherwise undifferentiated from the typical plant.

## SASA Makino & Shibata

A genus of about 50 species of woodland bamboos mainly from Japan but extending into Korea, China and the Kuriles. In cultivation in Britain their chief attraction lies in the leaf margins which bleach and wither, creating a variegated effect. Rhizomes monopodial or amphipodial, often aggressively invasive and capable of colonising large areas. Culms ascending, hollow, round in section; sheaths persistent, bristles rough and spreading; nodes prominent with a smudge of white, waxy bloom below. Branch complement 1 (rarely 3 and then one dominant at each node), lower nodes without branches. Leaves large, thick, visibly tessellated, hairless; bristles rough, whitish. Inflorescence paniculate. Stamens 6. Stigmas 3.

### *S.kurilensis* (Ruprecht) Makino & Shibata

This is a very hardy, semi-dwarf bamboo from high mountains in the Kuriles and now naturalised in the Honshu and Hokkaido districts of Japan. It is not common in cultivation, and is no more ornamental than any of the other sasas.

Rhizomes sympodial and ultimately far-running. Culms ascending, up to 3 m high and 30 mm in girth, dull green, unbranched in the lower half; sheaths thick, persistent but shattering, nearly hairless; nodes not prominent; branch complement 1, very rarely 3 and then one dominant; leaves up to 22 × 5 cm, visibly tessellated, shining dark green above, paler beneath, toothed on one side only, the veins conspicuous; leaf sheaths fugacious. H2.

### *S.k.* 'Variegata'

A form with well-marked, creamy-white striped leaves distributed by Kurt Blemnell. An effective and dramatic variegation.

### *S.palmata* (Burbridge) Camus

A vigorous bamboo with handsome leaves. It can look most ornamental when grown in the right setting, as beside a lake, and given plenty of space. It is easily distinguished from the similar *S.veitchi* by its much larger leaves — the second largest in the genus.

Rhizomes sympodial, far-running and forming extensive thickets. Culms erect, ascending or leaning, up to 2 m × 3 cm in girth, brilliant green maturing to dull green; sheaths long-persistent, often remaining till the third year by

182

which time they are very tattered; nodes not prominent, with some white, waxy bloom below; branches 1, rarely 3 but then one dominant; leaves large, up to 40 × 10 cm, bright, shining green above, paler and almost grey beneath, midrib prominent, yellow, the margins and tips withering in winter. H2.

### *S.p.* forma *nebulosa* (Makino) Suzuki
Differs only in the culms becoming mottled purple.

### *S.senanensis* (Franchet & Savatier) Rehder
Differs from *S.palmata* (q.v.) in its narrower leaves. H2.

### *S.tsuboiana* Makino
A species of little ornamental value. Rhizomes sympodial but not far-running. Culms up to 1.5 m and 1 cm in girth, erect or becoming erect, light becoming dark green; sheaths persistent, keeping their shape; nodes somewhat prominent; leaves up to 24 × 5 cm, bright, shining green above, greyish below. H2.

### *S.veitchii* (Carrière) Rehder
A very attractive, semi-dwarf bamboo, at its most attractive when the edges of the leaves have been bleached by cold weather. It is, however, treacherously invasive.

Rhizome sympodial and very invasive. Culms erect, or decumbent becoming erect, up to 2 m usually less and 2 cm in girth, first pale green then deep purplish-green, later dull purplish; sheaths covered with white hairs at first, long-persistent and scarcely tattering; nodes inconspicuous but with some white, waxy bloom below; branches solitary, often as long as the culms; leaves up to 25 × 6 cm, visibly tessellated, bluntly wedge-shaped at the base, coming to an abrupt point at the tip, broadly oval in outline, dull deep green above, paler below, soon developing bleached margins, the midrib prominent. H2.

### *S.v.* 'Nana'
A dwarf form with culms up to about 30 cm and leaves no more than 14 × 3.2 cm. Most ornamental and less invasive than the typical plant.

## SASAELLA Makino
A genus of about 12 species of wood-margin and meadow bamboos from Japan, differing from *Sasa* mainly in the more erect culms.

### *S.ramosa* (Makino) Makino
A rather invasive but otherwise pretty little bamboo. Differs from the similar *Pleioblastus pygmaea* in its greater stature, from *P.humilis* by the much hairier leaves and from *P.pumila* by the absence of a ring of hairs at the base of the culm sheaths.

Rhizomes sympodial, far-spreading, forming extensive colonies. Culms erect, up to 1.5 m × 1.5 cm in girth, bright green maturing olive-green. Sheaths persistent, pale green becoming parchment-coloured; nodes not conspicuous; branches usually 1, rarely 2, and one dominant; leaves up to 20 × 3 cm, edged with fine bristles on both margins, downy on both surfaces especially below, mid-green, withering at the margin in severe winters. H2.

### S.r. 'Nana'
A dwarf form growing to about 1 m.

### S.r. 'Variegata'
Has leaves longitudinally striped with bands of creamy-white, the bands varying much in width.

## SASAMORPHA Nakai
A genus of 4 species from Asia differing from *Sasa* in the greater height of the erect culms, 3 m as compared with 1.5 in *Sasa*.

### S.borealis (Hackel)
This bamboo is sometimes confused with *Pseudosasa japonica* (q.v.) from which it differs in its invasive habit, in the way in which the lower portion of the culm is unbranched while the upper part is densely branched, and in the bleaching of the leaf margins in winter.

Rhizomes sympodial and strongly running to form extensive thickets. Culms erect, up to 3 m often less × 6 cm in girth, dull purplish-green; sheaths partially tattering; nodes scarcely noticeable; branches 1 to 3, if 3 one dominant, mostly on the upper part of the culm; leaves up to 27 × 4 cm, glaucous, paler beneath with a purple tinge towards the base, the margins bleaching in winter. H2.

## SEMIARUNDARIA Nakai
A genus of 5 or 6 species from light woodlands in China and Japan. Rhizomes monopodial but not unduly invasive in the species usually grown. Culms stiffly erect, hollow, round in section or flattened on alternate sides in the upper internodes and gathered together in groups of clumps; sheaths soon shed, purplish-red, the inner surface highly polished, without bristles; branch complement 3–8, developing from the bottom upwards, lowest nodes without branches. Leaves visibly tessellated, with rough bristles. Inflorescence compound. Stamens 3. Stigmas 3.

### S.fastuosa (Mitford) Makino
*Fastuosa* means stately and that is just the word for this bamboo. It is a tall and decorative species that is neither really running nor caespitose. It forms small

groups of culms and then sends out a long rhizome and produces, at a distance of 1 m or more, another small clump. In time the rhizomes criss-cross, but the effect is always of well-spaced culms.

Rhizomes sympodial and not really running. Culms erect up to 6 m × 25 cm in girth, very thin-walled for their height, flattened below the nodes, olive-green at first, stained purplish at the nodes, maturing to dull yellow in sun; sheaths not enduring, thick, purplish, fading to parchment, highly polished on the inner surface; nodes quite prominent with some fugacious, white, waxy meal; branches in 2s or 3s, mainly borne on the top one-third of the culm; leaves visibly tessellated, 15 × 2 cm, constricted at the tip, bright green above, dull beneath, without auricles or bristles. H2.

## *S.f.* var. *yashadake* (Makino) Makino
Differs in having wider leaves, up to 15 × 4 cm, and fewer branches.

# SHIBATAEA Nakai
A genus of 3 species of woodland bamboos from the Himalayas to Japan. Rhizomes monopodial, producing culms in tufts and only running slightly. Culms erect, solid, slender, D-shaped in section; nodes prominent, 2-ridged. Sheaths persistent, hairless and without bristles. Branch complement 2–5. Leaves visibly tessellated, broad without bristles. Inflorescence paniculate. Stamens 3. Stigmas 3.

## *S.kumasasa* (Zollinger) Nakai
An enchanting little bamboo and especially desirable because it is slow to spread and quite distinct in aspect from any other bamboo. It has been cultivated in Japan since time immemorial.

Rhizome monopodial, slowly forming a dense clump of culms all of the same height. Culms nearly solid, triangular to nearly oval in section, up to 1.5 m × 0.6 cm in girth, rather zig-zag, pale green at first, becoming dull brown, produced much earlier than the new culms of most bamboos; sheaths purple at first fading to parchment colour; nodes prominent for the size of the culms, dark green; branches usually in pairs, rarely in 3s; leaves up to 11 × 2.5 cm, clearly tessellated, the upper surface dark green at first fading to yellowish-green, greyish below, the leaf stalk long. H2.

## *S.k.* 'Aureo-striata' (Regel) S.Susuki
This form with yellow stripes on the leaves is recorded and sounds interesting but I have not seen it.

# SINARUNDINARIA Nakai
A genus of a single species of woodland bamboo from China, formerly included in *Arundinarai*, but differing in its tufted habit of growth, the way in which the branches are all of the same length and also their horizontal presentation.

### *S.nitida* (Mitford) Nakai

A highly ornamental bamboo, similar to and sometimes confused with *Arundinaria spathacea*, from which it differs in its generally grey, overall appearance, in its smaller leaves and in its narrower, less noticeable culm sheaths. It makes an excellent lawn specimen or may be used as a screen. It is particularly sensitive to cold winds and is scarcely worth growing unless sheltered from them. It also needs some shade, having thin leaves. Several differing clones are cultivated.

Rhizome monopodial and slowly forming dense, caespitose clumps. Culms erect and ramrod stiff or whip-like and arching at the top, branchless in the first season, up to 6 m × 5 cm in girth, varying in colour from greyish to dark purplish; sheaths persistent, narrow, shorter than the internodes; nodes not prominent, with a distinct creamy-white ring; branches produced from the second season on, 4 or 5; leaves up to typically about 7.5 × 0.75 cm, occasionally as much as 10 × 1.4 cm, bright green, greyish beneath, edged with fine bristles on both margins. H2.

# 7 Sedges

The sedges are usually lumped together with grasses by gardeners because they have a generally 'grassy' appearance and broadly similar garden uses. In spite of their superficial similarities, however, they are really very different sorts of plants, separated by millions of years in evolutionary terms, the sedges being relatively ancient, the grasses among the most modern of plants. The sedges are also a very small family—some 80 genera— as compared with the grasses, which include some 650 genera and over 10 000 species.

The sedges differ from the true grasses in several ways, though they have many structural details in common. The first point of importance is that all sedges have a rhizomatous root system, like some of the perennial grasses. There are four distinct types of rhizome system in sedges, each giving rise to a characteristic mode of growth. There are sedges which have a sympodial rhizome system producing shoots and branches every few nodes, the general direction of growth being upwards; species with this root system are tussock-forming. There are sedges with a sympodial rhizome system in which the internodes between the shoots are few and short, radiating from the centre of the plant, in general, this type of root system also tends to produce a tufted plant, although because the root system is much-branched it frequently produces a plant that is more mat-forming in habit than tufted. Then there are sedges in which at least a few of the sympodial rhizomes are short or far-creeping, producing plants in which the shoots occur in loose or dense clumps, with outlying tufts beyond the boundaries of the main plant. Finally, there are sedges with monopodial rhizome systems in which leafy tufts are produced at regular intervals along a far-creeping rhizome.

The character of the rhizome varies according to whether a particular species is peat-loving or sand-loving. The rhizomes of peat-loving species are generally thick, with numerous root hairs, these often being present in such numbers as to form a 'felt' around the root. In the case of sand-loving or dry-habitat species, the rhizomes are generally wiry, much-branched and with few root hairs.

A characteristic of the sedges is that at every node on the rhizomes leaf scales arise. These are lanceolate or ovate, and keeled. The colour of both rhizomes and leaf scales can be diagnostic for a given species, but there are problems: when the plants are growing in anaerobic conditions, the colour can be masked by black derived from these conditions; when growing in acid conditions, the acidity can leach out the colour.

An important difference between the grasses and the sedges is that in the grasses there are usually many culms besides those which terminate in an inflorescence, but in the sedges the only aerial stem is that which terminates in an inflorescence, the leaves arising more or less directly from the rhizome.

The general leaf structure in sedges is similar to that of the grasses, though there are significant differences. The leaf, as in grasses, is composed of a sheath, a ligule and a blade. The sheath, particularly on the basal leaves, is very short in proportion to the blade, whereas in the grasses it is not uncommon for it to be longer than the blade. Whereas in the grasses the sheath is usually open, in the sedges it is usually closed. When it splits, it will do so in one or other of two ways: simple tearing is the most common, with the remains of the sheath either decaying soon after splitting or persisting as a pale, papery tissue, as in *Carex acuta*. The other method is for the sheath to split, producing a ladder-like effect. It is possible to determine which method of splitting occurs in any species found in the field by cautiously tearing the sheath open.

♂  male flowers
♀  female flowers

29  Flowers of a sedge: *Carex demissa*

The blades of the sedges are, at least in the basal leaves, longer than the sheaths and of a generally grass-like appearance. They may be flat, keeled, channelled or inrolled, although the flat and keeled types are probably the most common. If the blade is cut transversely with a razor blade and looked at end-on, it is very easy to see to which of these shapes the leaf conforms. In a very few species the blades are round or triangular in section. Where the blades are rough, this is usually the result of forward-pointing fine teeth, usually confined to the margins but occasionally also to the lower surface.

In the great majority of sedges, particularly those of the genus *Carex*, a ligule is present, as in the grasses, at the junction between the sheath and the blade. A very important difference between the grasses and the sedges is that in the sedges the ligule is usually fused to the blade for much of its length, which it is not in the grasses. Surprisingly, this makes it easier to see than in grasses.

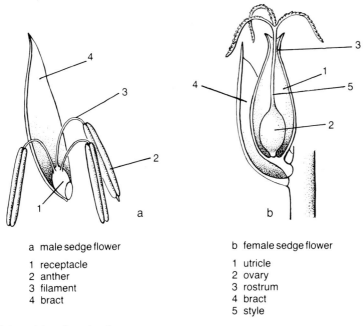

a  male sedge flower

1  receptacle
2  anther
3  filament
4  bract

b  female sedge flower

1  utricle
2  ovary
3  rostrum
4  bract
5  style

30  Male and female sedge flowers

It is in their inflorescences that the sedges differ most obviously from the true grasses. The inflorescence of the British species of sedge is a spike or panicle, the flowers being unisexual but both male and female flowers occurring on the same flower spike (except in the not very ornamental *Carex dioica*, which is truly dioecious as its name implies). Two arrangements of the unisexual flowers are found. The most common is that in which the terminal and occasionally the upper spikes are entirely male and the lower entirely female. Very occasionally, the higher female spikes have male flowers at the tip. The other arrangement is where the terminal spike is female at the top and male lower down: lower spikes on the same flowering stem may repeat this pattern, but in general are more likely to be entirely female.

A peculiarity of the sedges is that all the spikes except the terminal one are subtended by a bract. This may be quite small and appear to be like a large

189

glume, though in general these bracts become larger lower down the flowering stem, the largest ones appearing quite leaf-like. There is a considerable body of evidence to show that these bracts are homologous to the glume in grasses.

The actual flowers of the sedges are relatively simple affairs compared with those of the grasses. The male flower consists quite simply of three stamens arising from a low receptacle subtended on the lower side by a glume. As the anthers mature, the filaments elongate so that the stamens hang free from the enclosing glume. Once the stamens have dispersed their pollen, the anthers fall off but the filament remains. This is diagnostically useful since it indicates the position of the male flowers in specimens which are in fruit. The lower florets of the male spikelets are quite often sterile and have larger glumes than those which occur on the fertile spikelets.

The female flower consists of little more than a bottle-shaped *utricle* containing a single ovary and subtended by a single bract. The apex of the utricle (the neck of the bottle, as it were) is drawn out into a beak known as the *rostrum*. The length of this neck varies from species to species, and in a very few species is completely absent. The opening at the apex of the utricle may be split, bifid, notched, truncate or obliquely truncate. It is through this opening that the *style* protrudes. The style is usually swollen at the point of junction with the ovary, and usually persists in fruit. The style terminates in either two or three stigmas, which are papillate and fall soon after fertilisation.

The fruits of sedges are nuts, usually sessile in the base of the utricle, but occasionally short-stalked, and usually brown, sometimes yellowish or purple.

In general, the sedges are out-breeding, protrandry (the releasing of the male pollen before the female stigmas are receptive on any one plant) being the main device used to prevent self-fertilisation, although in some species this is only partial. Wind is the main agent of pollination, although pollen-eating beetles act as pollinating agents to a small extent. The stigmas usually remain receptive for as little as 24 hours, and very frequently all the stigmas on a spikelet or a plant are receptive during the same 24 hours. The stamens, on the other hand, take several days to discharge their pollen, groups of about a dozen florets being active in sequence. There are no records or apomixis or vivipary among the British sedges.

## A–Z of Sedges

### CAREX L.

A genus of perhaps as many as nearly 2000 species of superficially grass-like perennials from mostly wet habitats throughout the temperate and arctic regions, and occasionally mountains in the tropics. A few species are grown in gardens for ornament, variants with coloured leaves seeming to be the most popular. They are generally easily grown in damp to wet soil, and can readily be increased by division. Most species are also easily raised from seed.

Tufted or rhizomatous perennials with solid, 3-cornered stems and leaves in 3 rows, the sheaths closed, the inflorescences terminal, unisexual, in spikes, the male florets with 3 stamens, subtended by a bract or scale, the female made up of a single pistil enclosed in a thin sac (perigynum). Fruit a small nut enclosed in the persisting sac or utricle.

## *C.acuta* L.

Tufted to far-creeping species to 120 cm with rough, sharply 3-angled stems. Leaves to 140 cm by 7 mm, thin, glaucous, plicate, gradually narrowing to a pendulous tip. Sheaths brown or reddish-brown, persistent. Heads up to 10 cm long with 1–3 male spikes and 2–4 female spikes. An elegant and commonly occurring sedge of no particular ornamental value, though occasionally grown at the waterside.

The var. known variously as *variegata* or *foliis aureo-variegata* belongs under *C.elata* (q.v.). H1.

## *C.albula* Allan: Blond sedge

A highly ornamental sedge of most unusual colouring. Sometimes confused with *C.comans* but differing most noticeably in the almost white leaves. Forming tufts up to 35 cm tall. Culms smooth sometimes with a deep groove. Leaves about 1 mm wide up to 20 cm long plano-convex, grooved, rough to the touch. Sheaths dark brown to purple-red. Spikes 3–6, small, distant. H4.

## *C.atrata* L.: Black alpine sedge, Black sedge, Jet sedge

A diminutive sedge, having the general appearance of an iris, such as *Iris lacustris*, but topped by round, black, hard heads. A dwarf perennial with slow-creeping rhizomes to 50 cm, more usually about 15 cm or less. Leaves flat, iris-like, keeled, somewhat glaucous. Lower sheaths leafless, persistent, dark brown. Spikes 3–5, contiguous, the lower ones nodding, the upper one male only at the base. The lowest bract often longer than the inflorescence, the upper ones glume-like, heads oval or almost round; darkest brown seeming black. H1.

## *C.a.* var. *caucasia*

Easily grown in all but the driest soils, its size being mainly dependent on the amount of moisture at the roots, the more moisture the bigger. Probably at its best in a peat-bed; increase by division.

Differs in its smaller heads: less effective in the garden. H1.

## *C.berggrenii* Petrie

This species is quite distinct among carices in having flat leaves with blunt tips. I have grown plants whose leaves have varied from green to grey to reddish-brown, but these colour forms seem to be otherwise morphologically indistinguishable. Useful little plants for sinks or shelves in the rock garden. Occurs in bog conditions in the wild.

Small, tufted, shortly rhizomatous plants. Culms 2–3 cm long enclosed in light brown sheaths. Leaves 3–6 cm × 1–2.5 mm, linear, nearly flat, tip obtuse. Spikes usually 3, shortly pedunculate, crowded, conspicuous. H4.

### *C.brunnea* L.

A tender sedge from India and Australia which makes an attractive house or greenhouse plant.

Densely tufted, non-invasive sedge, growing up to 1 m, usually less than half that height. Leaves up to 60 cm long, 6 mm wide, sharply keeled, somewhat rough. Stems angular, slender. Spikes 4–8, slender, nodding, the whole inflorescence rather long and loose. Flowering season May to July.

### *C.b.* 'Variegata'

Generally small in growth, leaves broadly margined with a yellow band. Has been known, grown and treasured for a long time as a house or greenhouse plant, for which purposes its neat habit suits it well. H5.

### *C.buchanani* Bergg.

One of the most colourful of sedges, grown for its erect bright, reddish-brown foliage.

Densely tufted perennial without stolons or rhizomes, growing up to 60 cm. Leaves extremely narrow, 3-angled but appearing almost cylindrical; gradually tapering to an extremely fine, attenuated tip, a characteristic of which is the curious way in which they curl like a spring; leathery; richly glowing reddish-brown. Inflorescence, produced June to August, composed of 5 or more rather distant spikes, the lowest largest, those higher up becoming smaller; the largest up to 13 mm long, about 3 mm wide; the uppermost one staminate, buff. *C.petriei* and some *Uncinia* species have leaves of similar colouring. H4.

### *C.comans* Bergg.

An unusual New Zealand sedge, forming a mound of untidy, hair-like leaves.

A very densely tufted, evergreen perennial growing up to about 45 cm, usually rather less, without stolons or runners. Leaves up to 45 cm long, very narrow, thread-like; light yellowish-green or whitish-green; extremely flexible; at first erect, then arching to the ground. Spikes 5–7, oblong to cylindrical, the longest about 25 mm, about 3 mm wide, largely hidden by foliage. Flowering season June to August. H5.

### *C.c.* 'Bronze Form'

Has recently been introduced to cultivation: leaves dull brown. H5.

### *C.connica* Boot.

A densely tufted sedge with arching leaves. Rhizomes tufted, thinly covered in brown fibres. Culms up to 50 cm long, smooth. Leaf blades 2–4 mm wide, stiff, flat, dark green, rough to the touch. Spikes 3–5, erect, the terminal staminate, dark brown, the others pistillate, distant, densely flowered with long, inflated sheath. H5–G1.

### *C.c.* 'Hime Kansuge'

The form usually grown, with white margins to the leaves—a most elegant and agreeable sedge but not particularly hardy. The varietal name is merely the Japanese name for the typical, green-leaved form, all sedges being 'Kan-suge' in Japanese. H5–G1.

### *C.dipsacea* Bergg.

Forms dense, reddish tufts up to 75 cm tall. Culms up to 1.2 mm wide; basal sheaths yellow, red or dark brown; leaves up to 75 cm long, 2.5 mm wide, deeply channelled and with rough margins. Spikes 4–8, the terminal spike male. H4.

### *C.divisula* L.

A small-flowered sedge with graceful leaves. A densely tufted perennial with short rhizomes. Stems up to 75 cm, rough to the touch, with upward-pointing

31  *Carex divisula* subsp. *leersii*

teeth. Leaves up to 75 cm long flat or channelled, slightly rough beneath, evenly tapering to a fine point. Inflorescence up to 15 cm long; spikes 5–8, few-flowered, male flowers at the top, female flowers below. Utricles ovoid, shiny, pale yellowish-brown. H1.

### *C.d.* subsp. *leersii*
Differs in its larger, showier heads. H1.

### *C.elata* Allioni: Tufted sedge
Densely tufted perennial without stolons, or if with stolons, these being contained within the body of the plant, growing up to 76 cm. Leaves up to 76 cm long, about 6 mm wide, sharply keeled and rather glaucous; 3-angled; the lowest sheaths leafless. Inflorescence, produced May to June, composed of 3–5 spikes, the terminal one staminate, the longest up to 25 mm long, no more than 6 mm wide, the lower ones dark chocolate-brown. The typical plant has little, if any, garden merit. H5.

### *C.e.* 'Bowles's Golden'
Leaves the richest, most brilliant golden-yellow, with a very thin green margin. One of the most brightly coloured of all garden plants, and dramatic whether used singly or in drifts. It could well be used more widely in amenity plantings to give brilliant colour all summer. *C.reticulosa* 'Aurea' is similar in effect early in the year, but a paler, purer yellow with less orange in the colour, but the leaves soon become green.

### *C.e.* 'Knightshayes's Form'
A sport of Bowles's golden sedge that originated in Knightshayes's garden in Devon and differs in that the leaves are entirely rich golden-yellow without a green margin. Reputedly superior to Bowles's form. Any fertile soil in full sun, colouring fading to yellowish-green in shade. An abundance of moisture at the roots is desirable. H5.

### *C.firma* Host.
This tiny sedge is a gem for the rock garden or trough. It forms tiny cushions of spiky leaves. The typical plant is blue-green, but the variegated form is much more desirable, rather slower-growing but of the same habit.

Very dwarf, densely tufted sedge without stolons or runners, growing up to 10 cm after a great many years, plants usually being less than half that height. Leaves up to 25 mm long, about 3 mm across; 3-angled; rough, straight, very rigid, terminating in a sharp point. Inflorescence a short, compact series of tiny, dark chocolate-brown spikes. H1.

194

## *C.f.* 'Variegata'

Leaves boldly variegated creamy-yellow. Happiest in scree, with its head in the sun and its roots shaded by chippings. Increase by careful division, or by cuttings taken in spring and rooted under glass. H1.

## *C.flacca* L.

Probably the commonest sedge in the UK, frequent on chalk and limestone grasslands. Loosely tufted perennial with far-creeping rhizomes. Leaves up to 50 cm long, rigid, flat, tapering to a fine point, dull deep green above, glaucous beneath; sheaths dark red, to dark brown, persistent. Inflorescences up to 20 cm long, with 1–3 male spikes each up to 3.5 cm long, with 1–5 female spikes, cylindrical, the upper one erect, and male at the top, the lower ones more or less nodding: the utricle broadly ellipsoid, yellowish-green becoming nearly black. H1.

32  *Carex flacca*

## *C.fraseri* Andrews

This sedge is so unlike any other sedge that it is questionable whether it really is a sedge. In America it is known as *Cymophyllus fraseri*, and this may turn out to be the better name. Under whatever name, a charming and far too rare garden plant, grown as much for its leaves as for its flowers. The spikes emerge in early spring from the rolled, young leaves: the stems stand more or less erect, and the new leaves extend and gradually unroll once flowering is over. The little white, pompom flowers are a joy in early spring, and the very broad leaves exceptionally attractive. A woodland plant, probably at its most effective when massed or used as ground cover under rhododendrons, azaleas, camellias and so on. It comes from rich, moist woodlands and needs acid soil.

Densely tufted perennial growing up to 45 cm without stolons or runners. Short rhizomes. Leaves up to 30 cm long, 5 cm across; U-shaped in section; deep green; the margins toothed, the blades widening along their length, then terminating in a blunt, rounded tip. Inflorescence, produced April to May, a solitary globular, white spike up to 25 mm tall and across, borne among or above the foliage. H4.

## *C.hachijoensis* Akiyama

There is a considerable measure of confusion concerning the carices which have from time to time been called *C.morrowii*. There is confusion on the one hand as to which plant actually is *C.morrowii*, and confusion on the other as to *what* name should be applied to the plant now known in the trade as *C.morrowii* if it is not in fact *C.morrowii*.

*C.morrowii* is commonly represented in the trade in the cultivar 'Evergold', a form with a broad creamy-yellow median stripe.

The plant closely matches specimens in the Kew Herbarium (derived from material from the Royal Horticultural Society's Garden at Wisley) which has been determined as *C.oshimensis*. However, the very same cultivar is listed by Jelitt & Schracht in *Die Freiland Schmuckstauden* as *C.hachijoensis*. *C.hachijoensis* is close to *C.oshimensis*, but both are distinct from *C.morrowii* in that the beak of the utricle is short and scarcely notched, while in *C.morrowii* it is long and deeply bifid.

On balance, I think the cultivar 'Evergold' should properly be placed in *C.oshimensis*.

The other sedge known as *C.morrowii* is most familiar in the cultivar 'Variegata' which has a marginal (not median) variegation and straight, stiff leaves. I originally included this in *C.fortunei* but I now think it should be placed as a form of *C.morrowii*—which has a wide distribution in Japan giving it considerable variability.

## *C.morrowii* Boott.

A fine, dramatic sedge. Culms many, up to 40 cm long; leaves in bundles, the blades up to 10 mm wide, flat, thick very stiff, deep green, lustrous, the margins

196

rough to the touch, many-veined on the upper surface; the basal sheaths dark chestnut brown thinly covered with fibres when withered. H4. Ohwi comments that a white-striped form is common in gardens, and this is presumably *C.m.* 'Variegata' which is undramatically margined and marked white.

### *C.m.* 'Fishers Form'
A larger plant with a good cream variegation, an altogether superior plant. H4.

### *C.muskingumensis* Schw.: Palm sedge
Tufted perennial forming large patches. Sterile leafy culms numerous; fertile culms stout, up to 35 cm tall. Leaf blades up to 5 mm wide. Spikes 5–10, spindle-shaped up to 25 mm long, 6 mm wide, crowded together in dense clusters. Pistillate scales lanceolate, pale brown with clear margins. Nut narrowly oblong, up to 2.5 mm long. H4.

### *C.m.* 'Wachposten'
Has yellowish-green drooping leaves.

### *C.ornithopoda* Willd.
Densely tufted perennial with stems up to 15 cm long. Basal sheaths yellowish to dark reddish-brown, becoming fibrous. Leaves shorter than stems, up to 3 mm wide, pale green. Male spike up to 8 × 1.5 mm, stalkless. Female spike up to 10 × 3 mm, pendulous or semi-pendulous, stalkless or shortly stalked. Male glumes up to 3 mm long, yellowish to dark reddish-brown or nearly black. Utricles 2–3 mm, also yellowish to dark reddish-brown. H?

### *C.o.* 'Variegata'
The edges of the leaves conspicuously margined white. H?

### *C.oshimensis* Nakai: Japanese sedge grass
The variegated forms of this Japanese sedge are among the most desirable of all sedges, either for garden use or as pot plants. They are mound-forming.

Densely tufted, mound-forming perennial without stolons or runners. Leaves up to 30 cm long, about 6 mm wide, rarely more, evenly tapering to a fine tip; 3-angled or slightly U-shaped in section; arching; the margins bearing a narrow white band. Inflorescence, produced March to May, composed of 2–3 rather slender, foxy-brown spikes; the staminate flower terminal; fugacious. H5–G1.

### *C.o.* 'Aurea Variegata'
Has a very broad, deep golden stripe down the centre of each leaf. H5–G1.

### *C.o.* 'Aurea Variegata Nana'
Differs from the above only in its very dwarf, compact growth, the leaves being

197

no more than 7.5 cm long, and curled and twisted. Very charming and delightful. H5–G1.

### C.o. 'Evergold'
A name applied to a form with a creamy-yellow median stripe. H5–G1.

### C.o. 'Variegata'
Differs only in that the variegation is pure white instead of yellow. Equally fine. H5–G1.

### C.pendula Huds.: Weeping sedge, Pendulous sedge, Drooping sedge
One of the larger sedges, and, at least in the UK, where it is native, best grown in the wild garden where its arching and pendulous habit can be appreciated: it can also look very fine grown *en masse* in woodland, among foxgloves, lilies and so on.

Strong-growing, tufted perennial without stolons or runners, growing up to 1.2 m when in flower. Leaves up to 45 cm long, 22 mm wide; 3-angled, strongly keeled, evenly tapering to a fine point; yellowish-green above, blue-green beneath; the margins rough. Male spike terminal, obliquely set at the top of the arching stem, the stamens dependent, up to 10 cm long, female spikes 4 or 5; long-stalked, pendulous, up to 15 cm long; green or greyish. Flowering season May to June. H3.

### C.petriei Cheesem.
A delightful little New Zealand sedge that could pass, at a superficial glance, for a dwarf version of *C.buchananii* which it resembles in colour. It differs from *C.buchananii* in its smaller stature, its broader leaves, its generally less brilliant colouring and its fat, female flower-heads. The colour is quite variable in depth in plants grown from seed, and also varies according to whether plants are being grown in sun or shade, on acid or aklaline soil. Extremely effective in the garden planted in bold drifts, especially if grown in contrast to a blue grass.

Small, densely tufted perennial without stolons or runners. Leaves up to 30 cm long, about 3 mm wide; somewhat U-shaped in section; usually outward arching, evenly tapering to a narrow point; rich brown in colour. Inflorescence, produced June to July, composed of a terminal spike and up to 5 female spikes borne on short stalks, up to 2 cm long, usually less; rather fat, almost globose; extremely dark brown, becoming almost black. H4.

### C.phyllocephala T.Koyama
Dense, tufted perennial. Culms up to 45 cm long, 2.5 mm thick, erect, obtusely angled mainly hidden beneath the leaf sheaths. Lower sheaths without blades, darkest blood-red, the blades collected together at the top of the culm, the blades spreading, up to 20 cm long, 13 mm wide, the sheaths loosely clasping

198

the culm, minutely hairy. Inflorescence composed of 8–10 spikes making a capitate head: the terminal spikes up to 2 cm long, tawny, the others female, cylindric with rather small dark brown scales.

### C.p. 'Sparkler'

A form I first saw at Longwood Gardens, in which lime-green to dark green leaves are conspicuously marked with 1 to 4 longitudinal white streaks, the sheaths at the base of the leaf stalks being rich purplish. It is the showiest sedge I have ever seen and may well make a fine house plant. G2.

### C.pilulifera L.: Pill sedge

A delicate and diminutive sedge, with a limited natural range coming from poor, sandy or peaty soils with a pH of from 4.5 to 6.00. It is only grown in the highly decorative form C.p. 'Tinneys Princess', discovered by Gerald Mundy as a single tuft on a plant on his estate at Downton near Salisbury.

Densely tufted to about 30 cm. Leaves mid-green or yellowish, 2 mm by up to 20 cm long, rough above, abruptly tapering to a fine point; sheaths red-brown or purplish-red. Heads 2–4 cm long, with one male spike and 2–4 female spikes. H3.

### C.p. 'Tinneys Princess'

Has leaves with a broad, creamy-white stripe. H3.

### C.plantaginea Lam.

A most garden-worthy North American sedge grown mainly for its broad, plantain-like leaves. It is a densely tufted perennial to about 10 cm, strongly tinged red at the base. Leaves often longer than the culms, up to 25 mm wide: leaves of fertile culms bladeless and reduced to sheaths. Terminal spikes male, long-stalked, up to 2 cm long; female spikes 3 or 4 with only the lowest spikes stalked and exserted from the sheath. H4.

### C.riparia Curtis

I include this because it is often sold in its white-variegated form which indeed can look very pretty in a small pot. I have never seen it looking decorative in a garden. Once freed from its pot it runs in all directions, throwing up tufts at intervals as distant as 1 m, and becomes too diffuse to be showy.

The typical plant, though attractive in flower, with its golden stamens contrasting strongly with the dark brown glumes, is too fleeting in flower and far too aggressive. The variegated form is smaller and much finer, growing up to 37 cm, with superbly variegated leaves, but still with a strongly spreading habit.

An aggressively stoloniferous, tufted perennial, growing up to 1.5 m in flower. Stems rough. Leaves up to 1 m long, about 22 mm across; sharply

199

keeled, glaucous. Male spikes 5–6, the glumes dark brown with pale margins. Female spikes 1–5, distant; the upper ones erect, the lower ones nodding, up to 15 cm long; cylindrical to oval; the glumes light brown. Flowering season May to June. H3.

### C.r. 'Variegata'

Leaves dramatically variegated purest white, some leaves completely albino. H3.

### C.siderostica Hance

A striking broad-leaved, slowly running sedge, usually grown in its variegated form. Rhizomes slender, creeping; culms few, up to 40 cm long, with few basal sheaths. Leaves of sterile bundles with blades broadly lanceolate, up to 3 cm wide, thin, soft, smooth or thinly covered with fine hairs, the margins slightly rough to the touch. Spikes 4–8, androgynous, erect, short, cylindrical, with few flowers; up to 2 cm long, the bracts spathe-like, sheaths large, usually lacking blades. H4.

### C.s. 'Variegata'

Has the leaves thinly margined and streaked white. A good garden plant. H4.

### C.uncinifolia Cheesem.

An enchanting miniature sedge for troughs and rock gardens, grown for its pinkish-bronzy leaves. Very densely tufted, shortly rhizomatous perennial. Culms hidden by grey-brown membranous sheaths. Leaves up to 0.5 mm wide, pinkish or reddish-bronze, recurving, the margins somewhat incurled. Inflorescence a short, dense head of 3–4 spikes, the terminal spike male and shortly-stalked, the other female and stalkless. H4 or 5?

## CYPERUS L.

A genus of perhaps 500 species of perennial, grass-like plants from watery habitats mainly in the tropics and subtropics. Several species are ornamental, some being suitable for growing at the edge of water, others for cultivation as pot plants for the house or for growing as tub plants in a large greenhouse. They should be grown in ordinary soil, and all need abundant water. The pot plants will succeed in quite small pots. Most of the house plant and greenhouse species need a minimum winter temperature of 10°C. They are all usually increased by division, but seed is equally reliable.

Tufted or rhizomatous herbs, with narrow, grass-like leaves and flowers usually in umbels. Spikes many-flowered, bisexual, usually flattened; glumes many, distichous, usually fertile; bristles none, perianth absent; stamens 3. Fruit a 3-angled nut.

200

## *C.albostriatus* Schrader

Grown for the curious umbrella effect produced by the radial whorl of leaves at the tops of the stems. Usually grown as a pot plant, ideal for home or office decoration. Does best with the pot stood in a saucer of water. Can be increased by standing a head upside down in water until plantlets appear which can be detached and grown on.

Densely tufted perennial with tough, fibrous roots, growing up to 1 m when in flower. Stems several or solitary, up to 1 m long; smooth, angular, bearing at the top a whorl of leafy bracts. Basal leaves many, up to 45 cm long, about 6 mm wide, V-shaped, slightly rough on the margins. The leafy bracts up to 38 cm long, up to 13 mm wide, flat in section. Inflorescence produced above the radial whorl of leaves and composed of a few short-stalked, loose umbels; pale greenish or whitish. Flowering season July to September. G1.

### *C.a.* 'Variegatus'

Brilliantly variegated white on the leaves and stems. G1.

## *C.eragrostis* Lamarck

Of particular interest as the nearest thing to a hardy papyrus.

Vigorous, loosely tufted perennial without stolons or runners, growing up to 1.2 m, usually about half that height. Stems pale green, sharply 3-angled, stout, rough. Basal leaves up to 45 cm long, about 1 cm across, acutely V-shaped, evenly tapering to a point; finely veined above, somewhat rough on the margins. Inflorescence surrounded by many leafy bracts, up to 15 cm long, bright green, borne at right-angles to the stem; usually straight, sometimes somewhat drooping. Inflorescence, produced July to September, composed of a loose umbel of several densely packed, globular spikelets borne on stems up to 5 cm long; bright green or yellowish, becoming light brown. The curious umbrella-like inflorescence is excellent both in the garden and dried. Quite happy in ordinary garden soil so long as it does not dry out. H4.

## *C.involucratus* Rottboell: Umbrella plant, Nile grass

Often called umbrella plants because of the structure of their curious flower-heads. They are not hardy out of doors in the UK but make good pot plants for the home or conservatory. They seem to be tolerant of most room conditions, preferring a situation near a window but not where they will be scorched in hot weather.

Densely tufted perennial without stolons or runners, growing up to 75 cm. Culms erect, or erect becoming arching; naked, dark green, crowned by a whorl of leafy bracts. Leaves dark green, up to 30 cm long; basal 3-angled. Leafy bracts up to 15 cm long, variable in width, flat or almost flat in section; borne in a radial whorl at the top of the flowering stem and at right-angles to it, becoming drooping. Inflorescence, produced June to October, small, white,

globular heads borne on very short stems just above the whorl of leafy bracts.
H5.

### C.i. 'Flabelliformis'
A vigorous cultivar growing up to 1.2 m, differing from the type in having
spreading stolons and in its thickened, spongy leaves. H5.

### C.i. 'Gracilis'
A dwarf form to 45 cm tall, stems and leaves much narrower than in the typical
plant. H5.

### C.i. var. *nanus compactus*
Differs in its very dwarf, compact habit, growing to 30 cm. H5.

### C.i. 'Variegatus'
The most beautiful of the cultivars, unfortunately tending to revert and
difficult to keep. Dramatically variegated, white in leaf and stem. H5.

33  *Cyperus longus*

## *C.longus* L.

Interesting as the hardiest cyperus, often grown at the waterside but happy in any good garden soil so long as it never dries out.

Loosely tufted, rhizomatous perennial with smooth, sharply 3-angled, mid-green stems up to 1m. Inflorescence surrounded by several unequal, leafy bracts, usually longer than the inflorescence: primary branches unequal up to 10 cm; spikes about 10 mm long, linear, in loose racemes at the ends of the secondary branches. H3.

## *C.papyrus* L.: Papyrus, Moses grass, Egyptian paper reed

This is the true papyrus of antiquity, from which the earliest types of paper were made. Although now extinct along the banks of the Nile, it is still plentiful throughout Africa and in other parts of the tropics, where it often forms vast, almost impenetrable stands in swamps infested with snakes. The stems are used for the making of rafts, and the pulp is used, often illegally, for the making of a singularly powerful alcoholic beverage. It is also the 'bulrush' of Egypt, in which the baby Moses was found. It is a plant whose size really demands that it be given space in a large pond, where it will make a marvellous plant, growing upwards and arching somewhat under the weight of the rounded umbel of leaves at the top of the stem. Its tenderness, however, means that it usually has to be confined to a greenhouse pond, where there is sufficient room. It can be grown in a 30-cm or 38-cm pot, stood out in a garden pond through summer and brought in for the winter.

Vigorous perennial with strong spreading rhizomes growing up to 3 m. Stems extremely stout, up to 25 mm across; 3-angled, not jointed; smooth. Leaves borne in an umbel at the top of the stem, filiform or almost so; flexible, drooping, the whole head having a graceful appearance. Flowering season June to October. H5–G1.

### *C.p.* 'Nanus'

The variety most often offered by the trade, differing from the type in that the inflorescence is replaced by viviparous growths which form within the many-rayed head. H5–G1.

### *C.p.* 'Variegatus'

Slightly smaller-growing, boldly variegated white. Considered more tender than the typical plant. H5–G1.

## *C.ustulatus* A. Rich.

Robust perennial up to 2 m tall. Leaves polished grey-green with a dark grey, central midrib, crowded together at bases of culms, up to 120 × 1.5 cm, strongly keeled, the margins and keels finely toothed. Panicle a terminal umbel up to 14 cm long, composed of 6–12 rays, these usually unbranched, the

34  *Cyperus papyrus*

spikelets 8–13 mm, long, dark brown or ochrous forming dense spikes at the ends of the rays. An interesting sedge of exotic appearance, rather like a dwarf phormium. The form I introduced proved tender but it has recently been re-introduced by Graham Hutchins and his form may be hardier. H5–G1.

## DESMOSCHOENUS Hook.f.

A monotypic New Zealand genus sometimes included in *Scirpus* from which it is distinct by its harsh, stiff, narrow leaves and much-branching, stout, exceedingly long rhizome and its rather different inflorescence. It is a conspicuous element in the New Zealand flora because of its strange golden colouring. It is an effective sand-binder and is used by the Maoris to bind artefacts made from *Phormium tenax*. It makes a curious and colourful plant for the conservatory and may perhaps be hardy in the extreme south-west of the UK.

Perennial herb with thick, woody rhizome, 3-angled stems and leaves very rough to the touch. Inflorescence a contracted terminal panicle. Spikelets globose, many-flowered. Glumes spirally umbricate the lowest empty. Flowers hermaphrodite.

### *D.spiralis* (A.Rich.) Hook.f.

Description as for genus. The whole plant is rich golden-yellow, with leaves up to 90 cm long, 5 mm wide. H5–G1.

## ELEOCHARIS R.Br.

A genus of some 200 species world-wide, with 5 species in New Zealand of which one is endemic, the others also occurring in Australia. One species is sometimes cultivated for ornament. It forms a fine, creeping grass-like turf about 1.5 cm high, and is ideal in rock gardens, troughs and sinks but needs damp conditions, growing in the wild as a bog plant.

Annual or perennial, leafless herbs, stout or slender, sometimes rhizomatous, the culms in tufts or in linear series along a rhizome, each culm producing 1 or more leaf sheaths and a cluster of roots at the base. Inflorescence a solitary terminal spike. Flowers hermaphrodite.

### *E.pusilla* R.Br.

Carpet-forming perennial to 1.5 cm high. Rhizome very slender, pale brown, not exceeding 3 mm in diameter. Culms up to 12 cm long, densely tufted; sheaths thin and membranous, red-veined, transparent, the upper sheath colourless and somewhat inflated; spikelet few-flowered, up to 3 × 1 mm. H5–G1.

## ERIOPHORUM L.: Cotton-grass

A genus of about 12 perennial, grass-like plants from bogs throughout the north temperate and arctic regions. It is closely related to *Scirpus* but is distinct from it by the very numerous hypogynous bristles which extend far beyond the spikelets and create the effect of tufts of cotton—from which the genus derives its popular name cotton-grass and which give it such ornamental value. They are usually easily grown at the margins of ponds and in boggy ground, provided that the soil reaction is acid. They need controlling as they can colonise quite large areas. Increase by division.

### *E.angustifolium* Honck.

One of 4 British species of cotton-grass. The flowers are rather small and dull, but become interesting when the long, white, silken plumes attached to the seeds fluff out after flowering.

An extensively creeping perennial with far-reaching rhizomes, growing up to 60 cm when in flower. Stems subterete when fresh, smooth. Leaves up to 30 cm long, up to 6 mm wide, deeply channelled, narrowing to a long, 3-angled point, the uppermost leaf with a more or less inflated or funnel-shaped sheath. Inflorescence, produced May to June, composed of 3–7 nodding spikes, the bristles up to 3 cm long. H1.

### *E.latifolium* Hoppe: Broad-leaved cotton grass

Differs from *E.angustifolium* chiefly in its broad leaves, larger cotton-heads and more tufted habit. Grows to 60 cm. Stems sharply 3-angled, smooth. Leaves to 30 cm, flat except for a short, angular point, the uppermost leaf having a short, inflated or cylindrical, close-fitting sheath. Spikes 2–12. The garden merit is in the white, cotton-like seed-heads, the threads all tending to occur on one side of the head. Ideal in a container in a pond with only 2.5 cm or so of water over the roots. Easily grown in any damp soil; propagate by division. H1.

### *E.vaginatum* L.: Cotton-grass, Hare's tail

Abundant through the north temperate region. The smallest-flowered of the cultivated cotton-grasses, but has the merit of being tufted, virtually lacking runners. To 50 cm. Stems smooth, terete below, sharply 3-angled above. Leaves bristly, sharply 3-angled, to 30 cm long; stem leaves much shorter, the uppermost cylindrical, sheaths cylindrical, loose, narrowing at the mouth. Flower-heads solitary, bristles 2.5 cm long. Just as effective as the other species, but more desirable in the garden. Damp, acid soil; propagate by division. H1.

## GAHNIA J.R. et G.Forst.

A genus of some 40 species of perennials mainly centred on Australia and New Zealand, though other species occur in the Pacific Islands and Malaysia, China, Japan and Hawaii. Some species are occasionally offered by seedsmen and growers but none in my experience has proved frost-hardy. They are quite ornamental because of their large, nut-like fruits dangling at the tips of long filaments.

Perennials with harsh leaves and woody rootstocks, generally forming tussocks. Culms erect, smooth, round in section. Leaves mostly radical or almost all cauline. Panicle branched, spikelets many, 1-flowered and hermaphrodite, or 2-flowered the upper hermaphrodite the lower male. Nut hard and thick, showy.

### *G.procera* J.R. et G. Forst.

A high mountain species, probably hardy. Perennial forming stout, robust tufts. Culms up to 120 cm × 4 mm; leaves about as long and wide as the culms. Sheaths dull brown, up to 18 cm long. Panicle up to 20 × 5 cm, drooping, the spikelets 1- or 2-flowered; glumes 4–5, black, the outer glumes empty. Nut ovoid, brownish-orange or pale, smooth and shiny, up to 6.5 × 2.5 mm. H5?

### ISOLEPIS (Vahl) Roemer & Schultes

A genus of a single species—a segregate from *Scirpus*—of grass-like, often annual plant from Europe including Britain. It is a plant of delicate and pleasing appearance, sometimes grown as a pot plant for house decoration or in conservatories either in pots or as an edging. Easily grown in ordinary soil kept rather wet. Usually increased by seed.

### *I.cernuus* (Vahl) Roemer & Schultes

An attractive, bright green rush with a soft, semi-weeping habit. The general effect of a pot-growing plant is that of green hair. Useful in the conservatory.

Densely tufted perennial of very slender growth, growing up to a maximum of 15 cm, of arching, floppy habit. Stems filiform, smooth, bright green. Leaves up to 23 cm long, filiform. Spikelets solitary, greenish-white. Flowering season June to August. H4.

### MACHAERINA Vahl

A genus of about 25 species of perennials from the West Indies, South America and the Pacific Islands, with one species in New Zealand. This is of unproven hardiness but sufficiently ornamental to justify greenhouse or conservatory culture.

Tufted, virtually evergreen, grass-like plants with the flowers usually in cymes or panicles. Spikelets round in section, both terminal and axillary, 1–3 flowered; flowers bisexual; glumes few, overlapping.

### *M.sinclairii* (Hook.f.) Koyama

A really outstanding sedge. Grown for its unusual, iris-like leaves and huge, chocolate-brown inflorescences of considerable architectural value in leaf, the huge flower-heads a brilliant, bright, rich brown, borne high above the foliage.

207

Strong-growing, densely tufted perennial without stolons or runners, growing up to 1 m when in flower. Culms up to 1 m long; stout, smooth, laterally compressed. Leaves up to 1.2 m long, about 3 cm across, evenly tapering to a sharp point; flat in section, margins smooth; pale green. Inflorescence, produced July to August, a drooping, much-branched panicle up to 35 cm long, about half as much across; the whole head reddish-brown. H5–G1.

## OREOBOLUS R.Br.

A genus of about 12 species of perennial herbs mainly from the southern hemisphere, but also occurring in Malaya, Hawaii, Colombia, Panama and Costa Rica. Some species are grown as ornamentals but are not easy to cultivate, needing bog conditions to thrive yet perishing of winter-wet if grown in these conditions; but are worth every effort.

Perennials forming cushions, sometimes dense. Stems much-branched, very leafy, the leaves rigid. Spikelet solitary or with 1–2 laterial spikelets, the flowers hermaphrodite. Fruit and obovoid nut.

### *O.pectinatus* Hook.f.

Perennial forming light green cushions up to 10 cm tall. Stems densely packed, much-branched, especially at the base. Leaves in 2 ranks, in fan-like sprays. Spikelets usually solitary. H5–G1.

## SCHOENUS L.

A genus of about 100 species of rush-like perennials, natives of the temperate regions. One species is sometimes grown as an ornamental and is valued for its good reddish colouring. Undemanding in cultivation.

Perennials with or without creeping rhizomes. Culms erect or drooping, round in section, branched or unbranched, the leaves basal or cauline, rigid or flacid; the inflorescence paniculate or capitate.

### *S.pauciflorus* (Hook.f.) Hook.f.

Tufted, rush-like perennial, with a hard, woody rhizome up to 3 mm diameter; culms up to 87 cm × 1.5 mm; leaves reduced to very dark red-purple, basal sheaths, the uppermost up to 14 cm long. Panicle up to 3 cm long, with 2–6 spikelets at the tips of erect branches, the entire panicle subtended by a long bract taller than the panicle. The form in cultivation is rich reddish-purple all over, but in the wild red and green forms grow side by side and are morphologically indistinguishable. H5–G1.

## SCIRPUS L.

A genus of about 200 species of annual or perennial, grass-like plants from a variety of habitats in many parts of the world. Several species are grown as ornamentals, for different reasons. Those listed here are all perennials and can be increased by division. They grow well in ordinary garden soil provided it is really wet, but are generally best grown as marginals or in bogs.

Usually tufted plants, sometimes tall, stout and leafy but at the other extreme hair-like without stems, or in some species with the leaves reduced merely to the sheaths. Leaves few, at the base of the stems. Flowers bisexual, in heads or in spikes gathered into umbels; perianth usually reduced to 1–8-bristles; stamens 2–3. Fruit a lentil-like nut.

### *S.lacustris* L.: Bulrush, Clubrush

The typical plant is just a common bulrush (the term is a corruption of 'pool rush' — as distinct from woodrush), but the form with white stems is one of the most dramatic of all waterside plants — unique in appearance.

Stout, glabrous perennial with creeping rhizomes, growing up to 3 m at most. Rhizome very stout, somewhat knotty, producing tufts of often submerged leaves. Stems produced at more or less regular intervals along the rhizomes, up to 3 m tall, often less than that, up to 15 mm wide; terete, often with a few short leaves on the lower part, these leaves seldom more than about 5 cm long; green. Inflorescence, produced August to September, a dense head with several branches; light brown. H5–G1.

### *S.l.* Ssp. *lacustris*

Has green stems and a smooth glume below nut.

### *S.l.* Ssp. *tabernaemontani* (Gmelin) Palla

Smaller-growing with glaucous stems and biconvex nut. Two highly ornamental forms belong here. 'Albescens' with white stems with narrow, green, longitudinal stripes and 'Zebrinus', with the stems transversely striped creamy-white. H5–G1.

### UNCINIA Pers.: Hook sedges

A genus of perhaps 50 species mainly occurring in the southern hemisphere though absent from South Africa. They are typically sedges in most respects but differ most notably in their hooked rachillas. Most of the species occurring in New Zealand are endemic there, and some of these have coloured leaves of great ornamental value. No doubt several other species not yet introduced would be hardy and would extend the range.

Low, tufted or shortly rhizomatous perennials. Stems more or less 3-angled, with bract-like sheaths at the base. Leaves grass-like, linear, shallowly channelled, almost flat at the base, margins rough to the touch. Inflorescence a simple, terminal spike with unisexual flowers in 1-flowered spikes, male at the top, female lower; male with three stamens, female surrounded by a closed sac or utricle, the rachilla extending beyond the mouth of the utricle and terminating in a rigid glume which is sharply bent back to form a hook.

209

### *U.divaricata* Boott.

Loosely tufted or slowly creeping perennial; culms up to 16 cm × 1 mm, erect and rigid, the basal bracts yellow or brownish. Leaves up to 12 per culm, about 16 cm long × up to 4 mm wide, yellowish-green, rough on the margins. Spikes up to 4.5 cm long, 10 mm wide. Differs from other cultivated hook sedges in its generally yellowish colouring. H4.

### *U.egmontiana* Hamlin

Some years ago I was fortunate enough to receive seeds of this species from New Zealand. Seedlings were a most brilliant foxy-red and showed little variation. I gave plants to everyone who was interested and it is now offered by several nurserymen. It seems to be hardy south of London, and quite the brightest of the hook-sedges I have seen.

Densely tufted to 40 cm tall, the whole plant brilliant light foxy-red. Culms 0.5 mm × 30 cm; basal sheaths light brown. Leaves 4–6 per culm, 1–1.5 mm wide, up to 40 cm long, red. Spikes 9 cm × 3 mm with 10–20 rather distant female flowers. H5–G1.

### *U.rubra* Boott.

Generally similar to *U.egmontiana* but the whole plant is smaller and rich dark mahogany-red.

Tufted, to 35 cm. Culms rough to the touch, 3-angled. Leaves 2–3 to the culm, up to 2.5 mm wide, 35 cm long, tapering abruptly towards the tip, slightly rough to the touch. H5.

### *U.unciniata* (Linn.f.) Kuk.

Variable in colour in the wild, the form in cultivation in the UK is bright reddish-brown all over. Hardy in southern Britain.

A densely tufted, evergreen perennial growing up to 45 cm. Culms erect, up to 45 cm, about 2 mm across; glabrous, becoming slightly hairy just below the inflorescence. Leaf sheaths basal, dull brown. Leaf blades 5–10 to each culm, up to 30 cm long, 5 mm across, U-shaped in section; rough on the margins and towards the tip, upright or outward arching; dark green to reddish-brown, very variable in colour. Inflorescence, produced July to August, composed of several very slender, close spikes; light brown. H5–G1.

# 8 Rushes

The rushes differ from the true grasses in that the flowers are not arranged in spikelets, the bracts are not chaffy, the flowers are hermaphroditic, and they are presented in cymes, not in spikes or racemes.

They are much less closely related to the grasses than are the sedges. The two British genera embraced by the family Juncaceae are *Juncus*, the true rushes, and *Luzula*, the wood rushes. In both genera the flower is a cyme — an inflorescence in which each growing-point terminates in a flower. Although these flowers may look very tiny and insignificant, when they are examined under a hand lens or magnifying glass they can be seen to be very similar to what one is used to regarding as a 'normal' flower, with what look like three petals and three sepals. The two genera are very different in most other respects. The true rushes — *Juncus* — are mostly inhabitants of wet places, while the wood rushes — *Luzula* — are typically inhabitants of rich, moist woodlands. The leaves of *Luzula* are broad, flat and hairy to some degree; those of *Juncus* are frequently cylindrical.

## JUNCUS L.

A genus of about 160 species of annual or perennial, grass-like plants from marshy places throughout the world but especially in cold climates. They are mostly rather dull plants but a few are curious or ornamental. They are easily grown in moist soil and can be increased by seed or by division.

Generally rhizomatous perennials with tufted stems. Leaves flat or round, always with sheathing bases. Stems numerous, cylindrical, hairless. Flowers in heads or panicles, often made lop-sided by subtending bracts. Stamens usually 6.

### *J.capitatus* Weigel: Dwarf rush

A miniature rush of considerable charm, grown for the contast between the tininess of its leaves and the size and colour of its flower-head. Tufted annual to 5 cm, stems stiffly erect, branching only from the base, leaves to 4 cm long, all radial, more or less channelled, arising from a short, sheathing base; inflorescence a single, terminal head, green, becoming reddish-brown, subtended by radial bracts. Comes readily from seed sown in damp soil: probably best grown in a pan in an alpine house. Can become invasive grown as a pond marginal. H1.

### *J.effusus* L.: Soft rush

Stiffly growing, coarse, erect perennial growing up to 1.5 m. Stems up to 3 mm wide, rather soft, quite glossy; smooth along their length, pith continuous; bright green to yellowish. Sheaths reddish-brown, not glossy. Inflorescence, produced June to August, occurring about one-fifth of the distance from the top of the stem; seemingly lateral, many-flowered, lax or condensed.

The typical plant is a coarse-growing perennial of no ornamental value, but the following may be cultivated in suitable places. H1.

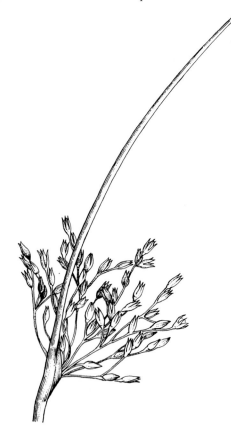

35 *Juncus effusus*

### *J.e.* 'Aureo-striatus'

Differs in its smaller growth, usually only to 1 m, and in its yellow colouring. The colouring is not outstanding, but is unusual among rushes. H1.

*J.e. compactus*
Differs in that the inflorescence is compact not lax: of no garden merit. H1.

*J.e.* 'Spiralis': Corkscrew rush
The stems are curled in a corkscrew fashion, often prostrate but in time forming clumps of upright as well as spreading stems. Curious rather than beautiful, well worth garden space. H1.

*J. glomeratus* 'Spiralis'
Leaves twisted and deformed. Similar to *J.effusus* 'Spiralis' but differs in having the overall appearance of a ball of wire-wool, whereas *J.e.* 'Spiralis' is more like a bunch of corkscrews.

*J.pusillus* Buch.
An enchanting dwarf rush introduced by Graham Hutchins and suitable for the rock garden or for troughs and sinks. Very small, slender, tufted perennial, stems 0.3 mm wide by up to 1.5 cm long, creeping and rooting. Leaves filiform, up to 0.2 mm wide. Inflorescence terminal, usually solitary, sometimes with 2–3 stalkless flowers. Flowers up to 2 mm long. Stamens 6. H5.

## LUZULA L.
A genus of about 40 species of perennial, grass-like plants from woods and dry places in the temperate regions mostly of the Old World. One or two species are grown for ornament, though they are not particularly decorative. Easily grown in ordinary soil and usually increased by division.

Tufted plants usually with rhizomes and stolons. Leaves flat, grass-like, with long white hairs. Flowers in cymes; perianth brown or green, with 6 scarious segments.

*L.alopecuros* Desvaux
A Falkland Island species recently introduced to the UK by Graham Hutchins. H5.

*L.banksiana* Meya
Robust, grass-like perennial with many-leaved tufts. Stem bases rhizome-like, covered with the fibrous remains of old leaf bases. Leaves flat, with long white hairs on the margins, especially towards the base, the tips not pointed, often thickened. Ornamental because of its hairiness. H5.

*L.celata* Edgar
Charming dwarf, cushion-like, tufted perennial with white-hairy leaves stained with rufous markings. Ideal for sinks and rock gardens. Stoloniferous. Leaves 10–30 mm long, the tip acute, the margins thickly clustered with white

hairs. Heads 6–16-flowered, in a single, nearly stalkless cluster. Differs from other cushion-forming *Luzula* species in the pointed tips to the leaves. H5.

### *L.luzulina*: Dwarf woodrush

The smallest of the cultivated woodrushes, its precise identity is not fully established. Originally released by Munich Botanic Garden, possibly merely a garden form and not a species. Very dwarf, tufted perennial with slowly spreading rhizomes gradually forming extensive mats, to 7.5 cm, often half that height. Leaves to 5 cm long, smooth above, rough below, evenly tapering to the tip, at which there is a small swelling; the undersurface covered in a few long hairs, pale, bright green; inflorescence a very loosely branched panicle borne well above the foliage. Makes dense, mat-forming ground-cover in shaded places: looks very neat if the inflorescences are clipped off. Any soil, sun or shade; propagate by division. H2.

### *L.luzuloides* (Lam.) Dandy & Wilmott

Not an outstanding plant as an individual, but highly effective—with its long-haired leaves and almost white inflorescences—if planted in large drifts; ideal ground-cover among shrubs in very large gardens. A loosely tufted perennial to 60 cm, with few, slow-spreading stolons. Leaves to 30 cm long, 10 cm across; grass-like, pale green, hairy; stem leaves much shorter. Flower stems slender, easily broken by wind or rain; inflorescence a loose, lax corymb of off-white flowers. Of sprawling habit. Any soil, sun or shade; seed or division. H1.

### *L.nivea* DC.: Snowy woodrush

Very similar to *L.luzuloides*, and the two are frequently confused. They can be told apart in that the flowers of this species are snowy-white, those of *L.luzuloides* greyish-white; leaves of this species dark green, those of *L.luzuloides* bright, light green. Generally similar to the foregoing species, and of similar garden use, but to be preferred for its whiter, more showy flower-heads. H2.

### *L.n.* 'Little Snow Hare' ('Schneehaeschen')

A form with very white, long-haired heads.

### *L.n.* 'Snow Bird'

Flower-heads pure white.

### *L.pilosa* Baumgarten: Hairy woodrush

Another woodrush that has no particular attraction as an individual plant, but makes good ground-cover among shrubs. A densely tufted perennial with a short, erect rootstock and slowly spreading rhizomes, to 30 cm. Basal leaves to 20 cm; grass-like, dark green; tapering to a truncate swelling at the tip; very hairy. Inflorescence a huge, lax cyme; flowers dark chestnut-brown. Woodland conditions; propagate by division or seed. Seeds freely when happy. H1.

### *L.p.* 'Greenfinch' ('Gruenfink')
Supposedly superior to the type.

### *L.pumila* Hook.f.
A tiny, cushion-forming species for sinks and rock gardens. Perennial cushion to 6 cm high. Leaves 1–4 cm long, up to 1.5 mm wide, margin slightly hairy, tip obtuse. Inflorescence a 4–10-flowered cluster. Flowers 2–3 mm long, the tepals dark brown. H3.

### *L.rufa* Edgar
A dwarf *Luzula* grown for its reddish leaves. The plant forms scattered, grass-like tufts. Leaves leathery, reddish-green, the margins slightly hairy, the tips obtuse. Heads single, compact, globose with up to 3 lateral clusters. Tepals pale reddish at first becoming dark brown. H5.

### *L.sylvatica* (Hudson) Gandin: Greater woodrush
By far the finest of the woodrushes for ground-cover in woodland or on the shaded side of a shrub, spreading persistently and making a completely weed-proof carpet.

Densely tufted perennial with a short, ascending rootstock and slowly spreading stolons, growing up to 76 cm when in flower. Basal leaves up to 30 cm long, 13 mm or more across; broadly linear, tapering to a fine point; sparsely hairy and somewhat filamentous on the margins. Flower stems erect or somewhat oblique, bearing a few short leaves. Inflorescence, produced April to June, a lax, terminal cyme, the branches wide-spreading, the flowers borne 3–4 together, chestnut-brown.

### *L.s.* 'High Tatra' ('Hohe Tatra')
Form from the High Tatra mountains.

### *L.s. marginata*
Has the leaf edges lightly banded white. H1.

### *L.s.* 'Tauernpass'
A low-growing form with broad leaves.

### *L.s.* 'Woodsman' ('Waldler')
Very broad leaves of a good, fresh green. Lovely in winter.

# 9 Cat-tails

These differ from the true grasses most characteristically in their monoecious flowers, borne in dense, cylindrical, terminal spikes, the male at the tip of the flowering stem, the female beneath it.

The cat-tails, of which there are no more than a dozen species in the world, belong to the genus *Typha* and the order Typhales and are of fundamentally different construction from the grasses, sedges, or rushes. Their most obvious distinguishing feature is their inflorescence, which is so distinct that it has given rise to not merely one but three common names—cat-tail, reed-mace or bulrush. The inflorescence is composed of two parts, both borne on the same axis. The upper part is the male, staminate inflorescence which is usually short-lived, and below this is the thickened pistillate female inflorescence, which is usually long-lived. Another difference lies in the thick, heavy, rhizomatous root system, and a further difference in the arrangement of the leaves, which arise in two ranks embracing the central flowering stem. There are no ligules.

## TYPHA L.

A genus of 12 or 15 perennial, grass-like, marsh plants widespread throughout the temperate and tropical worlds. They are indispensable ornamentals in lakes and ponds, unmistakable with their ramrod stiff stems and cylindrical, brown, fruiting heads. These are popularly picked and dried for indoor decoration but should be picked when immature to avoid their shattering. They are almost too easy to grow in any wet soil and need attention to prevent them from getting out of hand. They are usually increased by division, but can very easily be raised from seed sown in suitably wet soil.

Plants with stout, aggressively creeping rhizomes and erect stems. Leaves flat, mostly basal, in 2 ranks, with the sheath tightly enclosing the stem.

### *T.angustifolia* L.

More suitable for planting in gardens than the common *T.latifolia*, being somewhat more graceful in flower, smaller-growing, less vigorously invasive.

Vigorously spreading perennial, growing up to 1.5 m when in flower. Leaves green, somewhat arching, U-shaped in section, especially on the back; slightly channelled on the upper surface, smooth, up to 1 m long; generally about 6 mm across. Inflorescence borne on a stout, straight stem, the male spike terminal or nearly terminal, buff, fugacious; the female spike separated from the male by 3–8 cm; often interrupted, reddish to dark brown. Flowering season July to August. H1.

### *T.latifolia* L.: Cat-tail, Great reed-mace, Marsh beetle; also, erroneously, Bulrush

The familiar and ubiquitous reed-mace or cat-tail of the temperate and tropical world. The fluff from the seed-heads is still used in several parts of the world to stuff pillows; the Cossacks highly esteem the young shoots as green vegetables.

A coarse perennial with aggressively colonising rhizomes to 2.4 m. Leaves to 2 m, 4 cm across, somewhat U-shaped or nearly flat; glaucous. Inflorescence borne on a strong, straight stem; male inflorescence about 5 cm long, fugacious; female inflorescence contiguous, to 30 cm long, 2.5 cm across; dark brown. H1.

### *T.l.* var. *elatior*

Differs in its smaller, narrower leaves and shorter spikes. A fine and stately plant needing a lot of space to look good. Only suitable for the very largest gardens. H1.

### *T.minima* Funck: Dwarf cat-tail, Dwarf reed-mace

By far the finest of the cat-tails for garden ponds or bog gardens, very slender and graceful in all its parts. A slender perennial to 76 cm, with slowly but insistently spreading rhizomes. Leaves to 60 cm long, 2 mm wide; erect, slightly glaucous. Leaves of flower stems reduced to somewhat inflated sheathing bases, stem very slender, erect. Male spike up to 4 cm long; female spike contiguous, to 5 cm long, about 4.5 cm across; almost round, dark brown. H1.

### *T.shuttleworthii* Koch & Sonder.

A dainty species, but still invasive. Distinct in that the female spike matures a silvery-grey; otherwise similar to *T.latifoilia* but smaller. H1.

# Appendix 1 *Hardiness Zone Map*

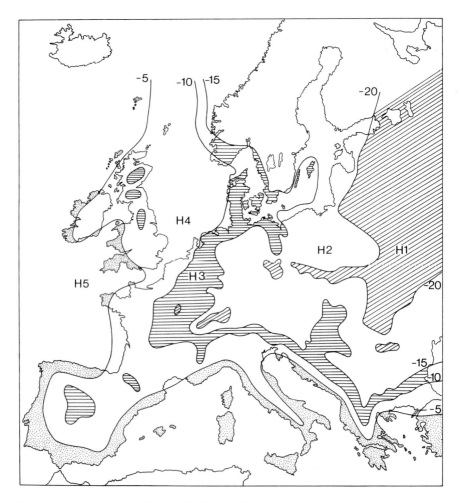

Map 1. Mean January isotherms for Europe (hardiness codes).
(After Krüssmann, *Handbuch der Laubgehölze*, 1960.)

# Appendix 2 *Conversion Tables*

| Celsius | Fahrenheit | Metric | Imperial |
|---|---|---|---|
| °C | °F | 2.5 cm | 1 in |
| −50 | −58 | 15 cm | 6 in |
| − 5 | 23 | 30 cm | 1 ft |
| 0 | 32 | 91 cm | 3 ft |
| 5 | 41 | 3 m | 10 ft |
| 10 | 50 | 6 m | 20 ft |
| 15 | 59 | 9 m | 30 ft |
| 20 | 68 | 18 m | 60 ft |

# Appendix 3 *Suppliers*

## Great Britain
Bressingham Gardens, Diss, Norfolk
Beth Chatto Gardens, White Barn Farm, Elmstead Market, near Colchester
Essex
Hoecroft Plants, Foss Lane, Welton, Midsommer Norton, Bath, Avon
Graham Hutchins, County Park Nursery, Essex Gardens, Hornchurch, Essex
Costin's Nurseries, Portgloriam, Kilcock, County Kildare, Ireland
Apple Court, Hordle, Lymington, Hampshire

### *Bamboos*
Drysdale Nurseries, 96 Drysdale Avenue, Chingford, London E4
Jungle Giants, Morton, Bourne, South Lincolnshire
Bamboo Nursery, Kingsgate Cottage, Wittersham, Kent

## West Germany
Dr Hans Simon, Georg-Mayr. Strasse, 70, D-8772, Markthiedenfeld
Staudengartnerie Grafin von Zeppelin, D-7811, Salzberg-Lausen

## United States
Kurt Bluemel Inc., 2740 Greene Lane, Baldwin, Maryland 21013

# Glossary

ACICULAR needle-like

ACUMINATE tapering to a narrow point

ADPRESSED lying flat against

ANNUAL a plant which completes its life-cycle in a single season

ANTHER the pollen producing part of the stamen

APICAL pertaining to the apex

APOMICTIC able to reproduce sexually, often by means of seeds which have not been fertilised by the normal pollinating processes

APPRESSED lying flat against

ARTICULATE jointed

ASCENDING of stems that at first grow horizontally and then curve upwards, continuing to grow more or less erect

ATTENUATE of leaf blades: drawn out to a fine point

AURICLE lobe; little ear, often occurring at the base of leaves

AWN a slender, usually stiff, bristle on a glume

AXIL the upper angle between a leaf or leaf-stalk and the stem that bears it

AXIS the central stem of a flower-head or of a part of a flower-head

BIDENTATE doubly toothed

BIENNIAL a plant which completes its life-cycle in two seasons

BIFID forked: dividing into two lobes, points or tongues

BISEXUAL with both sexes occurring on the same plant

BLADE the flat part of a leaf (as distinct from the petiole (stalk) or sheath)

BRACT a modified leafy structure accompanying an inflorescence and often occurring on the flowering stem

BRANCH COMPLEMENT used of bamboos to denote number of branches characteristic of the species

CAESPITOSE tufted: clump-forming

CALLUS thickened tissue formed over a wound or natural break

CALYX the sepals: the outer whorl of a perianth

CAPITATE of a flower-head that is compact and roughly spherical

CAPSULE a dry fruit usually containing many seeds

CARICES the plural of carex

CARYOPSIS a grain, as found in cereals: a dry, one-seeded indehiscent fruit with a thin pericarp

CAULINE pertaining to the stem

CHARTACEOUS papery

CHASMOGAMOUS having open, not cleistogamic (see below) flowers, allowing cross-fertilisation

CILIATE fringed with (usually fine) hairs

CLEISTOGAMOUS of a flower usually with a defective corolla, that does

220

not open properly but which sets seed by self-pollination

COMPRESSED flattened from side to side

CONNATE grown or growing together: so fused as to be inseparable without injury

CONTIGUOUS adjoining: touching

CONVOLUTE longitudinally rolled up

CORIACEOUS leathery

CORYMB a flat-topped raceme

CULM the stems of grasses (including bamboos)

CYME an inflorescence which terminates in a flower, this flower opening first, the other flowers arising from lower branches and opening later

DECUMBENT of a shoot which is horizontal, only becoming erect at the tip

DECURRENT of a structure that continues down a stem below the point of attachment as a ridge or ridges

DEFLEXED deflected; bent or turned abruptly downwards

DEHISCE of seeds splitting when ripe along a predetermined line

DICOT short for dicotyledons

DIGITATE of a flower-head: like the fingers of a hand spread out

DIMORPHIC having two forms or natures—i.e. a juvenile form and an adult one

DIOCEIOUS with male and female flowers on separate plants

DISARTICULATING of the heads of grasses, when they break apart for purposes of dispersal

DISTANT not close; standing apart

DISTICHOUS in two, opposite rows

ELLIPTIC about twice as long as wide and tapering equally both at the tip end and at the base

EMBRYO the part of a seed from which a new plant develops

EXSERTED thrust forth; protruding from; extending beyond

EXTRAVAGINAL of shoot innovations that occur outside the sheath

FILAMENT the stalk of a stamen, with an anther at its tip

FILIFORM thread-like

FLORET part of a spikelet made up of the flower or seed, the lemma and the palea

FUGACIOUS fleeting; soon falling

FUSOID shaped like a spindle

GENICULATE kneeling

GIBBOUS more swollen in one part than another

GLABROUS without hairs

GLAUCOUS bluish-green

GLUME small, scale-like bracts occurring in the flowers of grass

HERBACEOUS any plant whose above-ground parts are soft and juicy, not woody

HILUM the scar-like mark on a seed which shows where it was attached to the folicle

HISPID bristly: covered with short rigid erect hairs

HYALINE colourless; transparent

HYPOGYMOUS situated below the base of the ovary

IMBRICATE overlapping like roof tiles

INNOVATION the point of origination of a shoot

INTERNODE the section of a culm which occurs between the nodes

INTRAVAGINAL of short innovations that occur inside the sheath

INVOLUCRE a compact cluster of bracts at the base of a flower or inflorescence; in the grasses this is sometimes reduced to a mere ring of hairs

INVOLUTE rolled inwards

KEEL the narrow ridge that sometimes occurs along the midrib of a leaf, bract or glume

LANCEOLATE 3–4 times as long as wide, and tapering gradually towards the tip

LEMMA the outer of a pair of scale-like bracts in the spikelet. The other is the palea

LIGULE a small membranous flap arising where the blade meets the sheath and clasping the culm

LINEAR of leaves whose sides are parallel and far longer than wide

LODICULE specialised scale-like organs occurring in the flowers of grasses between the lemma and the palea which in due season inflate themselves with sap thereby forcing the lemma and palea to open exposing the flowers

MONOECIOUS with separate male and female flowers on the same plant

MONOPODIAL used mainly of the roots of sedges and bamboos, to describe a mode of growth whereby the tip of a rhizome continues to extend regardless of how many nodes arise along it: it is potentially far-reaching and fast running

NAVICULAR boat-shaped

NODE a joint on the stems of grasses and bamboos: the point at which in grasses one section of culm will break cleanly away from another

OBLONG of a leaf 2–5 times as long as broad whose sides are nearly parallel

OBOVATE proportions as for ovate, but attached at the tapering end

OBTUSE blunt

OVARY the lower part of a carpel containing the ovules

OVATE with approximately the outline of a hen's egg though usually pointed at the tip and attached at the broader end

OVULE the small, egg-shaped body from which a seed develops after fertilisation

PALEA the inner of a pair of scale-like bracts in the spikelet (the other is the lemma)

PALMATE lobed or divided in the manner of a hand with fingers spread out

PANICLE term used for the flower-head of a grass

PECTINATE in the form of a comb

PEDICEL the stalk of a single flower

PERENNIAL a plant which endures for more than two seasons

PERIANTH collective term for the calyx and corolla of a flower when taken together; all the outer parts of a flower which enclose the reproductive organs

PETIOLE a leaf stalk

PISTIL the collective term for the whole female part of a flower

PLANO-CONVEX shallowly curved

PLICATE folded into pleats

PLUMOSE feathery

POLLINATION the transference of the male pollen to the female stigma, however achieved

POOID grass-like

RACEME an inflorescence made up

of many stalked flowers arranged on a single axis

RACHILLA the joined axis in a grass floret

RACHIS the main stalk of an inflorescence

RHIZOME a horizontal stem above or below the ground acting as storage organ or for root extension growth, or both, with roots or stems arising from its nodes

ROSTRUM beak

RUNNER a stem usually above the ground making roots and shoots at nodes at intervals along its length

SCABRID rough to the touch

SCARIOUS of thin dry membranous texture

SESSILE stalkless

SETACEOUS bristle-like

SHEATH the part of a leaf which occurs below the ligule and which surrounds the culm

SPATHE bract enclosing one or several flowers

SPICATE bearing a spike or spikes

SPIKE an inflorescence composed of numerous stalkless flowers arranged on a single axis

SPIKELET an individual flower of grass occurring at the end of a pedicel and composed of rachilla, glumes, lemma, palea, lodicules, filaments, anthers, ovary, stigma and style

STAMEN the male generative organ, producing pollen

STIGMA that part of a style to which pollen adheres

STOLON a far-creeping above- or below-ground stem giving rise to a new plant at its tip and perhaps at the nodes as well

STYLE the upper part of a carpel or gynaecium, bearing the stigma

SUBTEND applied to any structure which occurs in the axil of any other structure

SUBTERETE less than circular in section

SYMPODIAL of the roots of sedges and bamboos: a mode of growth whereby the tip invariably turns upwards to become a leafy or flowering culm, further extension growth then arising from lateral buds; usually typifies plants of clump-forming habit

TEPAL floral organs similar to but not identical with petals and sepals and serving a similar function

TERETE about circular in cross-section and without grooves or ridges

TESSELLATION marked with a net-like pattern of veins

TOMENTUM a covering of soft hairs giving a woolly effect

TRUNCATE ending abruptly as if cut across

UMBEL an inflorescence in which all the flower-stalks arise together from the same point

UTRICLE a bottle-shaped organ

VILLOUS shaggy with long soft hairs

VISCID sticky

VIVIPAROUS of plants characteristically bearing young plants which can take root and when detached assume an independent existence; they may occur among or in place of normal flowers

# Index of Plant Names